Art and Objects

Art and Objects

Graham Harman

polity

The right of Graham Harman to be identified as Author of this Work has been asserted in accordance with the UK Copyright, Designs and Patents Act 1988.

First published in 2020 by Polity Press

Polity Press
65 Bridge Street
Cambridge CB2 1UR, UK

Polity Press
101 Station Landing
Suite 300
Medford, MA 02155, USA

ISBN-13: 978-1-5095-1267-6 (hardback)
ISBN-13: 978-1-5095-1268-3 (paperback)

A catalogue record for this book is available from the British Library.

Library of Congress Cataloging-in-Publication Data
Names: Harman, Graham, 1968- author.
Title: Art and objects / Graham Harman.
Description: Medford, MA : Polity, 2019. | Includes bibliographical
  references and index.
Identifiers: LCCN 2019008491 (print) | LCCN 2019017058 (ebook) | ISBN
  9781509512713 (Epub) | ISBN 9781509512676 (hardback) | ISBN 9781509512683
  (pbk.)
Subjects: LCSH: Aesthetics.
Classification: LCC BH39 (ebook) | LCC BH39 .H367 2019 (print) | DDC 111/.85--dc23
LC record available at https://lccn.loc.gov/2019008491

Typeset in 10.5 on 12 pt Sabon by Servis Filmsetting Ltd, Stockport, Cheshire
Printed and bound in Great Britain by TJ International Limited

The publisher has used its best endeavours to ensure that the URLs for external websites referred to in this book are correct and active at the time of going to press. However, the publisher has no responsibility for the websites and can make no guarantee that a site will remain live or that the content is or will remain appropriate.

Cover illustration: Beuys, Joseph (1921-1986): Telefon SE (Telephone T R), 1974. New Digitale (1)(A) York, Museum of Modern Art (MoMA). Multiple of two cans with paint additions and string, each 4 3/4 x 3 15/16" (12 x 10 cm); other (string): 70 7/8" (180 cm). Riva Castleman Endowment Fund. Acc. n.: 914.2005.© 2017. Digital image, The Museum of Modern Art, New York/Scala, Florence

Every effort has been made to trace all copyright holders, but if any have been overlooked the publisher will be pleased to include any necessary credits in any subsequent reprint or edition.

For further information on Polity, visit our website: politybooks.com

Contents

Abbreviations

GD   Graham Harman, "Greenberg, Duchamp, and the Next Avant-Garde"
HE   Clement Greenberg, *Homemade Esthetics*
HMW   Michael Fried, "How Modernism Works"
KAD   Thierry de Duve, *Kant After Duchamp*
LW   Clement Greenberg, *Late Writings*
MM   Michael Fried, *Manet's Modernism*
NO   Bettina Funcke, "Not Objects so Much as Images"
OAG   Rosalind Krauss, *The Originality of the Avant-Garde*
OC   Leo Steinberg, *Other Criteria*
OOS   Roger Rothman, "Object-Oriented Surrealism"
OU   Rosalind Krauss, *The Optical Unconscious*
PA   Jacques Rancière, *The Politics of Aesthetics*
RR   Hal Foster, *The Return of the Real*
TC   Arthur Danto, *The Transfiguration of the Commonplace*
TN   Harold Rosenberg, *The Tradition of the New*

. . . le chef-d'oeuvre qu'on regarde tout en dînant ne nous donne pas la même enivrante joie qu'on ne doit lui demander que dans une salle de musée, laquelle symbolise bien mieux, par sa nudité et son dépouillement de toutes particularités, les espaces intérieurs où l'artiste s'est abstrait pour créer.

Marcel Proust, *À l'ombre des jeunes filles en fleur*, p. 199

Preliminary Note

It is well known that Modernism in the visual arts finds an intellectual basis in Immanuel Kant's *Critique of Judgment* (1790), and more recently in the work of the pivotal American critics Clement Greenberg and Michael Fried. Kant is often called a "formalist" in his approach to art, despite not using the term in this connection. But he does speak of formalism in his ethical theory, and we will see that the reasons that motivate the term's appearance in one case apply to the other as well. Use of the word "formalist" to describe Greenberg and Fried encounters more resistance, at least in circles where these authors are viewed favorably, and special efforts are made to exempt Fried from this designation. Stephen Melville, for instance, laments "what is still far too often presented as Greenberg and Fried's Kantian formalism," while Richard Moran objects that formalism "seems an inapt term to characterize [Fried's] brilliant readings of French painting . . ."[1] The present book will nonetheless speak of Greenberg and Fried as Kantian formalists, though I am far more sympathetic to these authors than most who do so; indeed, I regard both authors as classics whose importance goes well beyond the sphere of art. Although I am well aware that Greenberg was cold to the word "formalism," and that Fried remains even more so, the term fits them perfectly well in the sense to be developed in this book. My goal in saying so is not to impose unwanted terminology on anyone, but to renew focus on what is living and what is dead in Kant's approach to art, and in his philosophical position more generally. No intellectual figure dominates the past two-and-a-half centuries like Kant, and previous attempts to get beyond him have never really gotten to the heart of the matter – the titanic efforts of German Idealism notwithstanding. Thus, we remain haunted by Kant's strengths and limitations to this day.

Beginning in the 1960s, the prestige of formalism in the art world was rivalled and then eclipsed by a general anti-formalist attitude that can be called "postmodern," for lack of a better term. This occurred through various practices that flouted the principles of modernist art: especially the formalist credo of the autonomy and integrity of the artwork reflected in the epigraph from Proust above. Yet the new generation of critics who lent their authority to the turn away from High Modernism were too quick to jettison formalism without safeguarding its most important insights. This has left the arts – like philosophy in its continental branch – in a wilderness defined in philosophy by misguided opposition to realism, and in art by a superannuated commitment to the now grandfatherly spirit of Dada. Object-Oriented Ontology (abbreviated OOO, pronounced "triple O") is in a good position to salvage treasures from the apparent wreck of formalism, because it *must* do so. As a philosophy committed to the autonomous existence of objects apart from their various relations, OOO endorses the basic formalist principle of the self-contained object, while flatly rejecting the further assumption that two specific *kinds* of entities – human subject and non-human object – must never be permitted to contaminate each other. This strict taxonomical segregation of humans from everything non-human stands at the center of Kant's revolution in philosophy, rarely for better and often for worse. The present book is meant as a challenge to both post-Kantian philosophy and post-formalist art, on the shared basis that both trends rejected their predecessor doctrine for the wrong reason. OOO remains allied to the formalist ban on *literalism*, though in a different sense from Fried's: one that I will also call "relationism." By literalism I mean the doctrine, or often the unstated assumption, that an artwork or any object can be adequately paraphrased by describing the qualities it possesses, which ultimately means by describing the relation in which it stands to us or something else. Nonetheless, OOO embraces *theatricality* despite Fried's intense – though disarmingly intricate – anti-theatrical sentiments. Stated differently, I will argue for a non-relational sense of the theatrical. I will also refuse Greenberg's unified flat canvas in favor of a model in which every element of an artwork generates its own discrete background.

It is often the case that philosophical books on art begin with expansive scruples about the respective meanings of such words as "art," "aesthetics," and "autonomy." Sometimes this is done with informative thoroughness, as in Peter Osborne's recent *Anywhere or Not at All* (ANA 38-46). While recounting the history of a term is never enough to justify etymological purism, it can certainly help shed light on what is lost through shifting meanings. The Greek word *aisthesis* refers, of course, to perception, and there was a specific historical process through which "aesthetics" came to refer to the philosophy of art, and yet another specific process through which various twentieth-century artists and theorists decided to reject the identification of art with aesthetics. Osborne takes sides in this story, as most others do: "The new, postconceptual artistic ontology that was established – 'beyond aesthetic' – came to define the field to which the phrase 'contemporary art' most appropriately refers, in its deepest conceptual sense" (*ANA* 37). At the same time, he accuses his opponents of a "confusion about autonomy" (*ANA* 37) that can only be cleared up through a historical account of the relation between Kant and Jena Romanticism. This recommendation is not philosophically neutral, since Osborne is inspired by Hegel – as mediated by Adorno – in a way that the present book is not. In particular, I reject Osborne's claim that not Kant but only the Romantics managed to argue for the autonomy of art, and I do so because Kant's isolation of art from conceptual paraphrase, personal agreeableness, and functional utility (as in his chilliness toward architecture) is sufficient to protect art from Osborne's assertion that "most of what has always been and continues to be of most significance about art . . . [is] its metaphysical, cognitive, and politico-ideological functions . . ." (*ANA* 42-3). The obvious downside of Osborne's approach is that it tends to drown what is most distinctive about art – and philosophy – in a swamp of arch disquisitions on mass media and the commodity-form. Art is autonomous for the same reason as everything else: however significant the relations between one field or object and another, most things do not affect each other in the least. Any attempt to explain art in terms of capital or popular culture shoulders a heavy burden of proof in explaining why these outside factors ought to outweigh what belongs to the artwork in its own right. It is not enough merely to assert that "all these relations [are] *internal* to the critical structure of the artwork" (*ANA* 46). Such claims face the doom of what Arthur Danto calls a "metaphysical sandpit" (*TC* 102), as will be seen in Chapter 6.

Nonetheless, to avoid any confusion in what follows, allow me to define briefly what I mean by the terms "autonomy," "aesthetics," and "art." By *autonomy*, I mean that while all objects have both a causal/compositional backstory and numerous interactions with their environment, neither of these factors is identical with the object itself, which might well replace or dispense with much of its backstory as well as its environment. By *aesthetics* I mean something even further afield than usual from its original Greek root: namely, the study of the surprisingly loose relationship between objects and their own qualities. This will be explained in what follows. By *art* I mean the construction of entities or situations reliably equipped to produce beauty, meaning an explicit tension between hidden real objects and their palpable sensual qualities.

This book was nearly complete for many months before I was able to add the final chapters; something in the argument felt wrong, for reasons hard to identify, and the publisher suffered patiently through the resulting delay. I was finally able to finish due to a lucky accident that requires a bit of personal history. In the late 1980s I was an undergraduate at St. John's College in Annapolis, Maryland, a classical liberal arts institution that hosts a stimulating Friday night lecture series. On one of those nights during my junior or senior year, a fiftyish Michael Fried made the short trip from Baltimore to give us a sparkling preview of what would soon become his 1990 book *Courbet's Realism*. Though I remember being blown away by Fried as a speaker, I had no sense at the time of his reputation or significance, and could not have foreseen that his work as an art critic and historian would become important to me as a philosopher many years later. Having long regretted my youthful lack of preparation to fathom the depths of his lecture on Courbet, I made sure to nominate Fried for the visiting speaker series at the Southern California Institute of Architecture (SCI-Arc) in Los Angeles after joining the faculty there in 2016. Less than two years later, the SCI-Arc administration delivered on my wish: Fried arrived on campus in early February 2018 for two lectures and a tireless Saturday masterclass, topped off with a marvelous Sunday talk on Caravaggio at the Getty Museum. It was a rare treat to see this living master at work for the better part of a week. More concretely, from hearing Fried speak and from asking a number of strategic questions, I was finally able to see my way through to finishing this book. He will not agree with most or even much of it, but I hope he will appreciate how his important body of work has sparked yet another parallel line of thought in philosophy. As witnessed by the recent appearance of Mathew Abbott's edited collection *Michael Fried and Philosophy,* I am not the first to owe philosophical thoughts to Fried, and am undoubtedly not the last.

Introduction
Formalism and the Lessons
of Dante

This is the first book to address in detail the relation between art and Object-Oriented Ontology (hereafter OOO), in the wake of a number of earlier publications on the topic.[1] For the purposes of this book, "art" means visual art, though the principles developed here could be exported – *mutatis mutandis* – to any artistic genre. What ought to make OOO's relation to art of especial interest to the reader is that this new philosophy treats art not as a peripheral subfield, but as the very heart of our discipline, as in the well-known OOO call for "aesthetics as first philosophy."[2] But what does it mean for aesthetics to serve as the basis for all philosophy, and why would anyone accept such an apparently deviant thesis? To develop these questions is the purpose of this book.

The title *Art and Objects* was recommended by an editor at Polity, and I could hardly refuse such a straight-to-the-point suggestion. Nonetheless, it could lead to one of two possible misunderstandings. The first is the verbal similarity of the phrase "Art and Objects" to the titles of two other works that lead in different directions from my own. One is Richard Wollheim's 1968 book-length essay *Art and its Objects*, a lucid piece of analytic philosophy not discussed directly in the pages that follow. The other similar title, no doubt more familiar to readers of this book, belongs to the provocative 1967 article "Art and Objecthood" by Michael Fried. This latter coincidence is more important, since Fried unlike Wollheim *has* had a significant impact on my thinking about artworks. Nonetheless, our respective uses of the word "object" have precisely the opposite meaning. For Fried, "object" means a physical obstacle literally present in our path, as he famously complains in the case of minimalist sculpture. For OOO, by contrast, objects are always absent rather than present. OOO's

1

real objects – as opposed to what we call sensual objects – can only be alluded to indirectly; they never take on literal form, and need not even be physical.

That brings us to the second and broader misunderstanding to which the title of this book might lead. Positive talk of "objects" in an arts context is often assumed to mean praise for mid-sized durable entities (sculptures, statues, glassworks, easel paintings) at the expense of what seem to be more free-form art media (performances, happenings, transient installations, conceptual works). In a OOO setting, however, "object" has a far broader meaning than solid material things. For the object-oriented thinker, anything – including events and performances – can count as an object as long as it meets two simple criteria: (a) irreducibility downward to its components, and (b) irreducibility upward to its effects. These two types of reduction are known in OOO as "undermining" and "overmining," while their combination – which happens more often than not – is called "duomining."[3] OOO holds that nearly all human thought involves some form of duomining, and tries to counteract it by paying attention to the object in its own right, apart from its internal components and outward effects. This is admittedly a difficult task, since undermining and overmining are the two basic forms of knowledge we have. When someone asks us what something is, we can answer either by telling them what the thing is made of (undermining), what it does (overmining), or both at once (duomining). Given that these are the only kinds of knowledge that exist, they are precious tools of human survival, and we must be careful not to denounce these three forms of "mining" or pretend we can do without them. Yet my hope is that the reader will come to recognize the parallel existence of forms of cognition *without* knowledge that somehow bring objects into focus, despite not reducing them in either of the two mining directions.

Art is one such type of cognition; another is philosophy, understood in the Socratic sense of *philosophia* rather than the modern one of philosophy as a mathematics or natural science *manqué*. As I wrote in "The Third Table," art has nothing to do with either of the famous "two tables" of the English physicist Sir Arthur Stanley Eddington: one of them being the physical table composed of particles and empty space (undermining), the other the practical table with distinct sensible qualities and the capacity to be moved around as we please (overmining).[4] For precisely the same reason, the celebrated distinction of the philosopher Wilfrid Sellars between the "scientific image" (undermining) and "manifest image" (overmining) cannot do

2

productive work for us.[5] Instead, art like philosophy has the mission of alluding to a "third table" that lies between the two extremes of cognition recognized by Eddington and Sellars. Already, those familiar with Fried will see that art in the OOO sense entails the exact opposite of the *literalism* that he associates with objecthood, though this is a mere difference in terminology that does not yet run counter to Fried's core principles.

It is well known that the OOO program emphasizes objects considered apart from their relations, which cuts against the grain of today's relational fashion in philosophy, the arts, and nearly everywhere else. By "relational" I mean the notion that an artwork (or any object) is intrinsically defined by some sort of relation with its context. In philosophy these are called "internal relations," and OOO upholds the counter-tradition that takes relations to be external to their terms: so that, in all but exceptional cases, an apple remains the same apple no matter the context in which it occurs. Now, to consider an object apart from its relations obviously sounds like the well-known "formalism" in art and literary criticism, which downplays the biographical, cultural, environmental, or socio-political surroundings of artworks in favor of treating such works as self-contained aesthetic wholes. In this connection, I have written some admiring things about the long unfashionable Greenberg, who deserves the title "formalist" despite his own resistance to the term.[6] We will see that the same holds for Fried, who is also a formalist in my sense despite his ongoing displeasure with that word. Robert Pippin's complaint that "there persists a myth that Fried's work is 'formalist,' indifferent to 'content'" certainly hits the mark, but only if we accept Fried and Pippin's definition of formalism as denoting indifference to content.[7] It is true that no one should accuse Fried of suppressing the content of paintings in the way that Greenberg usually does, but I will claim that there exists a more basic sense of formalism than this.

Given OOO's emphasis on the non-relational autonomy or closure of objects from their contexts, it is no surprise that there has been some wariness toward object-oriented thought in those aesthetic quarters where formalism is in low repute, even among those who feel sympathy for us on other grounds. Claire Colebrook, the prominent Deleuzean, worries aloud that OOO literary criticism will merely amount to a continuation of formalist business as usual.[8] My friend Melissa Ragona at Carnegie-Mellon University reacted as follows when I first posted the cover of this book on social media: "Excellent move from the old days of discussing Clement Greenberg to Joseph Beuys!"[9] Some months earlier, the Munich-based artist Hasan Veseli had interrupted an otherwise positive email to express the following reservation about my past writings on art:

> My art friends and I can't understand why you go on and on about Greenberg, although we do get your point (background, flatness). In retrospect it feels that his writings were already assigned an expiration date at the time that he wrote that stuff (probably because of his problems with subject matter, making art just a formalist exercise). Notable critics, from today's perspective, are the likes of Rosalind Krauss, David Joselit, Hal Foster, Arthur Danto . . .[10]

In my continuing fondness for Greenberg, I am outnumbered in the art world by his detractors. Nonetheless, I would respond by saying that there are perfectly good reasons to "go on and on" about him, even if his theories seem linked with a kind of art that lost its cutting-edge prestige a half century ago, and even if some of his theories can be shown to be wrong. The issue, as I see it, is that formalism was at some point simply denounced and abandoned rather than assimilated and overcome, as some literary critics have also argued in their own field.[11] A similar thing happened in philosophy to another theory that stressed the isolation of autonomous things: the unloved doctrine of the thing-in-itself beyond all human access. Here we have crossed into the long shadow of the German philosopher Immanuel Kant, whose three great *Critiques* sounded the formalist keynote in metaphysics, ethics, and aesthetics, respectively. We will see that Kantian formalism, conveniently centered in his recurring term "autonomy," consists of an intriguing combination of breakthroughs and deficiencies. Until the deficiencies are addressed and assimilated rather than circumvented by makeshift means, such as the vacuous claim that autonomy is inherently "bourgeois" or "fetishistic," there is a risk that philosophy and the arts – their fates more closely linked than is commonly believed – will continue to amount to little more than an ironic contempt for formalist claims.[12] I hold that this is exactly what happened in the first post-formalist philosophy (better known as German Idealism) and a century and a half later in post-formalist art. In both cases, important new possibilities were gained that had been foreclosed to formalism, but an even more crucial breakthrough was lost. One of the broadest claims of this book is that there will be no further progress in philosophy or the arts without an explicit embrace of the autonomous thing-in-itself. Moreover, we need to draw the surprising *theatrical* consequences of this point, despite Fried's understandable wish to banish theatricality from art. David Wellbery restates Fried's position with wonderfully flamboyant rhetoric:

4

The (essentially 'theatrical') instigation of a frustrated yearning, a vertiginous sense of transport toward the never-to-be-achieved completion of an additive series, elicits a form of consciousness that is essentially non-artistic. Thought, work-internal differentiation, lucidity, and self-standing achievement are sacrificed for the sake of the *frisson* of a mysteriously agitated, portentous emptiness.[13]

Let us all stand united against "mysteriously agitated, portentous emptiness" – though I still find much of aesthetic value in Richard Wagner's operas, which Wellbery seems to detest. The idea of theatricality defended in this book is not that of histrionic melodrama.

I took up these themes in 2016 in *Dante's Broken Hammer*, a book whose first part is devoted to the *Divina Commedia* of Dante Alighieri, and whose second part challenges the thought of that most un-Dantean figure, Kant.[14] As mentioned, *autonomy* is perhaps the most central of Kant's terms, unifying as it does the chief insights of all three of his *Critiques*. His metaphysics features the unknowable thing-in-itself, unreachable in any direct fashion; opposed to this noumenal thing is human thought, structured according to our pure intuitions of space and time and the twelve categories of the understanding.[15] Each of these realms is autonomous, even if Kant speaks in contradictory fashion of the thing-in-itself as *cause* of the world of appearance, an inconsistency on which the master was hammered by his first wave of converts.[16] In ethics, Kant's commitment to formalism is openly declared.[17] An action is not ethical if it is motivated by any sort of external reward or punishment: whether it be fear of Hell, the desire for a good reputation, or the wish to avoid a bad conscience. An act is ethical only if performed for its own sake, in accordance with a duty binding on all rational beings. Stated in technical terms, ethics must be "autonomous" rather than "heteronomous." Contextual subtleties play no role in Kant's ethics: in his most famous example, lying cannot be justified even when done with the best of intentions and yielding the most admirable results. Indeed, context is what must be rigorously excluded for an act to count as ethical at all.

This leads us to Kant's philosophy of art, another triumph of formalism, even if he does not use that exact word in this portion of his philosophy.[18] Beauty must be self-contained in the same manner as ethical actions, unrelated to any personal agreeableness. Here as in his ethics, what is at stake for Kant is not the art object, which cannot be grasped directly any more than the thing-in-itself, and cannot be explained at all in terms of criteria or literal prose descriptions. Instead, beauty concerns the transcendental faculty of judgment shared by all humans, which serves as the guarantor that anyone of sufficiently developed taste ought to agree on what is beautiful. The same holds for our experience of the sublime, whether it comes in the "mathematical" version of something infinitely large (the nighttime sky, the vastness of the sea) or the "dynamical" version of something infinitely powerful (a crushing tsunami, the discharge of a nuclear weapon). Here once more, Kant holds that the sublime is really about *us* rather than the apparently sublime entity, since the crucial feature of the sublime is that it overpowers *our finite selves* with an experience of infinite magnitude.

Nonetheless, Kant mixes two very different senses of formalism in a way that is fateful, in the negative sense, for modern philosophy and art theory. The important kernel of truth in his ethics should be clear enough: an action whose purpose is to gain rewards or avoid punishment is not really an ethical act, though we can never be entirely sure that any given act is free of ulterior motives. From here it is a small step toward recognizing the substantial truth of his aesthetics: an artwork is not beautiful just because it happens to please or flatter us in the manner of, say, Augustus Caesar reading Virgil's fulsome praise of his dynasty in the *Aeneid*.[19] Nonetheless, I hold that Kant is *overly specific* in his claim as to what must be separated from what in order to establish autonomy. For him as for nearly all modern Western philosophers, the two primary elements of reality are human thought on one side and everything else (a.k.a. "the world") on the other, and it is these two realms in particular that must be prevented from contaminating each other. In my opposition to this sentiment, I follow the French philosopher Bruno Latour's interpretation of modernity, in *We Have Never Been Modern*, as the impossible attempt to isolate and purify two distinct zones called human and world.[20]

At any rate, if the main problem with Kant is his formalist obsession with separating humans from everything else, we know which great figure in intellectual history resembles him least: that would be Dante, who wishes not to separate humans from world, but to fuse them together as tightly as possible.[21] Dante's cosmos is famously composed of *love*, in the sense of someone's passion for something: whether it be good, bad, or downright evil. The basic units of reality for Dante are not free autonomous subjects, but amorous agents fused with or split from the targets of their various passions, and judged by God accordingly. This is the sense in which Kant is the perfect anti-Dante: someone who promotes cool disinterest in ethics as in art, since to do otherwise would meld thought with world when, according to Kant, these two must be kept separate at all costs.

In his admiring critique of Kantian ethics, the colorful German philosopher Max Scheler looks very much like a twentieth-century Dante for philosophy. While Scheler insists Kant is right that ethics must be self-contained and not just a tool to attain certain "goods and purposes," he remains skeptical toward what he calls the "sublime emptiness" of Kant's call to universal duty.[22] Scheler's alternative model displays at least two salient features missing from Kant's theory. In the first place, ethics is less a matter of duty internal to human thought than an assessment of the things that one loves and hates, whether properly or improperly: an *ordo amoris* or rank order of passions.[23] In the second place, Scheler finds Kant's ethics too sweepingly universal, since any given person, nation, or historical period has a specific ethical calling that belongs to it alone. More generally, Scheler's theory entails that the basic unit of ethics is not a thinking human in isolation from the world; rather, the unit of ethics is a *compound* or *hybrid* (the latter is Latour's term) made up of the human ethical agent and whatever they take seriously enough to love or hate. Ethical autonomy thus gains a new meaning: no longer a clean separation of humans from world, but that of any specific human–world combination from all that surrounds it. Note that this does not amount to a regression into what the French philosopher Quentin Meillassoux has concisely termed "correlationism": a type of modern philosophy that focuses on the correlative relationship between thought and world, while denying us the right to speak of either in isolation. For one thing, both humans and the objects they love remain independent of their relations, since neither is fully exhausted by them. And more importantly, the ethical relation between human and object is itself a new autonomous object whose reality cannot be fully grasped by either of these elements or by any external observer. The real embraces us from above no less than eluding us below.

The relevance to art of this ethical detour will now perhaps be clear. It had seemed to me until recently that there was no Scheler-like figure in the arts to critique Kant's aesthetics on analogous grounds. But it now seems clear that Fried is the man for the job. True enough, his concept of "absorption" seems to perform the basically Kantian labor of keeping us at a distance from the artwork through the preoccupation of its elements with each other, resulting in a "closure" that ensures their obliviousness to the beholder. Yet even in Fried's account this is true only for a number of French painters of the eighteenth- and early nineteenth-century anti-theatrical tradition – as theorized by the philosopher Denis Diderot – along

7

with certain trailblazing forerunners such as Caravaggio.[24] For it is Fried himself who has shown that, no later than the work of Jacques-Louis David, it becomes increasingly difficult to read any painting as straightforwardly theatrical or anti-theatrical – and that in the crucial career of Édouard Manet, the need for a painting to face and acknowledge rather than negate and close off the beholder becomes unmistakable.[25]

In aesthetics no less than ethics, Kant insists on the separation of disinterested spectators from the objects they contemplate. It is noteworthy that Greenberg and Fried do it the *opposite* way from Kant, by asking us to focus on the art object while subtracting the human side of the equation. This can be seen in Greenberg's rejection of Kant's transcendental approach to art in favor of something closer to Humean empiricism and, of course, in Fried's vehement if qualified distaste for theatricality.[26] What Kant shares with Greenberg and Fried is the assumption that autonomy must mean one very specific autonomy in particular: that of *humans* from *world*. This probably explains Fried's unease with such recent philosophical trends as Latourian actor-network-theory, the vital materialism of Jane Bennett, and OOO itself, all of them committed in different ways to a flattening of the Kantian human–world divide.[27] The analogy in aesthetics for Scheler's anti-Kantian ethics would be the view that the basic unit of aesthetics is neither the art object nor its beholder, but rather the two in combination as a single new object. Despite Fried's probable hostility to such a notion on anti-theatrical grounds, we will see that he comes surprisingly close to adopting it in his historical work. Though I will end up endorsing something much like the theatricality that Fried condemns, this by no means ruins the autonomy of the artwork, since the compound entity made of work and beholder is a self-contained unit not subordinate to any external practical or socio-political purpose. This admittedly strange result will require that we jettison a number of typical formalist principles in aesthetics, though mostly not the ones that post-formalist art has seen fit to abandon. At the same time, we will be led to some new and important considerations for philosophy.

Chapter 1 ("OOO and Art: A First Summary") gives an overview of OOO aesthetic theory, which conceives of art as activating a rift between what we call real objects (RO) and their sensual qualities (SQ). This will return us to the long unfashionable phenomenon of beauty, which we grasp by contrast with its eternal enemy: not the ugly, but the literal. An examination of metaphor is the easiest way to see what is wrong with literalism, though metaphor also turns out to have a particularly clear *theatrical* structure, and this has important implications for the sphere of visual art no less than for literature.

Chapter 2 ("Formalism and its Flaws") offers a more detailed tour of Kant's *Critique of Judgment*. The goal of this chapter is to pin down the strengths and weaknesses of that foundational book of modern aesthetics, which in most respects remains unsurpassed. I will claim that despite abundant discussion of that book, the basic principle of Kant's aesthetic theory has been ignored more than overcome; for this very reason, it continues to draw us back into its midst, like a black hole capturing fugitive satellites. Among other things, I will claim that Kant's distinction between the beautiful and the sublime does not hold. There is in fact no such thing as the sublime, assuming we follow Kant in defining it as the *absolutely* large or powerful. As Timothy Morton has shown in *Hyperobjects*, there is something deeply anthropocentric about absolutes and infinities: which Kant might be the first to admit, given his surprisingly human-centered interpretation of the sublime.[28] Infinity has recently returned to philosophy in the works of Alain Badiou and his student Meillassoux, through their intriguing shared debt to the transfinite mathematician Georg Cantor.[29] Yet I am inclined to agree with Morton that very large finite numbers are of greater philosophical interest than infinity. Certain kinds of beauty can provide an experience of gigantic finitudes without making an ultimately impossible passage to the non-existent sublime, which is replaced in OOO by the notion of the "hyperobjective."

Chapter 3 ("Theatrical, Not Literal") considers the work of Fried, the most significant living figure in the formalist tradition despite his own continuing rejection of that term. I will claim that Fried's critique of literalism is uncircumventable, though he uses "literal" in a more restricted sense than OOO. Any art that ventures too close to the edge of the literalist crater must find some way to avoid it, at the risk of its dissolution as art: this is the major problem faced by Dada, though *not* – I will argue – with its supposed brother Surrealism. But whereas Fried pairs literalism with theatricality, I hold that the two are polar opposites. Indeed, we avoid the literalist destruction of art in no other way than through the theatricality which alone brings art to life. There is the added complexity that for Fried theatricality is not something that can be straightforwardly avoided, given that there is no art without a beholder. Nonetheless, when speaking as a critic of contemporary art, "theatrical" remains Fried's adjective of choice for works that fail to impress him, and I do not follow him in this usage.

In Chapter 4 ("The Canvas is the Message") we turn to Greenberg, focusing on the limitations specific to his powerful way of thinking. Turning away from an increasingly academic tradition of illusionist three-dimensional painting, the modernist avant-garde had to come to terms with the essential flatness of its medium: that of the background canvas. This shift to the flat background has at least two consequences. The first is Greenberg's consistent denigration of pictorial content, which he tends to dismiss as mere literary anecdote that continues to suggest an illusion of depth. The second, seldom if ever noted, is that the flatness of the canvas background medium is also treated as a *oneness* devoid of parts. On the latter point Greenberg has much in common with Martin Heidegger, that tainted but central philosopher, who often ridicules the surface of the world and its various visible entities as "ontic" rather than ontological. Heidegger also shows a nagging reluctance to conceive of Being as pre-dispersed into numerous individual beings, whose multiplicity he tends to portray as merely the correlate of human experience. It is Greenberg's version of this prejudice that prevents him from grasping the importance of pictorial content.

Chapter 5 ("After High Modernism") considers several of the most prominent ways in which the High Modernism championed by Greenberg and Fried has been rejected. I will focus here on those who do not play a significant role in other chapters of this book. Something should first be said about Harold Rosenberg and Leo Steinberg, two of Greenberg's contemporaries, often portrayed as his rivals. I then turn to the more recent figures T.J. Clark, Rosalind Krauss, and Jacques Rancière; though of necessity my treatment of each figure can only give a rough indication of where my views differ from theirs.

In Chapter 6 ("Dada, Surrealism, and Literalism") we turn to Greenberg's puzzling assertion that Dada and Surrealism are both forms of "academic" art. The problem with treating both movements in the same way is that, although they remain broadly linked in cultural history as overlapping currents of irreverent opposition, by Greenberg's own principles they lead in opposite directions. While the Surrealists retain the traditional medium of nineteenth-century illusionistic painting in order to call our attention to astonishing content, Duchampian Dada offers the most banal content imaginable (bicycle wheel, bottle rack) in an attempt to challenge our sense of what counts as a valid artistic object. Using an analogy from Heidegger's philosophy, I argue that Dada and Surrealism are diametrical opposites in how they go about dismantling literalism, while arguing further that they are not radical departures from the history of Western art.

Chapter 7 ("Weird Formalism") concludes the book. First, we consider the present state of art as surveyed by one well-informed observer: Hal Foster. Second, given that the most unusual claim of the first six chapters is that beholder and work theatrically constitute a new, third object, this chapter asks what the implications of this idea might be. As for the term "weird," it is no empty provocation, but a technical term drawn by OOO from the fiction of H.P. Lovecraft. Weird formalism is a kind that pertains neither to the object nor the subject, but to the unmapped interior of their union.

1

OOO and Art
A First Summary

Let's begin with an overview of the basic principles of OOO, since it cannot be assumed that all readers of this book are familiar with these matters. Object-oriented philosophy hinges on two major axes of division, one of which is usually ignored by our critics and sometimes even our supporters. The first and best-known axis concerns the difference between what OOO refers to as the *withdrawal* or *withholding* of objects. A hammer or candle is present to us, and yet they are also more than what is present to us. Though it may seem that this simply repeats the unpopular Kantian rift between noumena and phenomena, or the thing-in-itself and appearance, OOO adds the crucial twist that the thing-in-itself does not just haunt human awareness of the world, but is found even in the causal relations of non-human things with each other. While it is true that numerous thinkers since Kant have made room for an excess, surplus, or otherness of the world beyond our perception or theorization of it – Heidegger in particular – none to my knowledge have seen that such unformatted residue also exists in relations that do not involve human beings. The second and often forgotten axis concerns the connection between objects and their qualities, which OOO treats as being unusually loose. This counteracts the widespread empiricist tendency to treat objects as nothing over and above the bundles of their qualities, as if "apple" were merely a joint nickname for a set of tangible features bound together by habit, as in the philosophy of David Hume.[1] Joined together, these two axes yield a fourfold structure that OOO employs as a framework for illuminating everything that happens in the cosmos, whether in art or elsewhere. The best way to clarify these points is to begin with two of the most recent great European philosophers: the phenomenologist Edmund Husserl and his deviant heir Heidegger.

12

Heidegger's Insight: The Concealed and the Unconcealed

Kant launched a philosophical revolution with a trio of great works published in less than a decade: *Critique of Pure Reason* (1781), *Critique of Practical Reason* (1788), and *Critique of Judgment* (1790). The subject matter of these books can be summarized respectively as metaphysics, ethics, and art, though the third work also treats of themes in biology. For the moment, let's focus on the *Critique of Pure Reason*. Kant's central idea is his distinction between *phenomena* and *noumena*, also known as appearances and the thing-in-itself, though some scholars draw subtle distinctions between these pairs of terms. Kant sees his predecessors as having been devoted to "dogmatic" philosophy, which means the attempt to provide definitive answers about how reality is by means of rational argument. For example, this might involve attempts to prove that human freedom either exists or does not exist, that physical matter either is or is not made of indivisible particles, that time and space either have or do not have a beginning and an end, or that God must exist or need not exist. Kant covers these four themes under the heading of "antinomies," and concludes that it is pointless to attempt philosophical proofs for any of them, since their solution one way or the other lies beyond the limits of direct human awareness.

Kant's case against dogmatism hinges on his claim that human cognition is *finite*. All human access to the world seems to occur in three dimensions of space and one of irreversible time, and in a framework of twelve basic "categories" that define our human experience of reality: cause and effect rather than random events, the distinction between one and many, and other such rudimentary features of the world as we know it. But given that we are humans, and that we therefore encounter the world in a specific human manner, we have no way of knowing whether the conditions of our experience apply to the world as it is apart from our access to it. Perhaps God and angels experience a world without time and space or devoid of causal relations. Going beyond Kant's own remarks, maybe the same holds for hyper-intelligent alien beings or even for various animal species. Our imprisonment in human finitude means that we must limit the claims of reason; philosophy can no longer be about reality apart from us, or the "transcendent." Instead, philosophy must restrict itself to determining the basic conditions that hold for all human access to the world. Somewhat confusingly, Kant calls these conditions "transcendental," a word so unfortunately close to "transcendent," which we have seen means something entirely different. Whereas dogmatic philosophers claimed to address transcendent reality directly, Kant insists that we have access to the transcendental alone.

It is ironic that, although the career of virtually all major Western philosophers since the 1780s has been determined by their assimilation of Kant, his central idea of the thing-in-itself has been almost universally rejected. The unknowable noumenon has often been scorned as a residual form of Platonism or Christianity that slanders the world of bodies, pleasures, and life-affirming forces that we ought to celebrate instead, as in the philosophy of Friedrich Nietzsche. Yet Kant's more direct heirs, the so-called German Idealists running from J.G. Fichte through G.W.F. Hegel, make an important objection from within Kant's own framework. Namely, if we claim to think a thing-in-itself outside thought, this is itself a thought; seen from this standpoint, Kant seems to commit what would later be called a "performative contradiction."[2] Since thinking a thing outside thought is itself a thought, the distinction between appearance and the thing-in-itself itself turns out to be contained wholly within the sphere of thought. This line of argument is what allows Hegel to claim a new sort of "infinity" for his philosophy, replacing Kantian finitude with an ultimate reconciliation between subject and object through a dialectical movement of positing and negation. German Idealism has influenced many contemporary philosophers, and is most visible today in continental thought in the line passing through Slavoj Žižek and Badiou up through the latter's important disciple Meillassoux. None of these authors has any sympathy for the Kantian thing-in-itself: all of them claim, each in a different way, that the human subject is able to gain access to the absolute. We should note that OOO actively opposes this trend – which it designates as "neo-Modernism" or "epistemism" – and holds that reaffirmation of the thing-in-itself is the key to future progress in philosophy, though rather differently from how Kant imagined. Importantly for the present book, OOO also holds that the elimination of the thing-in-itself forecloses any effort to clarify the nature of artworks, since it robs us of the ability to disarm literalism.

A different way of rejecting the thing-in-itself and claiming direct access to the absolute is found in the phenomenology of Husserl. Born in Moravia in what was then the Austro-Hungarian Empire, Husserl's turn from mathematics to philosophy occurred in Vienna under the tutelage of the charismatic ex-priest Franz Brentano, who was also the teacher of psychoanalyst Sigmund Freud. Brentano's most famous contribution to philosophy was to revive the medieval concept of *intentionality*, which does not refer to the "intent" of a human action, as the term often falsely suggests to beginners. Instead, Brentano's concern was to ask how psychology differs from other sciences.[3] What is most characteristic of the mental realm, he claimed, is that every mental act is directed at an object. If we perceive, judge, or love and hate, then we perceive *something*, judge *something*, love or hate *something*. Now, it will immediately be remarked that we sometimes perceive things that are not really there: we hallucinate, make confused misjudgments, or go ethically astray by loving and hating imaginary things. What, then, is the relation between the objects of my mental acts and any "real" objects that might exist beyond them? Brentano gives insufficient guidance on this question. Intentionality, he says, is aimed at *immanent* objects, meaning objects directly present to the mind, and not – as frequent misreadings hold – at objects that may lie beyond it. Despite Brentano's Aristotelian heritage through his Catholic background, and his temperamental dislike for German Idealism, his philosophy shows a lingering idealist or at least agnostic attitude toward the outside world.

The numerous talented students of Brentano worked to clarify this cloudy point in his teaching.[4] One of the finest efforts in this direction was made by his brilliant Polish disciple Kazimierz Twardowski, in a provocative 1894 thesis entitled *On the Content and Object of Presentations*.[5] The most important claim of this work is that intentional acts are double, aimed both at an *object* outside the mind and a specific *content* inside the mind. Though Twardowski was seven years younger than Husserl, he was initially far more advanced than the latter, who had shifted from mathematics to philosophy relatively late in his student career. Indeed, much of Husserl's early work can be read as a protracted struggle with Twardowski's doubling of object and content. What worried Husserl is that under this model, there was no way to reconcile the two realms in such a way as to make actual knowledge possible: a variant of the issue that bothered the German Idealists when reading Kant. As Husserl put it at the time, how can there be *two* Berlins, one of them a content inside the mind and the other an object outside it? In that case, there would be no way for the two Berlins ever to come into contact, and knowledge of Berlin would not be possible.[6]

This question led Husserl to his philosophical breakthrough, which amounts to a radical idealism despite repeated denials by his followers even today. His solution, namely, was that Berlin itself is purely *immanent*: not because it exists merely in the mind, but because there is no important difference between what is in the mind and what is in reality. The thing-in-itself outside thought is for Husserl an absurd notion;

15

there is no object that could not be, at least in principle, the object of an intentional act by some mind. To speak of Berlin is to speak of Berlin itself, not just of a mental Berlin inside my mind. To be the real Berlin is not to be a Berlin-in-itself beyond access for all thought, and to be the Berlin-for-consciousness is not to be a mere mental figment with no objective correlate. Instead, the real Berlin and the Berlin in my mind are one and the same, both occupying the same ontological space. In short, Husserl rejects Kant's division between noumenal and phenomenal worlds. The major difference between Husserl and Hegel (another famous critic of the thing-in-itself) is that Husserl is far more interested in *objects*, which – despite being immanent in rational thought – nonetheless have shadowy contours and elusive profiles that must be carefully analyzed. This is why Husserl often *feels* like a realist adrift in a world of independent objects in a way that is never true of Hegel, even though Husserl rejects the noumena just as decisively as Hegel himself. Philosophy for Husserl must be phenomenology: not – as for Hegel – because we need to describe the various stages through which the thinking subject passes in becoming aware of the world more concretely, but because the phenomenal realm is filled with translucent objects that can only be illuminated through painstaking description. The world is already there before us for rational consideration, with no "absurd" noumenon lying beyond all possible mental access. Like Hegel, Husserl is an idealist and a rationalist; unlike Hegel, he is fascinated by all sorts of specific entities – mailboxes, blackbirds, imaginary battles of centaurs – that can be understood only when their concrete sensual profiles are analyzed and their essential properties sifted from their inessential ones. We will soon see that there is more to Husserl than this. But first, we should speak of his student Heidegger's effort to challenge and radicalize his phenomenology.

The young Heidegger felt called to philosophy after reading Brentano's early thesis on the different meanings of "being" in Aristotle.[7] He soon learned that Husserl was considered one of Brentano's leading disciples, and by sheer luck Husserl was called to a professorship at the University of Freiburg in Germany, where Heidegger was already enrolled. A close partnership formed between the two, despite their thirty-year age difference, and Husserl came to regard Heidegger as his intellectual heir. But Husserl's expectations would be disappointed, since it was not long before Heidegger put an independent spin on phenomenology. We have seen that the phenomenological method involves describing things as they appear to us, carefully sifting the wheat from the chaff so as to discover by intellectual means the essential features of every object in the world, as

16

opposed to their transient silhouettes as perceived by the senses. But in Heidegger's early Freiburg lecture course *Towards the Definition of Philosophy*, held when he was aged twenty-nine, his decisive break with Husserl is already visible.[8] Our primary way of dealing with the world, Heidegger tells his students, is not through direct consciousness of it as phenomenology holds. For the most part, we deal with things as *equipment*, meaning that we take them for granted unconsciously rather than encountering them sensually or intellectually. For example, the podium in the lecture hall is something the professor normally does not think about explicitly. We could make the same point about the oxygen in the room or the bodily organs of the professor and students, all of them normally invisible unless some environmental or health disaster leads us to notice them. In short, the phenomenal world that is primary for Husserl first arises for Heidegger from an invisible system of background entities. In most cases these are not directly observed by the mind, but are pre-theoretically relied upon or used. Our life-world is filled with equipment, all of it tacitly understood as useful for further human purposes. With this step, the basic assumption of phenomenology is rejected: it is simply not the case, Heidegger contends, that appearance in our mind is the primary way we encounter the world.

Over the next decade he continued to develop this model, culminating in his 1927 masterpiece *Being and Time*, regarded by many – myself included – as the most important philosophical work of the twentieth century.[9] Here, Heidegger gives an even more detailed version of his tool-analysis. A hammer is usually not noticed, but silently relied upon as it works to help us achieve some more conscious ulterior purpose. It helps us to build a house, and the house in turn assists our aspiration to remain dry and warm, which in turn provides support for more intricate family life and personal health. All the items of equipment in our environment are locked together in a holistic system, so that in a sense there are no individual pieces of equipment at all. This situation of unconscious holism can be disrupted in a number of ways, with the most famous such case occurring when equipment breaks or fails. If the hammer shatters into pieces, is too heavy, or is otherwise ineffective, our attention is suddenly seized by this individual utensil. Only at this late and derivative stage does the hammer finally become an individual phenomenon viewed directly by the mind in Husserl's sense.

Over the ensuing decades Heidegger has gained wide influence, and is now taken seriously even in analytic philosophy circles that tend to be allergic to philosophers from the heavily Franco-German continental tradition. Unfortunately, the mainstream interpretation of Heidegger limits his importance by reducing his insight to a trivial form of pragmatism. Heidegger's chief lesson is widely said to be as follows: prior to any theoretical or perceptual access to things, we deal with them through a set of unconscious background practices, one that is holistically determined by our total social-environmental context.[10] But there is a serious problem with this interpretation, and OOO first arose in the 1990s in direct opposition to it. For one thing, it should be clear that our *practical* contact with things is no more exhaustive than our theoretical or perceptual awareness of them. Heidegger is certainly right that our scientific objectification of a fish or flower fails to exhaust the full depths of these things. Perceiving something directly with the mind does not mean capturing the whole of its reality: no sum total of views of a mountain, for instance, can ever replace the existence of that mountain, any more than the set of all organic chemicals exhausts the existence of their key ingredient, carbon. Even if God could see all sides of a mountain simultaneously from every possible vantage point, this would not be enough: for the mountain is simply not a sum of views, as claimed tacitly by the idealist philosopher George Berkeley and explicitly by the phenomenologist Maurice Merleau-Ponty.[11] Quite the contrary: the mountain is the reality that makes all the views possible in the first place. In Heideggerese, we could say that the *being* of the chemical or mountain are not commensurate with any knowledge or perception of them; the mountain is always a surplus unmastered by all our efforts to grasp its properties. And yet, is the same not true of our *practical* dealings with an object? When we use a chemical in preparing a medicine or poison, or when we climb a mountain in a spirit of adventure, in these cases too we *abstract* certain features from these objects, which exist in their full and unexhausted plenitude quite apart from all our theoretical, perceptual, or practical encounters with them.

Another, harsher way of putting it is that the widely celebrated difference between the conscious theory or perception of a thing and the unconscious use of it is too superficial to count as a genuine philosophical insight. Far more important is the unbridgeable gap between the *being* of an entity and any human dealings with it at all, whether they be theoretical *or* practical. Another way of looking at it is that Heidegger, unlike Husserl, unwittingly revives a sense of the Kantian thing-in-itself. While it is true that Heidegger does not usually put it this way, there is a frequently overlooked passage where he directly invites this interpretation. In his important book *Kant and the Problem of Metaphysics*, published shortly after *Being and Time*, he writes as follows: "What is the significance of the struggle initi-ated in German Idealism against the 'thing-in-itself' except a growing forgetfulness of what Kant had won, namely . . . the original develop-ment and searching study of the problem of human finitude?"[12]

But ultimately, it is not Heidegger's own statements that authorize us to interpret his tool-analysis as leading back toward the Kantian noumenon. Thought experiments are often better understood by later figures than their original authors, as is clear from the history of science: Einstein's ingenious reinterpretation of the Michelson/Morley experiment on aether drag comes immediately to mind. As soon as we realize that unconscious practices fail to grasp the reality of things just as much as theory and perception do, we come to see that Heidegger's tool-analysis is not just a new theory of practical reason, but the demonstration of a noumenal surplus beyond all praxis no less than all theory. Furthermore, we must reject Heidegger's claim that the system of tools is *holistic*, with all tools linking together in a totality that is determined by the purposes of some human being. For we must never forget that one of the chief features of tools for Heidegger is that they can *break*, and that nothing would break if it were seamlessly assigned to other tools in its environment. A hammer can break only because it has more features – such as feebleness or fragility – than the current practical system takes into account. While Kant seemed to place the noumena in another world far from human everyday life, Heidegger shows that the thing-in-itself enters and disrupts all thought and action in this world. We are always merely caressing the surface of things, only half-aware that they are more than our theory or praxis takes them to be at any moment. To summarize, what Heidegger bequeaths to philosophy is a model of individual beings impenetrable to the human senses and intellect, but equally opaque to everyday human use. Though he was too focused on the internal drama of human being ever to read his own tool-analysis in quite this way, I believe it would be possible to convince him of this interpretation if he were still alive.

This was the original motivating insight of OOO, dating to the early 1990s. The next one, coming a half-decade later, concerns a point on which there would be no hope at all of convincing Heidegger.[13] For if it is true that no human theoretical, perceptual, or practical encounter with objects can ever exhaust the surplus reality of things, the same is true even of non-human objects in their relations with each other. Ultimately, the rift between things and our encounter with them is not the contingent product of a human, alien, or animal "mind," but occurs automatically in any relation at all. When a stone strikes the surface of a pond, the stone is real, and so too is the pond. Through their interaction, they have either one-way or two-way effects on each other. But clearly the stone does not exhaust the reality of the pond, and neither does the pond encounter the full reality of the stone. In other words, it is not just humans that are finite, but objects more generally. The stone encounters the pond in a "stony" way even if it has no trace of anything like consciousness, and likewise, the pond encounters the stone in a "pondy" way. The same is true of any relation. Critics of OOO are often bothered by this point in particular, because this is where we break with the Kantian framework of modern philosophy, and also where our critics – wrongly – think that we stray into a form of disreputable panpsychism. For on this level we are speaking merely of the finitude of all relations, not claiming that this requires anything worthy of being called mental life.

Nonetheless, OOO does have a certain moral authority stemming from a largely forgotten aspect of the post-Kantian landscape. German Idealism continues to receive lavish praise for demolishing the thing-in-itself, yet it is rarely noted that the noumenon is not Kant's only major principle, and hence not the only one that might have been reversed. The other, more claustrophobic element of Kant's thought is the assumption that the only relations we can talk about must involve a human being. That is to say, for Kant as for his successors there is no way to speak of the relation between fire and cotton, but only of the human cognition of both as the first burns the second. This is the Kantian prejudice that German Idealism unknowingly preserves, despite its self-congratulatory murder of the noumenon. OOO holds, by contrast, that the German Idealist radicalization of Kant was not just contingent, but wrong. What should have happened instead, from the 1790s onward, is that Kant's notions of finitude and the thing-in-itself should have been retained, while simply removing their restriction to cases involving human beings. For in fact, the entire cosmos is a dramatic strife between objects and their relations. The first principle of OOO is now on the table, the only one that most critics bother to take into account: the withdrawal of real objects from all relation. To discover the second, we must leave Heidegger and return to Husserl, doing more justice this time to his misunderstood legacy.

Husserl's Insight: Objects and Qualities

When we last encountered Husserl, his emphasis on the direct mental awareness of objects had just been overthrown by Heidegger's appeal to our mostly tacit dealings with entities in the world (which OOO then developed into a theory of objects withdrawn from their relations with humans or anything else). Most arguments over the difference between Husserl and Heidegger remain stalled on this single point, with one side triumphally affirming Heidegger's maneuver and the other claiming that Husserl already knew about the hidden being of things. The latter camp is simply wrong, since Husserl is perfectly clear in his rejection of any thing-in-itself beyond direct access by the mind, though this is precisely what Heidegger champions if we read him properly. Nonetheless, there is an important side to Husserl that Heidegger seems to grasp only hazily: not the rift between accessible beings and their hidden being, but a different one between beings themselves and their own shifting qualities.

Empiricist philosophers, who urge us to restrict our attention to what we experience directly, have generally been skeptical of any notion of "objects" as something beyond their palpable qualities. For example, Kant's admired predecessor Hume famously treats objects as just bundles of qualities: there is no proof of any "horse" over and above its countless visual appearances, the sounds it makes, and the various ways it can be ridden, tamed, or fed.[14] Husserl's greatest contribution to philosophy, despite his idealism, was to show how much tension is already underway *within* the phenomenal realm between an object and its qualities.[15] Let's stay with the example of a horse: we never see it in exactly the same way for more than a passing, flickering instant. We see the horse now from the left side, now from behind, now from an oblique angle, and at other times even from above. It is always at a specific distance from us when standing, walking, or running, and is always found to be peaceful, agitated, or in some other mood. If we take the empiricist view, then it is never strictly the "same" horse in each of these instances. There is merely a sort of family resemblance between the horse at each specific moment: after all, the empiricist holds that we only encounter a set of qualities at every moment, never an enduring unit called "horse" over and above such qualities. Husserl's view, like that of the entire phenomenological tradition after him, is the exact opposite. Whatever the horse is doing from one moment to the next, however close or far away it is and however subtly different its colors become as the sun sinks toward the horizon, what I encounter is always *the horse*. All its shifting qualities are inessential, and merely pass from one moment to the next in a kaleidoscopic manner. For empiricism, the qualities are all-important and there is no enduring horse-unit apart from them; for phenomenology, there is only the horse-unit, and all its shifting qualities (which Husserl calls "adumbrations," *Abschattungen*) are merely passing decorations atop its surface. To summarize, Husserl gives us a new rift – barely present in Heidegger, outside a few important early traces – between the intentional object and its shifting, accidental qualities.

But there is even more going on than this, because Husserl actually discovered that the intentional object has *two* kinds of qualities. Along with those that pass quickly from one moment to the next, there are also the essential qualities that the horse needs in order for us to keep considering it this horse, rather than deciding it is really something else. In fact, this is the major task of phenomenology according to Husserl: by varying our thoughts and perceptions, we should ultimately come to realize which of the horse's features are essential rather than accidental. Unfortunately, he also holds that the *intellect* grasps the essential qualities of an object while the *senses* grasp the accidental ones: though Heidegger later shows that the difference between the intellect and the senses is simply not that important, given that both reduce entities to presence before the mind. Yet we should not understate the complexity of what Husserl discovers. Although we must reject Husserl's limitation of objects to the sphere of consciousness as being too idealist to account for the thing-in-itself, there is more going on here than mere idealism. What arises in Husserl is a double tension in which the intentional object – such as the horse I perceive in the meadow – has *accidental* qualities, despite being different from them, and also has *essential* qualities despite being different from them, given that an object is a unit over and above its essential features no less than above its accidental ones.

The time has come to restate everything in the standard OOO terminology that will occasionally be used in this book. For objects and qualities, we use the simple abbreviations O and Q. For Heidegger's realm of real objects, withdrawn from all relation and descended ultimately from Kant's noumena, we use R. For Husserl's realm of appearances, which do not withdraw but are always directly present, we do not use the ugly and ambiguous term "intentional," but call it "sensual" instead, abbreviated as S – even though it includes cases of access to things via the intellect rather than the senses. Just as genetics analyzes DNA in terms of the chemical abbreviations G, C, A, and T, OOO has a basic alphabet of O, Q, R, and S, with two types of objects (R and S) and two of qualities (again R and S), with the difference that we allow both R and S to pair with either O or Q, giving us double the number of possibilities found in genetics. Objects can be either present (SO, from Husserl) or irredeemably absent (RO, from

Heidegger, with the proviso that objects hide from each other no less than from us). The same holds for the qualities of objects, which can either be present to the senses (SQ, Husserl's "adumbrations") or forever withdrawn from direct access (RQ, like Husserl's "essential qualities," with the proviso that Husserl is wrong to think the intellect can grasp them directly).

Furthermore, since there are no bare objects without qualities or free-floating qualities without objects, none of these four abbreviations can exist in isolation, but must be paired with one of the opposite type. This yields four possible pairings in all. Let's consider Husserl once more. Though we reject his notion that the real qualities of things can be known by the intellect, we agree with him that real qualities exist: his analysis is perfectly convincing when he shows that any sensual object (such as a horse) has essential qualities no less than inessential ones. In OOO terminology, Husserl shows that when dealing with sensual objects we have both SO-SQ (inessential qualities) and SO-RQ (essential ones). Turning to Heidegger's case, in which the broken tool announces its qualities while remaining forever withdrawn, we have the interesting hybrid form RO-SQ, which proves to be the most important of the four tensions for art. I say four rather than three because we must also speak of the RO-RQ tension, one that is admittedly hard to talk about, since both of its terms are withdrawn from direct consideration. But without RO-RQ, withdrawn objects would all be the same: interchangeable substrata that would differ only insofar as each displayed different sensual qualities at different times to some observer. Since this would preclude any inherent difference between a hammer-in-itself, a horse-in-itself, and a planet-in-itself, there would be no way to account for the special character of each withdrawn object. Thus, the existence of an RO-RQ tension must also be affirmed. Leibniz already saw this in *Monadology* §8, where he insists that his monads are each one, but that each must also have a plurality of traits.[16]

Metaphor and its Implications

We are now ready to turn to art. Although this book deals primarily with the visual arts, there are good reasons to start with a discussion of metaphor, which shows us the workings of art more generally in lucid form. How so? Because metaphor is easy to contrast explicitly with *literal* language, and it turns out that whatever else art may be, it cannot have traffic with any form of literalism. This is the point of closest approach between OOO's theory of art and that of Fried, to be discussed in Chapter 3 below. This does not rule out considering, say, Marcel Duchamp's ready-mades as art, but merely requires that we find a non-literal element in them if they are really to qualify as art.

By *aesthetics*, OOO means the general theory of how objects differ from their own qualities. Given that there are two kinds of objects and two of qualities, there are four separate classes of aesthetic phenomena: RO-RQ, RO-SQ, SO-SQ, and SO-RQ. Generally speaking, RO-RQ is the tension at stake in causation of every type; the old philosophical topic of cause and effect is thus brought for the first time under the banner of aesthetics, where it rightfully belongs.[17] RO-SQ is a less surprising aesthetic tension, the one that deals with our perception of objects under constantly changing appearances and conditions, of the sort that Husserl meant whenever he talked about adumbrations; we will soon see that this tension was noticed by Kant in the *Critique of Judgment* as well, under the name of "charm." SO-RQ, which again owes so much to Husserl, concerns the tension between the objects that appear to us and the real qualities that make them what they are; it is here that we find "theory" in the sense of cognitive understanding. It is only with the RO-SQ tension that we find *beauty*, which I do not hesitate to insist is the domain of art, even if most artists today want nothing to do with beauty, but would rather sidestep that question in favor of some socio-political topic or other, given that emancipatory politics is the great intellectual piety of our era. On this score, the situation described by Dave Hickey in *The Invisible Dragon* has not significantly changed, despite his misleading mention of politics: "If you broached the issue of beauty in the American art world of 1988, you could not incite a conversation about rhetoric – or efficacy – or pleasure – or politics – or even Bellini. You would instead ignite a question about the marketplace."[18] For OOO, the meaning of beauty is not some vague appeal to an ill-defined aestheticism, but is explicitly defined as the disappearance of a real object behind its sensual qualities. For reasons soon to be explained, this always has a theatrical effect, and beauty is therefore inseparable from theatricality – despite Fried's understandable insistence to the contrary.

In any case, the OOO theory of metaphor owes much to an important but neglected essay on the topic by the Spanish philosopher José Ortega y Gasset, who was more widely read during the heyday of existentialism than is the case today.[19] Here I will not repeat my interpretation of Ortega's essay, but will simply present the revised

OOO theory that emerged from it.[20] In the past, I have always used metaphors from renowned poets; this time I will choose a homely anonymous example found at random in a Google search. It comes from a poem that most intellectuals would scorn as sentimental greeting card verse, though it works perfectly well for our purposes:

A candle is like a teacher
Who first provides the spark
That kindles love of learning
In children's minds and hearts.[21]

If it helps the reader to take it more seriously, we can pretend that this is simply the first stanza of a morbid poem by the Austrian expressionist Georg Trakl, one that soon takes a darker turn toward cocaine, incest, and extinction. Let's also simplify the exercise by limiting ourselves to the first line: "a candle is like a teacher." Next, we should contrast this statement with the dictionary definition of a candle. When I enter "definition of candle" into Google, here is what comes up first: "a cylinder or block of wax or tallow with a central wick that is lit to produce light as it burns." For good measure, let's also use Google to look up the definition of "teacher." This is the first result: "a person who teaches, especially in a school." If we combine the two definitions to replace the original metaphor, the result is perfectly ridiculous. Namely:

A candle is like a teacher.

becomes

A cylinder or block of wax or tallow with a central wick that is lit to produce light as it burns is like a person who teaches, especially in a school.

While somewhat amusing, the second statement is not only unwieldy, but utterly absurd. Yes, we might imagine a master poet of Dada who could pull off this line in a poem, and therefore we hesitate to exclude it from art for all eternity. Yet barring the rare appearance of such a master, there is nothing but sheer literality when we read "a cylinder or block of wax or tallow with a central wick that is lit to produce light as it burns is like a person who teaches, especially in a school." Like every definition taken in isolation, this joint definition is structured as a literal identity. But since under normal circumstances the combined identity is patently false, we are not sure what to make of the statement. Though we mentally repel the second statement in the same way that we hold all nonsense at a distance, we do not

25

do the same with the original poem, even if we regard it as cloying kitsch. "A candle is like a teacher" is somehow able to draw us into its atmosphere to a sufficient extent that we take it with at least provisional seriousness. We see immediately that this is not a literal statement of the sort we expect from scientific or other knowledge. But what makes the two cases different?

A literal statement treats objects, explicitly or not, as interchangeable with a list of the qualities it possesses.[22] Imagine speaking with someone who had somehow managed to go through life without ever hearing the word "candle," despite a relatively large overall English vocabulary. In such a case, we could repeat the dictionary definition and instruct this person that a candle is a cylinder or block of wax or tallow with a central wick that is lit to produce light as it burns. This definition gives *knowledge* about what a candle is. It does this by deflecting our attention away from the candle itself in two opposite directions. First, it undermines the candle by telling us what it is made of: "a cylinder or block of wax or tallow with a central wick." Next, it overmines the candle by telling us what it does: "[it] is lit to produce light as it burns." In the effort to instruct our ignorant acquaintance, the candle is treated as purely equivalent to the sum of its physical composition and its external effects on the world at large. The same holds for the definition of a teacher. If somehow our friend also does not know what "teacher" means, we can give him this knowledge by moving in the same two directions. Looking downward (undermining) we find that a teacher is "a person," since human beings are the raw material from which all teachers so far have been made. We can also look upward (overmining) to learn that the teacher is someone who "teaches, especially in a school." Here once more we gain knowledge, and knowledge always entails that an object is replaced by an accurate description of its components, apparent properties, or relations. No aesthetic effect occurs, and hence there is no beauty. We have nothing but paraphrase: nothing but *literalism*. There is no sense of any surplus in the candle or the teacher that goes beyond what we get from adequate definitions of them. Even if these definitions leave out numerous additional details about candles and teachers, we are already on the right track, and cease defining them further only because we have already conveyed enough information for the person to grasp what we mean.

Literal descriptions sometimes fail, of course. It is possible to define a candle or teacher incorrectly, however rare this may be with such widely familiar objects. Yet I remember a moment of youth when someone asked me the meaning of "concierge" and I gave them an incorrect definition: not as an impish prank, but because at that age I misunderstood what the word meant. When this happens, we have simply ascribed the wrong qualities to the object named. We saw this occur earlier in more bizarre fashion when the definitions of candle and teacher were absurdly combined: "A cylinder or block of wax or tallow with a central wick that is lit to produce light as it burns is like a person who teaches, especially in a school." Failure also occurs when we replace just one of the definitions and say either "a candle is like a person who teaches, especially in a school" or "a cylinder or block of wax or tallow with a central wick that is lit to produce light as it burns is like a teacher." Such combinations fail because the literal similarity of candles to teachers is not especially compelling. But this is precisely what makes their *metaphorical* union possible, which leads to some important insights.

Consider the following three statements: (1) "A professor is like a teacher." (2) "A candle is like a teacher." (3) "The demographic makeup of Los Angeles at the time of the 2010 census is like a teacher." Which of these is a good candidate to work as a metaphor? Number 1 is out of the question in most cases, since it is merely a literal statement that points to numerous banal properties shared in common by teachers and professors. With number 3 we have the opposite problem. The two terms appear so unrelated that no aesthetic effect occurs when we hear the sentence: though again, perhaps a poet or comedian of genius could make it work, given the right set-up. Number 2 seems closer to a happy medium, one in which candle and teacher have some connection, though it is not entirely clear what that might be. Perhaps it has something to do with the way that both "bring light" in different senses of the term. But once this is made too explicit, we have again entered the realm of the literal comparison of qualities, and the metaphor immediately falls apart. Imagine the following lines by a poet who should have quit while she was ahead: "A candle is like a teacher, because candles literally bring light to a room, and teachers figuratively bring light to the minds of students." We now have little more than an annoying platitude. For metaphor to occur, there must be a connection between its two terms, but it must be non-literal and should not be made too explicit.

To learn another important property of metaphor, we can simply *reverse* each of the three statements from the previous paragraph and see what happens. (1) "A teacher is like a professor." (2) "A teacher is like a candle." (3) "A teacher is like the demographic makeup of Los Angeles at the time of the 2010 census." In Number 1 there is really no change from the previous version. A professor is like a teacher,

27

and a teacher is like a professor; reversing the order of the terms makes no difference to the palpable if tedious truth of the statement. Since the two objects share similar properties, it hardly matters which is mentioned first. In Number 3 there is also no real difference when the terms are reversed: an already highly implausible description has been flipped around, and it is no more or less plausible than it was in original form. It is still difficult to see any connection between a teacher and the demographic makeup of Los Angeles in 2010; this comes off as merely a failed literal description in which the properties of the two terms do not match. But notice how different things are with Number 2: "A candle is like a teacher" and "a teacher is like a candle" both work as metaphors, even if not as especially brilliant ones. Yet the important point is that the metaphors are completely different in the two cases. In the first, we have a candle that seems to impart some sort of teacher-like wisdom and prudence as we sit with it vigilantly through the night, or something along those lines. In the second, we have something like a teacher who somehow illuminates young minds or sets them aflame, though no such literal paraphrase can ever exhaust the metaphor, any more than a globe can be successfully rendered in a two-dimensional map without certain distortions. In the first case the candle is the subject and somehow acquires vague teacher-predicates; in the second, the reverse is true. Literal description or paraphrase simply compares the qualities of whatever two objects are discussed side by side, and hence the order is easily reversible. In metaphor, however, it is a case of translating qualities from one object to another, and thus it is either a teacher with candle-qualities or a candle with teacher-qualities, each completely different from the other.

This has philosophical importance. Imagine a literal statement of the following sort: "a teacher leads the classroom, prepares lesson plans for each day, assigns homework, grades student performance, and lets parents know how their children are faring academically." We need not interpret this statement in empiricist fashion as just a bundle of qualities. We may be well aware – like Husserl himself – that teachers do many other things besides these, and that the teacher remains a teacher no matter what limited things they are doing at this very moment. If that is the case, then we are already aware of a certain tension between the teacher and his or her currently manifest qualities. In OOO terms, we are dealing with the teacher as SO-SQ, an accessible sensual object with numerous shifting sensual qualities. Yet something different happens with "a teacher is like a candle." Here, the teacher takes on candle-qualities rather than the expected

28

teacher-qualities. We have no clear idea what a teacher with candle-qualities would be like, and for this reason the teacher is no longer an SO teacher presented directly to our minds, but an RO teacher: a withdrawn object, a kind of black hole around which the candle-qualities mysteriously orbit. Here we have the (Heideggerian) RO-SQ tension that is the basis of all art. Even if we know that the sensual teacher is different from his or her sensual qualities, in principle he or she can always be described in terms of an accurate qualitative description. But no such paraphrase is possible when the teacher becomes a real object, one that mysteriously withdraws behind the sensual candle-qualities it is now said to possess. Elaine Scarry is on to the same insight when she tells us of metaphor that "when one term ceases to be visible (either because it is not present, or because it is dispersed beyond our sensory field), then the analogy ceases to be inert: the term that is present becomes pressing, active, insistent, calling out for, directing our attention toward, what is absent" (*BBJ* 96).

But this also raises a significant problem: in what sense do we direct our attention toward what is absent in the metaphor? That which is absent is said to be inaccessible in any direct way to human cognition, like a Kantian thing-in-itself or Heideggerian tool-being. Just the same, it makes no sense to think that an object might withdraw and leave behind purely detached qualities, given our acceptance of the phenomenological axiom that objects and qualities always come as a pair. In the metaphor "a teacher is like a candle," the teacher becomes an RO withdrawn object that leaves behind insistent candle-qualities. And since these candle-qualities cannot attach themselves to a with-drawn teacher, and cannot reattach themselves to their original candle without collapsing into a merely literal statement, there is only one remaining option. Namely, it is *I the reader* who am the real object that performs and thereby sustains the candle-qualities once they are stripped from their usual candle-object. As strange as this may sound, it really just expresses the obvious fact that if the reader is not truly engrossed in the poem, then no aesthetic effect can occur amidst the literalizing boredom. Stated differently, *all aesthetics is theatrical*, as we will see again in Chapter 3 when partially disagreeing with Fried. Nonetheless, the withdrawn teacher does not lose *every* role in the metaphor, since it guides or steers the way in which we perform the candle-qualities it leaves behind in its wake. This becomes clear if we consider alternative metaphors such as "a policeman is like a candle" or "a judge is like a candle." If it were merely a question of the reader performing candle-qualities in place of the absent subject term, then all of these "like a candle" metaphors would be the same, though clearly they are not. One metaphor asks us to perform candle-qualities in the manner of a teacher, another in that of a policeman, and the third in that of a judge. What exactly does this mean? I propose that in such cases, the missing object performs the same role of guidance as the *title* in the case of paintings, poems, or pieces of music. But I leave this theme for another occasion.

At any rate, this is the point at which opponents of OOO generally complain about "negative theology," by which they mean a gratuitous positing of mysterious hidden objects to which no access is possible. But our claim is not that *no* access is possible to the shadowy teacher with candle-qualities. Instead, we insist that one can *allude* to this personage: speaking of him or her indirectly or obliquely, rather than by literal paraphrase in terms of qualities. It is true that we can never attain *knowledge* of the candle-like teacher, since knowledge is always literal mastery of what a thing is made of or does, and we have no idea how to paraphrase a candle-teacher; in fact, we really know nothing more than its name. Here we broaden our point beyond metaphor and expand it to cover any art at all. The minimal negative condition for something to count as an artwork is that it cannot *primarily* be a form of knowledge, whether of the undermining or the overmining sort. This does not exclude the possibility that artworks might also communicate certain literal truths, but it does entail that anything that solely communicates such truths is not an artwork. We gain little from describing what an artwork is physically made of (undermining), and miss the point just as badly if we replace the work with a description of how it affects or is affected by its socio-political context (overmining). For if it is actually an artwork, then it must be a surplus capable of many other possible effects or even of none at all. An artwork, of no matter what genre, is unparaphraseable.

Art, then, is a cognitive activity without being a form of knowledge, which to repeat does not exclude the possibility that artists and beholders can also obtain knowledge from artworks as a kind of side-effect.[23] It is perhaps more surprising that the same is true of philosophy. When Socrates and perhaps some earlier Pythagorean figures spoke of *philosophia*, or love of wisdom, they meant that actual knowledge was attainable only by a god and not by a human. There is no passage in Plato's Dialogues in which Socrates claims to have attained knowledge, though there are several in which he openly declares that he knows nothing. His famous search for definitions of justice, love, friendship, and virtue always fail to obtain the desired definitions. Socrates is not just being ironic when he says that he has

30

never been anyone's teacher, or that the only thing he knows is that he knows nothing. This point has been forgotten largely due to philosophy's jealous modern emulation of mathematical physics, today's model of knowledge *par excellence*. Philosophy has aspired to be like science or deductive geometry in attaining knowledge, even though this is the exact opposite of its mission. After all, knowledge means the literal paraphrase of a thing by its qualities, and philosophy has more to do with objects than with qualities. This is the abiding sense in which philosophy is much closer to the arts than to the sciences, and the opposite assumption is the flawed central principle of analytic philosophy, for all its clarity and rigor.

Aesthetics is first philosophy because aesthetics relies on the non-literal character of its objects, by which I mean that they are unparaphraseable in terms of qualities. Knowledge always amounts to a downward or upward paraphrase, but art – like Socratic philosophy – is not a form of knowledge. That is why the relation between OOO and the arts is so strong, and it probably explains why artists and architects have responded to it even more warmly than other disciplines. For in both cases it is a question of withdrawn or inscrutable objects that need to be approached from the side rather than head-on. The reader now has enough background in object-oriented philosophy to be able to follow its theory of art. Given the importance for us of the debate between formalism and anti-formalism, we turn to the godfather of formalism in aesthetics and everywhere else: Immanuel Kant.

2

Formalism and its Flaws

Given that OOO emphasizes the autonomy of objects from all relations, it has a certain obvious kinship with what is called aesthetic formalism, though this turns out to be more complicated than it seems. Since "formalism" can have different and even opposite meanings in different intellectual contexts, it is worth explaining what we mean by it here. Formalism sometimes refers to an emphasis on "form" at the expense of "content." Whenever this is the case, formalism refers to a theory that tries to "formalize" the structures of a system or situation that hold good no matter what content those forms may contain at any given time; a good example would be the theoretical current known as structuralism. In architecture, "form" is generally opposed to "function" or "program," so that architectural formalism often prioritizes the appearance of a building while downplaying its social purposes, as in the writings and designs of Peter Eisenman.[1] But formalism in the arts always means, at a minimum, that the artwork is taken to be an independent and self-contained unit largely autonomous from its biographical, economic, cultural, and socio-political context. This is why many critiques of formalism have a political basis, and have generally come from the Left, which loves to embed aesthetics and indeed all culture in some purportedly more basic social antagonism. It is often claimed, for instance, that only those with secure or privileged positions in society can afford to play formalistic games with the arts; others, more threatened, must pay special attention to artworks that call for social justice, or which were created by those on the demographic margins of society. From a OOO standpoint, there is no reason to exclude social or political content *a priori* from artworks, and in this respect it is not a formalist doctrine in the traditional sense. Where we agree with formalism is in its view that the artwork, like any object, must be treated to a large degree as an autonomous unit cut off from its surroundings. It does not make rampant contact with *all* aspects of its context, but allows some to enter while rigorously excluding others. If this were not the case, we would reside in a holistic cosmos where everything mirrors everything and all interpenetrates all. More concretely, it would be impossible for artworks to travel between different centuries, nations, or galleries, or even to pass from one minute to the next without being utterly shaken to their cores. I see no reason to adopt such a cataclysmic ontology, no matter how righteous its political implications may currently and falsely seem.

What OOO opposes in formalism is one *specific* aspect of the doctrine to which Kant is committed, and after him Greenberg and Fried. I refer to the formalist emphasis on one sort of autonomy in particular: that of humans from world, or world from humans. Here OOO follows Latourian actor-network theory (ANT) in holding that a great many objects are actually impure human–world hybrids. The ozone hole, animals fitted with tracking devices, or even the Mississippi River – once it was dredged and opened to commerce along its entire length – are all difficult to classify as either natural or cultural. Our significant difference from ANT concerns its implicit tendency to assume that all objects are hybrids, thus *requiring* a human as one of their elements. This sometimes leads ANT to insupportably anti-realist conclusions: as in the infamous claim that the Pharaoh Ramses II cannot have died of tuberculosis, since in ancient Egypt that disease was not yet discovered.[2] Nonetheless, Latour is right that there are countless hybrid objects in the world, even if not all objects meet this description, though I will argue that art itself is always such a hybrid. The point will return later when we consider how Kant's aesthetics – like the rest of his philosophy – requires an artificial separation between humans and objects, and the way this prejudice infects the aesthetic formalism of high modernist criticism.

Beauty

It is rare these days to hear artists speak of beauty, a point which suggests that the insights of formalism have been forgotten along with its excesses. To lose the "sense of beauty," as the philosopher George Santayana terms it in his book of the same name, is to generate a confusion of boundaries between art and something else: usually either political emancipation or a commitment to wry intellectual stunts.[3] Scarry rightly laments the near-banishment of beauty from the humanities in recent decades (*BBJ* 57). Žižek, in one of his more perceptive cultural remarks, observes that the traditional roles of art and science have been reversed:

> One is supposed to enjoy traditional art, it is expected to generate aesthetic pleasure, in contrast to modern art, which causes displeasure – modern art, by definition, *hurts* . . . In contrast, beauty, harmonious balance, seems to be more and more the domain of the sciences: already Einstein's relativity theory, this paradigm of modern science, is praised for its simple elegance – no wonder the title of Brian Greene's bestselling introduction to string theory is *The Elegant Universe*.[4]

From a OOO standpoint, unlike that of traditional formalism, there is no need to exclude all socio-political considerations, jokes, or brute encounters with the real from the sphere of art. Yet insofar as these do manage to enter artworks, they must clear a certain hurdle in order to belong to the world *of art* rather than to political pamphlets, stand-up comedy, or mere scenarios of shock and repulsion. Let us feel no shame in calling this hurdle "beauty," an old but still sparkling term. While the meaning of beauty is often left hopelessly vague, OOO defines it very precisely: as an RO-SQ split, the opening of a fissure between a real thing and its sensual qualities. Since this particular rift is the central topic of all OOO writing on art, the reader can expect it to recur for the rest of this book.

We return now to Kant. His chief ethical writings – *Critique of Practical Reason* and *Groundwork of the Metaphysics of Morals* – are openly formalist through their emphasis on autonomy. In an ethical context, this means that an action should not be guided primarily by non-ethical concerns such as rewards, punishments, or other consequences, all of which make ethics heteronomous rather than autonomous. As we have seen, the wish to avoid Hell after death may count as admirable in religious life and lead to positive civic results, but is not an ethical motivation in the strict sense. While "autonomy" is not a key term in Kant's *Critique of Pure Reason*, it is clearly at work in this *magnum opus* as well, in the sense of the finite human's autonomy from the thing-in-itself and vice versa. As for the *Critique of Judgment*, its topic is not just art, but our ability to judge purposiveness in the world more generally. Thus it is divided into two parts, the first dealing with *aesthetic* judgment (and hence with the arts) and the second with *teleological* judgment (and hence primarily with biology). In Kant's own words: "By [aesthetic judgment] I mean the power to judge formal purposiveness (sometimes called subjec-

34

tive purposiveness) by the feeling of pleasure or displeasure; by the second I mean the power to judge the real (objective) purposiveness of nature by understanding and reason" (*CJ* 33). But artworks for Kant do not actually have a purpose, and merely present us with a *form* of purposiveness. Since the present book is focused on the arts and not biology, we will not be concerned with Kant's distinction between subjective and objective purpose. Yet we will pay considerable attention to another, more famous distinction he makes within aesthetics itself: that between the beautiful and the sublime. It is well known that for Kant the sublime, unlike the beautiful, is a matter of that which is "absolutely large" (the mathematical sublime) or "absolutely powerful" (the dynamical sublime). For now, we need only be aware that "not all aesthetic judgments are judgments of taste, which as such refer to the beautiful; but some of them arise from intellectual feeling and as such refer to the *sublime* . . ." (*CJ* 32).

One of the best-known aspects of Kant's theory of art is the strong role it grants to disinterested contemplation, which alone preserves the autonomy of aesthetic experience from extraneous personal motives. The point is not whether the content of a given artwork is personally likable to us or not. Instead, in questions of beauty we are concerned only with "how we judge it in our mere contemplation of it." (*CJ* 45) If I am asked whether a particular palace is beautiful and proceed, "as [Jean-Jacques] *Rousseau* would, to rebuke the vanity of the great who spend the people's sweat on such superfluous things" (*CJ* 46), then I have missed the point completely. For when it comes to making judgments of taste, "we must not be in the least biased in favor of the thing's existence but must be wholly indifferent to it" (*CJ* 46). Perhaps Kant summarizes it best when he says that "*taste* is the ability to judge an object, or a way of presenting it, by means of a liking or disliking *devoid of all interest*. The object of such a liking is called *beautiful*" (*CJ* 53). Although OOO agrees with Kant that personal interests of every sort must be excluded from aesthetic judgment, it turns out that one pivotal interest is nonetheless required: an interest in the RO-SQ rift between the aesthetic object and its sensual qualities, one that makes it impossible for disinterested contemplation to count as the aesthetic demeanor *par excellence*. This is due to what we saw briefly in the previous chapter as concerns metaphor: the need for the aesthetic beholder to step in and replace the vanished real object. In every other sense, however, we can agree with Kant that "all interest ruins a judgment of taste and deprives it of its impartiality . . ." (*CJ* 68).

Above all, it is important to distinguish taste from what Kant calls the agreeable, meaning "what the senses like in sensation" (*CJ* 47; emph. removed). We are already familiar with the need to distinguish this from the good. For example, when "a [culinary] dish stimulates our tasting by its spices and other condiments, we will not hesitate to call it agreeable while granting at the same time that it is not good [for our health]" (*CJ* 50). Since we can already make such distinctions as this, we are in a position to grasp the difference between the agreeable and the beautiful. As Kant shows in some wonderfully clear examples: "To one person the color violet is gentle and lovely, to another lifeless and faded. One person loves the sound of wind instruments, another that of string instruments" (*CJ* 55). Only a dogmatic boor would condemn his fellows for being fond of the color violet or wind instruments: for when it comes to the agreeable, we all speak for ourselves. Yet in matters of beauty we are not so tolerant: "we permit no one to hold a different opinion, even though we base our judgment [of beauty] only on our feeling rather than on concepts; hence we regard this underlying feeling as a common rather than as a private feeling" (*CJ* 89). Whereas a green lawn or the sound of violins (*CJ* 70) may count as agreeable and hence as belonging to a merely personal sort of preference, the taste for the beautiful excludes all such interest, and therefore must "involve a claim to being valid for everyone . . . a claim to subjective universality" (*CJ* 54). Kant goes so far as to say that "it would be ridiculous if someone who prided himself on his taste tried to justify [it] by saying: This object (the building we are looking at, the garment that man is wearing, the concert we are listening to, the poem put up to be judged) is beautiful *for me*" (*CJ* 55). Whereas the agreeable is a private matter, the beautiful is universal and therefore inherently public (*CJ* 57-58).

We now come to a point on which OOO differs from Kant in terminology while accepting his underlying insight: "a judgment of taste is not a cognitive judgment" (*CJ* 44). What Kant means is that the beautiful is not something that can be determined according to any of the rules or criteria that dominate the other prominent spheres of mental life. Whereas Kant uses "cognitive" to refer solely to the procedures of knowledge and conceptual rationality, OOO uses the word more broadly to include both aesthetics and what we take to be a cousin of the arts: *philosophia* itself. Nonetheless, OOO agrees with Kant that aesthetics is not a matter of the conceptual, which always means the literal and hence the directly accessible. The differences between the aesthetic and the conceptual are both numerous and important, and prevent the attempts of fanatical rationalists – who are still with us today – to wish aesthetics out of existence as a central theme of philosophy. For instance, Kant says that beauty can only be a *feeling* (*CJ* 48). While it is obvious that the agreeable has no concept, being purely personal, the beautiful is universal but *still* has no concept (*CJ* 56). There is no definition, no criterion, and no rule for beauty: "No one can use reasons or principles to talk us into a judgment on whether some garment, house, or flower is beautiful. We want to submit the object to our own eyes . . ." (*CJ* 59). Whereas clean logical judgments can be made in a snap, "we *linger* in our contemplation of the beautiful, because this contemplation reinforces and reproduces itself." Against the often robotic assumption that to "make a science" of any given topic is to improve it, Kant notes rightly that "there is no science of the beautiful . . . there is no fine science, but only fine art" (*CJ* 172). While the Kant of the first *Critique* mocked the need for examples as the sign of a weak theoretical mind, when it comes to aesthetics he insists on their importance: "Among all our abilities and talents, taste is precisely what stands in most need of examples regarding what has enjoyed the longest-lasting approval in the course of cultural progress, in order that it will not become uncouth again and relapse into the crudeness of its first attempts . . ." (*CJ* 147). We might also say something about the respective virtues and vices of art and science. One often encounters a smug triumphalism concerning the precision and reliability of the sciences versus the fuzzy self-indulgence of the arts. Kant answers this sentiment in advance by noting that logical judgments can go wrong no less than aesthetic ones (*CJ* 156).

We have already seen that Kant regards the beautiful – unlike the merely agreeable – as universally binding. But this does not make it "objective," as if beauty were a property of the objects we contemplate. People do "talk about the beautiful as if beauty were a characteristic of the object and the judgment were logical," but nevertheless, "the judgment is only aesthetic and refers the object's presentation merely to the subject" (*CJ* 54). In other words, beauty is both universal *and* subjective. The field that deals with objects for Kant (though not for OOO) is *logic* (*CJ* 45). By contrast, aesthetics "does not connect the predicate of beauty with the concept of the *object*, considered in its entire logical sphere, yet it extends that predicate over the entire sphere *of judging persons*" (*CJ* 59). We can phrase this in terms of the old chestnut about beauty being in the eye of the beholder, as long as we add that Kant thinks all beholders ought in principle to agree. We should also note that Kant means a *human* beholder. For, continuing modern European philosophy's general lack of finesse in dealing with animals, Kant ignores an enormous amount of anecdotal and empirical evidence concerning the aesthetic prowess of birds, beasts, and insects: "Agreeableness holds for nonrational animals too; beauty only for human beings, i.e., beings who are animal and yet rational . . ." (*CJ* 52). Having stated that beauty belongs to all rational animals and *only* to all rational animals, he nonetheless requires that each one be responsible for their own judgments of taste: "Taste lays claim merely to autonomy: but to make other people's judgments the basis determining one's own would be heteronomy" (*CJ* 146).

There is an additional Kantian point about beauty that separates it decisively from anything conceptual: namely, beauty always belongs to an individual experience rather than to a class of experiences. After a sufficient number of years on the planet, many of us conclude that all roses are beautiful. And yet: "if I compare many singular roses and so arrive at the judgment, Roses in general are beautiful, then my judgment is no longer merely aesthetic, but is a logical judgment based on an aesthetic one" (*CJ* 59). Kant returns to this point later, changing nothing but his flower of choice: "Only a judgment by which I find a singular given tulip beautiful . . . is a judgment of taste" (*CJ* 148).

Another loose end concerns Kant's intriguing discussion of what he terms the difference between *free* and merely *accessory* beauty. Free beauty is unconnected to any concept or purpose. He gives some disarming examples: flowers, parrots, hummingbirds, crustaceans, wallpaper ornament, and musical fantasias (*CJ* 76-77). Yet the beauty of other important things is not free, for an interesting reason: "the beauty of a human being . . . or the beauty of a horse or of a building . . . does presuppose the concept of the purpose that determines what the thing is [meant] to be, and hence a concept of its perfection, and so is merely [accessory] beauty" (*CJ* 77). I call special attention to the case of buildings, given that OOO has become especially entangled in recent years with architecture.[5] It is hard to imagine Kant giving this field the respect it deserves: he seems to interpret architectural function as the contamination of aesthetics by ulterior motives. As he puts it: "*Architecture* is the art of exhibiting concepts of things that are possible *only through art*, things whose form does not have nature as its determining basis but instead has a chosen purpose, and of doing so in order to carry out that aim and yet also with aesthetic purposiveness" (*CJ* 191). Although Kant does not openly proclaim allegiance to any particular style of architecture, he does leave a certain number of clues as to his taste. His major concern seems to be that architects must avoid the two extremes of excessive order and disorder. Concerning the first, Kant rejects the widespread belief that regular geometrical figures are inherently beautiful (*CJ* 92). Indeed: "Everything that [shows] stiff regularity (close to mathematical regularity) runs counter to taste because it does not allow us to be entertained for long by our contemplation of it; instead it bores us . . ." (*CJ* 93). As for the second, although he prefers the greater freedom displayed by English gardens and baroque furniture, he concedes that these genres "[carry] the imagination's freedom very far, even to the verge of the grotesque" (*CJ* 93).

Let's speak in closing about Kant's notion of *charm*, so different from the OOO sense of the term as described in my book *Guerrilla Metaphysics*, where it was treated as a close neighbor of the even more important term "allure."[6] Kant's own notion of charm is of great interest to us, both because it shows his surprisingly keen eye for the delights of the sensual world, and because it touches on a philosophical theme of direct importance to OOO. Kant says that charm is at stake, for instance, whenever we are concerned not with beautiful objects, but simply with beautiful *views* of them. Recall that we encountered this distinction between objects and their various profiles earlier, when drawing attention to the sensual world as theorized by Husserl. Kant's version of this concept runs as follows:

> In beautiful views of objects, taste seems to fasten not so much on what the imagination *apprehends* in that area, as on the occasion they provide for it to engage in *fiction*, i.e. on the actual fantasies which the mind entertains itself as it is continuously being aroused by the diversity that strikes the eye. *This is similar to what happens when we watch, say, the changing shapes of the flames in a fireplace or of a rippling brook*: neither of these are beauties, but they still charm the imagination because they sustain its free play. (*CJ* 95; emph. added)

Here Kant makes advance discovery of Husserl's distinction between intentional objects and their shifting adumbrations, defined by OOO as the SO-SQ tension between a sensual object and its sensual qualities. Kant had already come close to doing so in the *Critique of Pure Reason* with his discussion of the "transcendental object=x" as distinct from the thing-in-itself, though ultimately his "transcendental object" is too close to Hume's "bundle" to count as a sensual object in the OOO sense. But in the block-quote passage just cited, Kant gets it right: the constant arousal of a difference between the phenomenal object and its qualities is something very close to beauty without quite clearing the hurdle. He even holds the line on this point with some insistence: "the view that the beauty we attribute to an object on account of its form is actually capable of being heightened by charm is a vulgar error that is very prejudicial to genuine, uncorrupted, solid taste" (*CJ* 71). Now that we have a fairly clear sense of what Kant means by beauty, let's turn briefly to his theory of the sublime, which in recent years has received more than its share of attention.

The Sublime

Having just spoken of Kant's insightful remarks on the difference between charm and beauty, we turn now to his powerful if obvious point that charm has nothing to do with the sublime. As he puts it: "liking [for the sublime] is incompatible with charms, and . . . the liking for the sublime contains not so much a positive pleasure as rather admiration and respect, and so should be called a negative pleasure" (*CJ* 98). Restated in OOO terms, since charm is a purely SO–SQ sensual phenomenon while the sublime has an unmistakable connection with the ungraspable depth of the real, the rippling delights of charm cannot have the least connection with the ominous foghorn of the sublime. Indeed, it is almost comical to try to imagine the differing charms of a tornado or landslide as viewed from separate safe vantage points.

We now discuss the sublime more generally. Kant begins by telling us that "the beautiful and the sublime are similar in some respects" (*CJ* 97). Both are unconnected with any form of interest, and hence are liked "for their own sake" (*CJ* 97). Both must also be singular, in the sense that "starry skies are always sublime" would be a merely logical judgment, just as "all roses/tulips are beautiful" turned out to be. The sublime can only be experienced with respect to a specific experience of a starry sky, not to the entire class of stargazing experiences *a priori*. It should also be obvious that no experience of the sublime can be replaced by a literal description of it, any more than beauty can be replaced in this way. Yet there are differences between the two as well. Most importantly for us: "the beautiful in nature concerns the form of the object, which consists in [the object's] being bounded. But the sublime can also be found in a formless object, insofar as we present *unboundedness* . . ." (*CJ* 98). It is strange that Kant says the sublime "can also" be found in a formless object, as if it were possible to find it anywhere else. For whereas "in the case of the beautiful our liking is connected with the presentation of *quality* . . . in the case of the sublime [it is connected] with the presentation of *quantity*" (*CJ* 98). The sublime for Kant is always that which exceeds us absolutely and immeasurably, and which therefore cannot

40

be bounded without immediately ceasing to be sublime. As he puts it: "the sublime in nature can be regarded as entirely formless or unshapely" (*CJ* 142). In fact, it *must* be regarded in this way.

Another important difference is that whereas beauty is positive, the sublime is always negative, since it restricts our freedom by giving us a sense of being overwhelmed:

> Thus any spectator who beholds massive mountains climbing skyward, deep gorges with raging streams in them, wastelands lying in deep shadow and inviting melancholy meditation, and so on is seized by *amazement* bordering on terror, by horror and a sacred thrill; but, since he knows he is safe, this is not actual fear . . . (*CJ* 129)

One consequence of the amazement drawn forth by the sublime is that while beauty leads to restful contemplation, the sublime is accompanied by an agitated mind (*CJ* 101). "This agitation (above all at its inception) can be compared with a vibration, i.e., with a rapid alternation of repulsion from, and attraction to, one and the same object" (*CJ* 115). Kant holds that the alternating pleasure and displeasure brought about by the sublime both stem from the same cause. For the displeasure "arises from the imagination's inadequacy" (*CJ* 114) in dealing with it, while the pleasure arises from the simultaneous realization of the fact that "every standard of sensibility is inadequate to the ideas of reason" (*CJ* 115). Another key difference is that our experience of the sublime is not universally binding on others the way beauty is. In Kant's words: "Beautiful nature contains innumerable things about which we do not hesitate to require everyone's judgment to agree with our own . . . But we cannot with the same readiness count on others to accept our judgment about the sublime in nature" (*CJ* 124). An odd consequence is that our ability to respond to the sublime depends even more on our cultural training than does our sense of the beautiful. Generally speaking, when an uncultured person is confronted by the sublime in nature, he or she "will see only the hardship, danger, and misery that would confront anyone forced to live in such a place. Thus . . . the good and otherwise sensible Savoyard peasant did not hesitate to call anyone a fool who fancies glaciered mountains" (*CJ* 124). Paradoxically, then, while the sublime seems to be something massive or mighty and utterly beyond human measure, our sense of which situations count as sublime is for Kant largely an artifact of social construction.

We come at last to his famous distinction between the mathematical and dynamical sublime. The mathematical variety pertains to vast size that outstrips us completely: "We call *sublime* what is *absolutely large*

41

... what is large beyond all comparison" (CJ 103). There is another way of putting it: "*That is sublime in comparison with which every-thing else is small*" (CJ 105). We have seen that there are several ways in which the sublime differs from the beautiful, but here we encounter a possibly surprising point they share in common. Given that Kant treats the sublime as something shapeless and overwhelming, com-pletely beyond our ability to grasp it, we might expect him to treat the sublime as *objective* where beauty was presented as *subjective*. But we soon find that with the sublime no less than the beautiful, the object plays no role at all – as we might already have guessed from Kant's point that tourists adore glaciered mountains while the peasants of Savoy merely loathe them. "What is to be called sublime is not the object, but the attunement that the intellect [gets] through a certain presentation that occupies reflective judgment" (CJ 106). And again: "true sublimity must be sought only in the mind of the judging person, not in the natural object the judging of which prompts this mental attunement" (CJ 113). This is true even when we are confronted with "monstrous" or "colossal" objects (CJ 109), such as "shapeless moun-tain masses piled on one another in wild disarray, with their pyramids of ice, or the gloomy raging sea" (CJ 113). Yet no matter how far we venture toward the infinite, Kant assures us that the infinite is really a matter of our own mental power in pointing toward it. In this way, he exposes himself to the critical force of Morton's observation that large finite numbers are actually more threatening than infinite ones. As Morton puts it: "There is a real sense in which it is far easier to conceive of 'forever' than very large finitude. Forever makes you feel important. One hundred thousand years makes you wonder whether you can imagine one hundred thousand anything."[7]

With the dynamical sublime, we turn from absolute size to absolute power. Naturally, we cannot experience this if the absolute power is one that currently threatens us; in that case our attention is swal-lowed up by our terrified interest in personal safety, leaving no room for sublimity at all. In Kant's words: "When in an aesthetic judgment we consider nature as a might that has no dominance over us, then it is *dynamically sublime*" (CJ 119). And further: "We can ... consider an object *fearful* without being afraid *of* it, namely, if we judge it in such a way that we merely *think* of the case where we might possibly want to put up resistance against it, and that any resistance in that case would be utterly futile" (CJ 119-120). But from the moment we take something to be a serious threat, we have left the realm of the sublime. Just as beauty must exclude all personal interest, the sublime must exclude all personal fear (CJ 120).

42

OOO and Kantian Formalism

To bring this chapter to a close, let's summarize the major points of agreement and disagreement between OOO and Kant's *Critique of Judgment*, the foundational work of aesthetic formalism. The first point of agreement – though we have already hinted at a significant qualification – is that beauty has nothing to do with personal interest. That is to say, our judgment of quality should not be swayed by considerations of what is merely agreeable to us. On a related point, OOO agrees with the Kantian claim – as seen in his dismissal of Rousseau's political rejection of a palace – that works of art cannot be judged primarily in terms of their beneficent or malevolent socio-political effects. Numerous important artists have been of a reactionary, racist, or criminal cast of mind. In some cases, this has done permanent damage to their legacies, while in others the effect on reputation has been more limited. Formalism will always have a tendency to downplay the moral or political credentials of works and their authors. The primary difference in OOO is that it does not exclude political or other external factors *a priori* from judgments of an artwork, and argues only that the work itself acts in such a way as to admit or exclude external forces of various sorts.

OOO also agrees with Kant that aesthetic judgments are not primarily intellectual in character. The sole difference on this point is terminological: whereas Kant says that aesthetic judgments are not "cognitive," OOO would say that art is cognitive without being conceptual. Despite the difference in terms, the same thing is meant: there can be no science of beauty. In other words, there are no principles of beauty that can be stated in clear prose terms; if there were, it would be possible to use these principles to create outstanding works of art simply by following them diligently, an absurd expectation refuted by all experience. If this were the case there would be infallible teachers of aesthetics, able to turn students into artistic giants at will: a point refuted for similar reasons by Socrates in Plato's *Meno* when denying the existence of teachers of virtue.[8] One cannot say, for example, that great art must be symmetrical, or asymmetrical, or some perfect mixture of the two. We cannot even assent to Aristotle's dictum that great drama must be unified as to action, time, and location, since there are too many great counterexamples that ignore these very rules.[9] Nor can we say that great art ought to exemplify moral virtues, though Kant himself seems to brush up against such a claim in his Third Critique (*CJ* 232). There is nothing the least bit moral about

43

the writings of Sade or even the paintings of Picasso. If many continue to view Lovecraft as a hack pulp horror writer, this lives or dies on the question of inherent aesthetic merit rather than any consideration of his repellently racist views.[10]

Our major departure from Kantian formalism is as follows. Kant clearly states that beauty has nothing to do with the object, but only with the transcendental faculty of judgment shared by all human beings. Here the "subject" side of the world is cleanly severed from the "object" side, in accordance with the basic taxonomical distinction of modern philosophy that treats these two as mutually dangerous animals that must never be placed in the same cage. In one sense it is true that Kant is a "correlationist" – to use Meillassoux's term – who holds that we can never speak of humans without world or world without humans, but only of a primordial correlation between the two.[11] I agree that this assumption remains an obstacle to philosophical progress. Nonetheless, the problem with correlationism is not – as Meillassoux holds – that two things are combined so that we never have either in pure form. Instead, the problem is that the primary correlation at the basis of philosophy is taken to consist of *two* and *only two* entities, one of them mind and the other world: with the latter category sloppily including all the trillions of kinds of non-human entities. How absurd that *here alone* no combination should be permitted: as if human plus world were utterly different in kind from any other compound, whether hydrogen plus oxygen, or the meeting of the Eurasian and North American tectonic plates. This is the point where Latour rightly criticizes Kant for the opposite reason: an excessive *purification* of thought from world, not an impermissible mixing of them.[12]

Please note that the problem is not just that Kant views aesthetics as "subjective" rather than "objective," as if we merely needed to reverse the polarity to set things right. For it turns out that Fried and Greenberg already perform this very reversal without addressing the root of the problem: Greenberg by favoring Hume's "empirical" approach over Kant's "transcendental" one, and Fried by demanding that human theatricality be banished as much as possible from art. Here the same difficulty remains: it is still assumed that this single mixture of subjective and objective poles is enough to ruin aesthetic experience. OOO's rather different approach is to treat the artwork as a *compound*, one that always contains the human being as an essential ingredient. Then how can OOO claim to be formalist at all, given our insistence that the artwork cannot be autonomous from humans?[13] Does this leave us with just another post-formalist *rela-*

tional theory of art, as advocated by Nicolas Bourriaud?[14] The answer is that we draw an important distinction between the human being as an *ingredient* of art and as a privileged *beholder* of it. The autonomy of artworks does not mean that they would remain artworks even if all humans were exterminated, any more than hydrogen alone would still count as water if all oxygen were sucked from the cosmos. What it does mean is that, despite being a necessary ingredient of every artwork, the human beholder cannot exhaustively grasp the artwork of which he or she is the ingredient. Consider the following worry, as expressed by Moran:

> unlike mathematics or morality, the artwork is defined by internal requirements which themselves include a relation to some beholder . . . [and] this inclusion threatens to compromise the very idea of aesthetic autonomy, as if aesthetic autonomy and independence themselves included a fatal dependency, and among art's internal requirements themselves was a necessary relation to something outside it.[15]

My response is that the artwork is actually a compound made up of myself along with the independent object outside me that common sense thinks of as the artwork. This compound exceeds both parts individually and is not exhaustively knowable by the human beholder who forms part of it. Rembrandt's *Nightwatch* is not a painting if no one experiences it, yet it does not follow that *Nightwatch* is nothing more than whatever I or some other person might make of it; this is enough to ensure its autonomy, despite its need for a beholder. One implication of the human ingredient in art is that theatricality must not be excluded from aesthetics, but is one of its necessary conditions. Among other things, this entails that OOO does not share formalism's usual *a priori* hostility to performance art, conceptual art, land art, "happenings," interactive installations, or other hybrid genres that have flourished since the 1960s at the expense of more traditional media. There can certainly be junk performance and banal conceptual or land art, just as there is kitsch painting and sculpture. But this must be determined on a case-by-case basis, never by dismissing entire genres: as Greenberg and Fried themselves emphasize in principle, if not always in critical practice.

What remains to be considered is what to make of Kant's distinction between the beautiful and the sublime. An important objection to OOO on this point has been penned by Steven Shaviro, always the most fair-minded and stimulating critic of object-oriented thought. He does so in a wonderful article entitled "The Actual Volcano," in which he defends his favorite philosopher Whitehead against OOO;

45

I answered his charges at the time in an accompanying piece.[16] The point of contrast between the two philosophies could hardly be more obvious: while OOO argues for a non-relational model of objects, Whitehead contends that a non-relational object would be a mere "vacuous actuality."[17] Actual entities, he says, must be analyzed into their relations, which he terms "prehensions." Much of the disagreement bears on ontology rather than art, and can be left aside for now. What makes Shaviro's discussion relevant to art is that he defends Whitehead's emphasis on beauty against what he takes to be OOO's obsession with the sublime. To begin with, I find Whitehead's account of beauty unsatisfying in its own right. Namely, he defines beauty as a matter of "patterned contrasts": a shot in the night that strikes a mixture of deserving and undeserving targets. The theory of beauty-as-patterned-contrasts faces immediate difficulties, since it implies without qualification that (a) *all* patterned contrasts are beautiful and (b) *only* patterned contrasts are beautiful. The former claim is obviously wrong, since there is nothing inherently beautiful about a patterned contrast of rich and poor neighborhoods across a large urban area, or a map of bomb damage in a wartime nation. Whitehead would need to add a qualifying condition to tell us exactly *which* patterned contrasts lead to beauty. But I am equally skeptical of the latter claim that *only* patterned contrasts can be beautiful, since this excludes *a priori* such art as minimalist sculpture or an Ad Reinhardt black square (the more famous one of Kasimir Malevich at least shows minimal contrast between the square and its white border). While it is certainly possible to critique such works for their lack of internal diversity, it is not clear that they fail – if they do – through their lack of either patterns or contrasts.

More interesting for us is the way Shaviro links Whitehead's theory with beauty while identifying OOO with the sublime. Shaviro's key passage is worth quoting at length:

> The difference between Whitehead and Harman is best understood, I think, as a difference between the aesthetics of the beautiful and the aesthetics of the sublime. Whitehead defines beauty as a matter of differences that are conciliated, adapted to one another, and "interwoven in patterned contrasts," in order to make for "intense experience." Harman, for his part, appeals to notions of the sublime: although he never uses this word, he refers instead to what he calls allure. This is the attraction of something that has retreated into its own depths. An object is alluring when it does not just display particular qualities, but also insinuates the existence of something deeper, something hidden and inaccessible, something that cannot actually be displayed. Allure is

properly a sublime experience, because it stretches the observer to the point where it reaches the limits of its power, or where its apprehensions break down. To be allured is to be beckoned into a realm that cannot ever be reached.

It should be evident that beauty is appropriate to a world of relations, in which entities continually affect and touch and interpenetrate one another; and that sublimity is appropriate to a world of substances, in which entities call to one another over immense distances, and can only interact vicariously.[18]

Shaviro goes on to claim that the sublime has already been thoroughly exploited by aesthetic Modernism, and that the new landscape of the twenty-first century would benefit from an aesthetic return to beauty instead. My first complaint is that he provides no demonstration of the supposed link between the sublime and Modernism, and hence is unable to prove that OOO is working an already exhausted mine. But that is less important than another consideration. Namely, even if we were to concede Shaviro's historical point that Modernism is too much about the sublime, what makes him so sure that OOO itself is connected with it? It is certainly true that allure occurs for OOO when an object "does not just display particular qualities, but also insinuates the existence of something deeper, something hidden and inaccessible, something that cannot actually be displayed." It might also seem true that this holds for the Kantian sublime, whose absolute largeness or power entails a formlessness that does not display particular qualities and cannot be directly accessed. Yet Shaviro's account omits a crucial difference between the two philosophies. For although the OOO object is deep and hidden and cannot be displayed, it is by no means quantitatively or qualitatively "absolute," as seen from my agreement with Morton that the finitude of hyperobjects is more pertinent than absolutes.

In fact, OOO does not really distinguish between the beautiful and the sublime at all. Rather, it could be said that the alluring real object has features of both. For OOO as for Kant, beauty always appears in the case of a *specific* thing, despite Kant's further argument – which I have rejected – that beauty lies in our judgment rather than in the object itself. And for OOO as for Kant, there is an inexhaustible depth to the world that never takes on fully palpable form. What we deny is that there are two different *kinds* of experience, one of the beautiful and the other of the sublime. From the object-oriented standpoint, aesthetics must treat the apples of a still life and the awesome power of a tsunami in precisely the same way.

47

3

Theatrical, Not Literal

It is still common to hear blanket dismissals of Greenberg, of whom Fried rightly states: "I am not alone in regarding [him] as the foremost art critic of the twentieth century" (*AO* xvii). If someone is a plausible candidate for the foremost critic in one of the most eventful centuries in art history, and was nonetheless subject to professional ostracism well before that century had ended, we are faced with an intellectual puzzle. A related puzzle is presented by Fried himself. Despite his close intellectual and – at one time – personal connection with Greenberg, and his staunch defense of a conception of art almost equally at odds with post-1960s fashion, Fried has never quite been met with the extremes of derision with which the deceased Greenberg is still booed off the stage. I am not entirely sure why this is so, though it may be because Fried's reputation is based only in part on the High Modernist criticism that earned Greenberg several generations of artistic enemies. Although Fried is hardly less blunt in expressing his critical views than was Greenberg at his peak, he is also the author of a respected art-historical trilogy, and of later books that extend his ideas back in time to Caravaggio and his school.[1] And while these historical books do cover themes related to his more acerbic early critical work, they deal with the pre-history of Modernism; this puts him at a safer remove from the present than Greenberg, who focused his often savage attention on the latest exhibitions of sensitive living artists rather than distant historical figures. There is also the fact that Fried has turned his attention once more to important contemporary artists, including photographers, and in a more optimistic spirit than previously. This recent nod to contemporary art may partly redeem him in the eyes of some opponents.[2] Whatever the reasons, I have never been hissed when mentioning Fried's name in public, though

48

this did happen once when I uttered the words "Clement Greenberg" during a lecture.[3]

Turning now to Fried in his own right, his career-long engagement with the paired themes of "absorption" and "theatricality" is of the greatest importance not just for art history, but for philosophy as well. Though he means absorption and theatricality as opposite terms, his historical works interweave them in ways that are sometimes difficult to pin down. In any case, the deep importance of these two concepts makes Fried's collected works among the most important intellectual resources of recent decades. But since I continue to call Fried a "formalist" despite his impatience with those who do so, let's begin by tackling this topic head-on. One of his clearest rejections of this label comes early in *Courbet's Realism*, the second book of his widely read Diderot–Courbet–Manet trilogy:

> I don't think of my approach in this book (or in *Absorption and Theatricality*) as in any sense "formalist," an epithet that has tended mechanically to be affixed to my work ever since the 1960s when I wrote about recent abstract painting and sculpture in terms of particular issues that, having come to the fore in the abstract painting and sculpture of the immediate past, were inevitably issues of abstraction. Basically, I understood formalism in art history or art criticism to imply an approach in which: (1) considerations of subject matter are systematically subordinated to considerations of "form," and (2) the latter are understood as invariable or transhistorical in their significance (the second of these points is often left implicit). (*CR* 47)

The subtext of this passage is that by the criteria listed here, Greenberg *is* a formalist, and thus Fried takes a distance from his former close associate. I find this attitude more justified on the first point than the second. For as concerns point 1, it is clear that Fried has a superior capacity for dealing with subject matter. Whereas Greenberg tends to suppress the content of artworks altogether, to the point of rarely having anything illuminating to say about it, Fried gives us marvelous interpretations of pictorial detail ranging from subtleties of clothing, to the exact position of tea cup handles, to the way a pig's floppy ears cover its eyes. On a related note, Greenberg is relatively useless when discussing any art prior to Manet or after Jules Olitski, who mark roughly the beginning and provisional end of modernist art in his conception. By contrast, Fried's focus on absorption rather than flatness allows him to range as far back as Caravaggio and as late as the Albanian video artist Anri Sala (b. 1974), and one has the sense Fried still plans to move further in both temporal directions. But as for Fried's point 2, although he often claims that Greenberg was wrongly committed to a trans-historical principle of flatness in art, and while this conception has influenced such admirers of Fried as the well-known Hegel scholar Pippin, I think this interpretation is misleading for reasons to be discussed below.[4]

In short, I gladly admit that Fried is not a formalist in his own sense of the term, since he is a great master at handling subject matter and also has a keen historical sense of how art has developed. Yet there is a more obvious sense of formalism that fits Fried perfectly. In the Introduction to *Absorption and Theatricality*, addressing those who view the painting of eighteenth-century France through its relations to the declining *Ancien Régime* and the rising bourgeoisie, Fried adopts an elegant if familiar position: "I should also say that I am skeptical in advance of any attempt to represent [the] relationship [between painting and beholder] and [the 'internal' development of the art of painting] as essentially the products of social, economic, and political forces defined from the outset as fundamental in ways that the exigencies of painting are not" (*AT* 5). This is not to say that Fried wishes to do the opposite and subsume all politics under aesthetics: in his Courbet book he tells us he "wants no part" of such a claim (*CR* 255). But by insisting on the relative autonomy of painting's internal development from socio-political factors, Fried invites the ire of those full-time political moralists who have flooded the humanities, and who solemnly reject claims for the autonomy of art from politics as a grave failure of human obligation. To this extent, I salute Fried as a formalist in the beneficial sense. But for the purposes of this book, there is an even more important sense in which he is a formalist, and it is one that OOO considers harmful. I refer again to the Kantian formalism that insists on separating two and only two terms: (1) humans, and (2) everything else. We need only consider Fried's key opposition between absorption and theatricality, the former usually treated as good and the latter as bad. For it will turn out that absorption and theatricality would be one and the same if not that Fried separates them by means of Kantian formalism, even if his historical work shows how difficult it is to know whether a given painting is theatrical or not.

But let's take a few steps back to Fried's famous 1967 essay "Art and Objecthood," which continues to capture attention even if it has few ardent defenders among younger artists. Its key terms "literalism" and "theatricality" are no longer at the explicit center of aesthetic debate, though I will try to place them near the center of philosophy. The essay's attack on Minimalist art also still manages to feel contemporary, though the face-off it stages between Modernism and an early brand of Postmodernism might have made it seem like a period piece by now. The probable reason that "Art and Objecthood" still seems fresh today is that its arguments were merely sidestepped rather than overcome. Looking back at his article from a distance of nearly three decades, Fried writes in 1996 that "the *terms* of my argument have gone untouched by my critics, an unusual state of affairs in light of the antagonism 'Art and Objecthood' has provoked." (43) In what follows, I too will accept the terms of Fried's argument, though without quite leaving them untouched. The reader might expect me to focus on Fried's use of the term "object," but this point is actually of little interest, given that Fried (like Heidegger) simply uses this word in the opposite sense from OOO's own. It is a different matter with "literalism" and "theatricality," two terms that have also become central for Object-Oriented Ontology thanks to Fried's article. But whereas for Fried the two have the same meaning, OOO sees them as opposites, or even as the twin sisters – one good, one evil – that we might encounter in a fairytale.

Art and Objecthood

Fried often uses the term "literalist" to describe the kind of art that most everyone else calls "Minimalist," Greenberg included. Here I will follow the mainstream terminology and speak of Minimalism: not just because this usage is more widely known, but because "literalist" has another, less restricted meaning for Fried that we will also have cause to employ. "Art and Objecthood" appeared in *Artforum* in 1967. Since this sounds like a late date for High Modernism, it might be thought that Fried was attacking Minimalism in the spirit of a rear-guard action. He assures us that this was not so: "today it is often assumed by writers who weren't actually there that with the advent of Minimalism in the mid 1960s the high modernist group was put on the defensive – in fact 'Art and Objecthood' is sometimes read in that light. But the mood in 1967-68, artistically speaking, was distinctly upbeat [for modernists]." (13) As evidence of this, Fried mentions going in the same year to see Kenneth Noland's first horizontal stripe paintings, along with his general awareness of Anthony Caro's modernist masterwork *Prairie* and his burgeoning new genre of table sculptures, as well as the then-recent spray paintings of Olitski. We know that Noland, Caro, and Olitski were also great favorites of Greenberg; Fried omits any mention here of his Princeton undergraduate friend Frank Stella, the contemporary artist about whom he

51

and Greenberg disagreed most. But if the mood in Fried's Modernist circles in 1967-68 was still upbeat, he admits that the situation soon changed for the worse, leading in short order to his abandonment of criticism in favor of art history. For we will see that Fried is nothing if not anti-theatrical, and "no one with even the sketchiest awareness of recent history needs to be told that 'theatricality,' not just in the form of Minimalism, went on to flourish spectacularly while abstraction in my sense of the term became more and more beleaguered" (*AO* 14). Here he refers in particular to the 1970s and 1980s, though even in 2019 art remains saturated by a spirit of theater in the sense he detests.

As Fried sees it, Minimalism is not a random accident that occurred on the outside of advanced art; it came to High Modernism from within, like an autoimmune disease. Unlike Pop or Op art, he says without elaborating, the "seriousness [of Minimalism] is vouched for by the fact that it is in relation both to modernist painting and modernist sculpture that literalist art defines or locates the position it aspires to occupy" (*AO* 149). This makes it a form of "ideology" (*AO* 148), by no means a compliment coming from Fried. Yet however "ideological" the Minimalists may or may not be, Fried is right that they overlap with Modernism on some important points. For instance, they share Greenberg's concerns about the pictorial illusion of three-dimensional space that dominated Western painting from Cimabue and Giotto until at least Manet. Fried quotes leading Minimalist Donald Judd as sounding like a zealous Greenbergian when Judd expresses a wish to "[get] rid of the problem of illusionism and of literal space ... which is riddance of one of the salient and most objectionable relics of Western art" (*AO* 150). The difference is that Judd seems to think that painting *per se* is inherently guilty of illusionistic contamination, which Greenberg and Fried do not, being intensely devoted to the continued good fortune of such painters as Morris Louis, Noland, and Olitski.

But an even more interesting topic here is *relationism*, a theme that is central not only for the Minimalists, but for Kant, Greenberg, and Fried (who do not make use of the term), and more explicitly for OOO. We saw in the previous chapter that Kantian formalism, in aesthetics no less than ethics and metaphysics, is centered in the notion of *autonomy*. While a "heteronomous" ethics or aesthetics would relate these fields to some external function – rules, rewards, and punishments for ethics, agreeable sensations for aesthetics – autonomy requires the opposite procedure. In Kant's case we saw that aesthetics was located in the faculty of judgment shared by all human beings, quite apart from the object itself. Greenberg and Fried invert this position and prioritize the object side over the subject side, though without rejecting Kant's demand for the autonomy of one from the other. Ultimately, to speak of autonomy is to speak of something that has reality apart from its relations, as in Kant's unpopular model of the thing-in-itself or OOO's withdrawn objects. At first glance, the Minimalists also seem to be anti-relationists, since Judd complains about the inherent relationality of painting no less than about its illusionism. But this is misleading. While the Minimalists do wish to exclude any relations between the separate parts of an artwork, this is only so that they can better focus their attention on the artwork's relation *to us* when encountered in a specific situation. And that is precisely Fried's complaint when he condemns the theatricality of the Minimalists. Aimed solely at provoking a reaction from the beholder, theatricality abandons the internal complexity of the artwork and replaces it with something whole, single, and indivisible: such as a simple white cube or wooden rod (*AO* 150). Against this excessive internal simplicity that screams out for relation with a beholder, Fried prefers the Modernist sculpture of Anthony Caro, which he famously describes as "syntactic" due to the "inflections" and "juxtapositions" of its individual components (*AO* 161). Caro's syntax of sculptural elements engaged in mutual relation is opposed by the Minimalists for its supposed anthropomorphism: a charge that Fried will throw back in their faces, given their evident craving for a theatrical relation with the beholder.

Although Fried emphasizes the problem of literalism by using the very name "literalist" to describe the practitioners of Minimalist art, it is striking how seldom he mentions this term in his article in comparison with "theatrical." Clearly, he is much more impassioned about this latter enemy. We have already seen that the literal must be the mortal enemy of any formalist approach to art – such as Kant's – and that the literal amounts in effect to the *relational*, given that the literal meaning of anything is always a meaning for someone or something, thereby effacing its autonomy. And while Fried like Greenberg engages in plenty of self-distancing from the term "formalist" (*AO* 19), the work of both critics makes sense only as a continuation of the Kantian insistence on the autonomy of aesthetics from all that threatens it: personal interest, subjective preference, situational context, conceptual justification, linguistic paraphrase. Despite their surface diversity, all these anti-Kantian aesthetic principles can be summarized as relational conceptions of art. Recalling our earlier example, when a candle is defined literally as "a cylinder or block of wax or tallow with a central wick that is lit to produce light as it burns," this gives us not what the candle is in its own right, but only its relations with its parts and its effects. By contrast, the candle that appeared in metaphor was figurative: a kind of "third candle" irreducible to either its components or its uses. Thus the *literal* is the true death of art, a role that Fried will ascribe instead to the theatrical, which he takes to be its deadlier synonym.

In fact, Fried speaks of the literal in his essay almost solely in connection with a single topic: that of *shape*. The theme is of great importance to him, not least because "shape" is the point on which he first found his own footing as a critic, independent of the older Greenberg, who did not emphasize it to the same degree. This can be seen most easily in Fried's greater appreciation for the work of his friend Stella, who did not look like a great innovator from Greenberg's standpoint. As Fried would put it in 1996: "['Shape as Form: Frank Stella's New Paintings'] was an important piece for me, because in it for the first time I took issue with Greenberg's theorization of modernism . . ." (*AO* 11). For Greenberg, as we will see, the key to modern painting is its recognition of the inherent flatness of its canvas medium, and its corresponding rejection of the three-dimensional illusionism dominant for centuries in European painting. But while Greenberg and Fried agreed on the importance of Noland and Olitski as painters, Fried shook up the Greenbergian canon by adding Stella, whose use of irregular polygon framing shapes allowed Fried to read recent Modernist painting in a way Greenberg could not have attempted. As we hear in further retrospective remarks by Fried from 1996: "I saw [Barnett Newman and Stella's attention to the framing edge in painting] as a new development and related it to the recent tendency toward opticality, on the grounds that the latter took pressure off flatness (a tactile feature) while putting pressure on shape, the other major physical or literal characteristic of the picture support" (*AO* 23). For as Fried notes in "Art and Objecthood," Modernist painting from about 1960 began to sense the danger of producing nothing but literal objects. In his own words: "modernist painting has come to find it imperative that it defeat or suspend its own objecthood, and that the crucial factor in this understanding is shape, but shape that must belong to *painting* – it must be pictorial, not, or not merely, literal" (*AO* 151). Unlike Stella, whose pictorial content either incorporates or counteracts the shape of its frame, Minimalist art "stakes everything on shape as a literal property of objects" (*AO* 151). This is why Fried sees such ominous stakes in the emergence of Minimalism: "[for by contrast with] modernism's self-imposed imperative that it defeat

54

or suspend its own objecthood through the medium of shape . . . the literalist position evinces a sensibility not simply alien but antithetical . . . as though, from that perspective, the demands of art and the condition of objecthood were in direct conflict" (AO 153). This brings Fried into collision with what he regards as his true enemy:

> What is it about objecthood as projected and hypostatized by the literalists that makes it, if only from the perspective of recent modernist painting, antithetical to art?... The answer I want to propose is this: the literalist espousal of objecthood amounts to nothing other than a plea for a new genre of theater, and theater is now the negation of art. (AO 153)

What exactly, in Fried's eyes, is wrong with "theater" in the arts? Here again he combines two features as enemies that we wish to separate, one as foe and the other as friend. For just as OOO wants to join Fried's condemnation of the literal while defending the theatrical from his attacks, we also find *two separate halves* in his concept of the theatrical, one deserving of censure but the other well worth preserving. If the reader pays close attention, the distinct halves can already be seen in the following passage: "Literalist sensibility is theatrical because, to begin with, it is concerned with the actual circumstances in which the beholder encounters literalist work" (AO 153).

The two halves in question are "the actual circumstances" and "the beholder," which Fried identifies while OOO claims they are different things altogether. Fried continues: "[The minimalist artist Robert] Morris makes this explicit. Whereas in previous art 'what is to be had from the work is located strictly within [it],' the experience of literalist art is of an object in a *situation* – one that, virtually by definition, *includes the beholder* . . ." (AO 153). We know what a beholder is. But what counts as part of the "situation" of an artwork? Fried seems to fear a rampant holism that would dissolve the work into its total context: "Everything counts – not as part of the object, but as part of the situation in which its objecthood is established and on which that objecthood at least partly depends" (AO 155). The title *Relational Aesthetics* has already been taken by the famous short work of Bourriaud, though he does not mean "relational" in the full sense of the term. He is primarily interested in artworks that spark conversations between otherwise reticent gallery visitors through works that, for example, encourage them to prepare food together. I do wish someone had written a more comprehensive, ultra-holistic work called *Relational Aesthetics*, one which claimed that every artwork is completely devoured by the whole of its surroundings.

As an object-oriented theorist who defends the autonomy of objects from their contexts, I would be as appalled by such a work as Fried himself; still, a book of that sort would be a powerful counter-wizard worth engaging in repeated combat.

In any case, Fried wants to exclude two different things from the sphere of high-quality contemporary art: (a) the work's total situation, and (b) the work's beholder, the spectator who encounters it. But Fried never lays it out this way, because he sees the situation and the beholder as basically the same thing. As he puts it, while summarizing the Minimalist or literalist view he abhors: "The object, not the beholder, must remain the center or focus of the situation, but the situation itself *belongs* to the beholder – it is *his* situation . . . But the things that are literalist works of art must somehow *confront* the beholder – they must, one might almost say, be placed not just in his space but in his *way*" (AO 154).

Despite Fried's squeamishness about the term "formalism," we have seen that he endorses both the central insight and central dogma of this basically Kantian way of looking at art. The insight concerns the formalist insistence on *autonomy* in art, which ultimately means its non-literal and hence non-relational depth. Here OOO endorses the position of Kant, Greenberg, and Fried against misguided attempts to say that everything is in relation, everything affects everything else, or that everything is art. We even draw the line in terms that Fried might appreciate: the literal can never be aesthetic, because the literal is what reduces objects to bundles of qualities, and the relational – being a broader form of the literal – does nothing other than this. The main difference is that Fried is not committed to anything like the ungraspable thing-in-itself, which is central for OOO. But as we saw when discussing the *Critique of Judgment*, Kant simply assumes that autonomy is destroyed the moment we have cross-contamination between humans and the world. No one would say that water is not an autonomous thing just because it is formed of both hydrogen and oxygen, yet somehow the mixture of thoughts and inanimate objects is supposed to be ruinous for autonomous non-relationality. That this is not so is clear from countless examples. The nation of China is made up of numerous individuals, institutions, geographical features, agricultural seasons, flora and fauna, and so forth. Yet only a nominalistic pedant would deny our ability to speak of "China" as a unified thing due to the number of changing heterogeneous pieces of which it is composed. Clearly we can speak of China and its characteristic features just as we can speak of water and its typical traits, even if the former seems less mechanically predictable than the latter.

By the same token, it is not clear why the artwork has autonomy only if both the situation of the work *and* the beholder are excluded. Fried is surely correct – and this is where OOO loves formalism – that all is lost if we sink into holistic laziness and contend that nothing can be disentangled from anything else, as implied by Osborne's Frankfurter Hegelianism. Even the most purportedly interconnected installation piece or architectural design does not exist in relation to *the whole* of its environment. The exact pattern of grains of dust in a gallery or museum need not affect an artwork in the least. True, we can imagine an installation that is constructed in such a way as to interact intimately with the precise configuration of the dust – yet this would take a great deal of conceptual and mechanical work to pull off, and even in that case much else would still be excluded. In short, the supposed holism of any situation is usually just an exaggeration of a *finite* number of feedback mechanisms, ones that can sometimes even be enumerated in exact detail. For instance, it is often assumed that the fragility of the earth's climate now means that *everything* affects *everything else*, that all is related to all, that each tiny hiccup of an individual human will somehow contribute to the degeneration of the planet. The relevance of this point to Fried's article is that he immediately seems to worry that once the situation of a work is considered, it will contain absolutely *everything* surrounding it, thereby entailing the dissolution of the artwork into a literal situation of everyday objects just sitting around in a room. Yet to worry about this – and I speak here as a great admirer of Fried – is to yield to two separate fallacies.

The first is the assumption that we have an all-or-nothing question when it comes to an artwork's relations, though an artwork is usually constructed with several relations in mind: not zero, and not infinitely many. Even Fried – and Greenberg, for that matter – would presumably agree with an important anti-formalist point made in literary studies by Harold Bloom, whose theory of the "anxiety of influence" contends that works are produced as deliberate "misreadings" of strong predecessors rather than arising from nothing.[5] Indeed, part of Fried's case against the Minimalists is that, despite their widespread influence, they are not "legitimate successors" to the paintings of Noland and Stella, a claim entailing that no work exists in a historical vacuum (*AO* 19). Though I agree with Fried that no artwork should be thought to include the whole of its situation, this is no reason to make a worried separation between any individual artwork and *everything* that surrounds it. The artwork is not impenetrable to the outside world, though it does have significant firewalls and cannot make links without a good deal of labor. Otherwise, it would vanish whenever the surrounding world changed even to a limited extent, a prediction not borne out by the history of art or anything else. In the memorable words of literary theorist Rita Felski: "Context stinks!"[6]

The second difficulty is with Fried's wish to exclude *the beholder* from the artwork, an even more damaging Kantian prejudice, one to which Fried does add considerable nuance in his historical work. It is true that Kant seems to have done exactly the opposite, making the beholder's faculty of judgment the very center of art while excluding the object itself. But as mentioned earlier, though Greenberg and Fried seem to invert Kant's subjectivist aesthetics in favor of a focus on the object, all three share the notion that subject and object must not be mixed: a claim diagnosed by Latour as the central prejudice of modernity in every field.[7] But here my objection to Fried is stronger than in the case of "situations." For while it is true that many, even most aspects of an artwork's situation are closed off from the inner confines of that work and leave no trace on it, the beholder cannot be excluded from the work at all. This point is partly conceded by Fried in *Absorption and Theatricality*, when he admits that the supposed non-existence of the beholder in anti-theatrical painting is a "supreme fiction" (*AT* ch. 2) OOO certainly agrees that an artwork ought to be closed off from the ulterior personal interests of the beholder, and that the work cannot be exhausted by the beholder's attempts to describe or conceptualize it. It does not follow that there need not be a beholder at all, as if there could still be artworks after all aesthetically capable creatures were exterminated by plague or war. In fact, the human is not primarily part of the artwork's situation, but is an ingredient of the work no less than paint or marble. To ask "what would art without humans – or other capable beings – be like?" has no more sense than the question "what would water without hydrogen be like?" Hydrogen is a necessary but not sufficient condition for water, and human beings are necessary but not sufficient conditions for an artwork. It follows that what Fried dismissively terms "theater" is essential to the arts, a point we will discuss shortly. Nonetheless, *literalism* must be coldly refused entrance into the aesthetic realm, except as a special case requiring some sort of non-literal basis – as we will see in Chapter 6 in connection with Dada.

Allow me now a brief digression to discuss an intriguing point raised by Fried in connection with Robert Morris. Namely: "Morris believes that [our] awareness [of our own physical relationship to the minimalist artwork] is heightened by 'the strength of the constant, known shape, the gestalt,' against which the appearance of the piece from different points of view is constantly being compared" (*AO* 153). What makes this of interest is that Morris uses the term "gestalt" to mean exactly what Husserl means by "object": a constant shape that endures no matter what perceptual details its beholder might encounter at any given moment. This is what we called the SO-SQ tension, and what Kant gave the name "charm": the rippling variations that enhance an artwork without themselves rising to the level of art. If Minimalism were as purely devoted to literal, surface objecthood as Fried claims, then such charm would be all that it has to offer. Yet Fried is aware that some of the minimalists at least claim to offer more than this, since he quotes Tony Smith as saying: "I'm interested in the inscrutability and mysteriousness of the thing" (*AO* 156). It is also worth noting that newcomers to OOO often assume a link between this philosophy – which is devoted to the withdrawn or non-literal character of things – and Minimalism. If we take Smith's claim about the mystery of the thing seriously, then perhaps Minimalism is less about "what you see is what you get" than about eliminating the object's needless detail in order to focus on an inner spirit or soul of the thing that exceeds its relatively impoverished surface.

The phrase "spirit or soul of the thing" is meant here in a deliberately provocative sense, since this formulation touches on what Fried considers to be the "anthropomorphism" of Minimalist art. Yet this very complaint should raise a red flag, since the charge of anthropomorphism is most often made by those who want everything to hinge on a single taxonomical rift between humans and everything else. This includes philosophers of the stature of Kant, but we have already seen – with the example of the object "China" – that there is no reason why an autonomous object could not be made from a motley assortment of human and non-human elements; in fact, Latour shows that such hybrid entities are widely produced on a regular basis. There is no good reason why metaphors from the human sphere should be forbidden to describe non-human objects: for example, when Latour speaks of two non-human actors "negotiating" their relationship, it would be puritanical and ridiculous to complain that inanimate things cannot really negotiate. That would be analogous to rejecting the "candle is like a teacher" metaphor for the reason that candles cannot literally enter a classroom and teach. Of course not: the non-literality is the whole point, the very factor that makes it a metaphorical statement. There is no reason why anthropomorphic metaphors should be cause for special intellectual horror, unless one is excessively devoted to the utter uniqueness of humans by contrast with everything else in the cosmos: the key dogma of modern philosophy since René Descartes.

Fried, who like Kant and Greenberg is overly taxonomical in his outlook, insisting on something like an absolute segregation of humans from non-humans, has no sympathy for art that smells even vaguely anthropomorphic. But while the Minimalists rejected Caro for the supposed anthropomorphism of his sculptures, Fried contends that the shoe is really on the other foot: "the heart of Caro's genius is that he is able to make radically abstract sculptures out of concepts and experiences which seem – which but for his making are and would remain – inescapably literal and therefore irremediably theatrical . . ." (*AO* 180-1). Therefore, it is actually the Minimalists who are guilty of anthropomorphism. Their works make us feel a certain distance, and "in fact, being distanced by such objects is not, I suggest, entirely unlike being distanced, or crowded, by the silent presence of another *person*" (*AO* 155). Fried even lists three specific factors that prove the anthropomorphism of Minimalist work: "First, the size of much literalist work . . . compares fairly closely with that of the human body" (*AO* 155). When Tony Smith tells an interviewer that his aim in constructing a six-foot cube was neither to make it large like a monument nor small like an object, Fried shrewdly remarks that "what Smith *was* making might be something like a surrogate person – that is, a kind of statue." This brings us to what Fried calls the second anthropomorphic factor in Minimalism: "the entities or beings encountered in everyday experience in terms that most closely approach the literalist ideals of the nonrelational, the unitary, and the holistic are *other persons*" (*AO* 156). Third and finally, "the apparent hollowness of most literalist work – the quality of having an *inside* – is almost blatantly anthropomorphic. It is, as numerous commentators have remarked approvingly, as though the work in question has an inner, even secret, life . . ." (*AO* 156). It is interesting that this should be the place where Fried cites Tony Smith's remarks on the inscrutability and mysteriousness of the thing: as if secretiveness were obviously just a human quality improperly projected onto non-human things. Here OOO disagrees, given its conception of every object as having a withdrawn inner dimension.

Nonetheless, Fried thinks that anthropomorphism is merely a symptom, while theatricality is the disease: "what is wrong with literalist work is not that it is anthropomorphic but that the meaning and, equally, the hiddenness of its anthropomorphism are incurably theatrical" (*AO* 157). Non-theatricality vs. theatricality is, for the Fried of 1967, the basic strife separating the legitimate Modernist avant-garde of Noland, Olitski, and Stella from the illegitimate, literalist, and anthropomorphic theater of the Minimalists. Here, a dismayed Fried quotes Smith's excited recollection of sneaking onto the unfinished New Jersey Turnpike in the early 1950s and sensing the end of art as he knew it:

> It was a dark night and there were no lights or shoulder markers, lines, railings, or anything at all except the dark pavement moving through the landscape of the flats, rimmed by hills in the distance, but punctuated by stacks, towers, fumes, and colored lights . . . The road and much of the landscape was artificial, and yet it couldn't be called a work of art. On the other hand, it did something for me that art had never done. (cited *AO* 157)

Now, I find it hard to be as appalled by this passage as Fried himself. Smith is simply recalling an aesthetic experience, at a surprisingly early date, of a kind that is readily familiar to anyone living in the early twenty-first century. He evokes the sort of quasi-sublimity we all know from urban infrastructure, advanced architecture, and many videogames, with the advance of virtual reality promising even more of the same. Many of us will agree with Smith that, although not quite "artworks," experiences of this kind have an aesthetic character that deserves the serious philosophical treatment it has never received – unless the widely mocked efforts of Jean Baudrillard at an ontology of simulacra are considered a step in the right direction, as they probably are.[8] But Fried sees nothing profound in all of this, just more theater enlisted in a war against high-quality art. In his view, Smith's recollection gives us nothing more than literalism: "what was Smith's experience on the turnpike? Or to put it another way, if the turnpike, airstrips, and drill grounds [of Nuremberg] are not works of art, what are they? – What, indeed, if not empty, or 'abandoned,' *situations*?" (*AO* 159). What Fried overlooks is that while most situations do not have an aesthetic character at all, some of them clearly do. While writing these words, I am keeping my wife company late at night in her academic department, as banal a situation as most such places: filled with books, staplers, a coffee maker, a photocopier, and loud forced-air heating. I would certainly agree with Fried that this situation flouts every valid criterion of what ought to count as aesthetic, but do not see that the same holds for Smith's renegade cruise down the unfinished Turnpike. For we saw earlier that an artwork need not exclude *all* aspects of its situation, and there are even cases in which an entire situation takes on an aesthetic character; this often happens when a film or novel transports us to some other era of history.

In opposition to Smith's vision of an ostensibly post-art aesthetics, Fried – who speaks so bitingly of literal objecthood – insists nonetheless on the importance of *objects* as against mere situations. As he puts it: "In each of the above cases [described by Smith] the object is, so to speak, *replaced* by something: for example, on the turnpike, by the constant onrush of the road, the simultaneous recession of new reaches of dark pavement illumined by the onrushing headlights, the sense of the turnpike itself as something enormous, abandoned, derelict, existing for Smith alone and those in the car with him . . ." (AO 159). Readers familiar with OOO will already sense that Fried is using "object" in too limited a sense, though he now speaks of it positively whereas his earlier remarks on objecthood were pejorative in tone. With the shift from object to experience, Fried seems to think we lose something precious, whereas OOO would regard Smith's night-time drive as consisting of *nothing but* a multitude of objects. Fried's negative view is expressed as follows: "what replaces the object . . . is above all the endlessness, the objectlessness, of the approach or onrush or perspective" (AO 159). And further: "in each case being able to go on indefinitely is of the essence" (AO 159). This reference to indefinite continuation might seem to come from nowhere, yet it is closely linked to what Fried will say at the conclusion of his article. There, he will claim that duration is inherently theatrical, and that we ought to insist that genuine art be wholly manifest to the beholder at every moment: "it is by virtue of their presentness and instantaneousness that modernist painting and sculpture defeat theater" (AO 167). We are now on the doorstep of the article's famous final sentence: "Presentness is grace" (AO 168).

But let's close this account of "Art and Objecthood" by turning back a few pages, to where Fried gives an important list of three principles that characterize his approach to art, at least as of 1967. This should give us a clearer sense of where Fried and OOO agree and disagree. The principles are as follows, with italics removed for ease of reading:

(1) The success, even the survival, of the arts has come increasingly to depend on their ability to defeat theater. (AO 163)
(2) Art degenerates as it approaches the conditions of theater. (AO 164)
(3) The concepts of quality and value – and to the extent that these are central to art, the concept of art itself – are meaningful, or wholly meaningful, only within the individual arts. (AO 164)

As for the first principle, we need to replace "theater" with "literalism" to produce a statement with which we can wholeheartedly agree. No literal situation – meaning a situation constituted purely by our *relations* with things – can count as aesthetic, let alone as art in the more restricted sense. As we saw in the case of metaphor, the only way to avoid literalism is to bring a real object (RO) into play. Yet there is nothing *inherently* more literal in a situation than in an object. Situations can be aesthetic, hyperobjective, or disquieting no less than a durable object made of canvas or marble. There is no reason to exclude multi-object situations as artworks in advance; this can only be decided on a case-by-case basis – by *taste*, Kant would say. The fact that installations, performances, land art, conceptual art, or happenings are now established genres in a way that was not true in the 1950s no doubt means art has become more theatrical, but does not automatically entail the disaster that it has become more literal. We would say much the same thing about Fried's second principle: agreeing that art degenerates as it approaches the conditions of the *literal*, but not as it approaches those of the theatrical.

Fried's third principle follows directly from the second. The concepts of quality and value, he says, have meaning only within the individual arts. This idea comes from Greenberg, who opposed the nineteenth-century trend toward giant Wagnerian agglomerations of the different arts, preferring instead what he saw as the modernist tendency for each genre to focus on its own equipment: Stéphane Mallarmé and James Joyce dealing primarily with the inherent capacities of language, Anton Webern as the composer's composer, Antonin Artaud rejecting theater as storytelling in favor of theater for primal theater's sake, and so forth. Thus, Fried speaks sarcastically of the notion that "the real distinctions ... are displaced by the illusion that the barriers between the arts are in the process of crumbling ... toward some kind of final, implosive, highly desirable synthesis" (*AO* 164). Now, it is not entirely clear what constitutes an individual art, but surely Fried would admit there is no permanent natural list of genres. Opera is less than a thousand years old, despite Nietzsche's failed effort to trace it back to Greek tragedy.[9] Jazz is even younger, and perhaps even more heterogeneous in its list of contributing influences and its typical range of instruments. There is admittedly a tendency in our time to overvalue mixtures and hybrids for their own sake, and even those readers who think Fried is unfair to the music of John Cage and the art of Robert Rauschenberg will concede that there are numerous other cases where genre-busting goes astray. Even so, there is no reason to exclude fusions of genre *a priori*. A great deal of work has always been needed to make *plausible* fusions between painted scenery and singing, or any other pre-existent genres. Many such efforts fail laughably, but sometimes they strike the target, in such a way that a new form of art is born. On a related note, Fried complains that the Minimalists want to replace the notion of "quality" in art with the idea that it need only be "interesting," to use Judd's word (*AO* 165). Yet it is not clear that these terms need be opposed. As I will argue shortly, there is no art unless the beholder is interested. And even if numerous artworks are of interest to us, this merely constitutes them all as artworks; the question of relative quality still remains.

Theatrical Aesthetics

OOO has been identified at various times as both compatible and incompatible with Minimalism. In September 2011, in conjunction with a roundtable discussion between me, Jane Bennett, and Levi R. Bryant at the CUNY Graduate Center in New York, the art show "And Another Thing" was curated by Katherine Behar and Emmy Mikelson. It included work by Carl André, and otherwise had a rather Minimalist feel to it. The implied link between OOO and Minimalism did not bother me, since I am not entirely convinced by Fried's dismissal of the Minimalist style as irredeemably literal-ist. More recently, I have been called upon to denounce Minimalist architecture by Patrik Schumacher, who contends that "Minimalism is alien to the spirit and thrust of OOO because it delivers hardly any virtuality."[10] Though unlike my colleague Bryant I have no special fondness for the Deleuzean concept of the virtual, Schumacher's point is that Minimalism is so simplistic in surface articulation and potential program that it cannot harbor the rich layers of withdrawn architectural surplus required by OOO.[11] Yet there are more positive readings of Minimalism available, including that of Marc Botha, who plausibly argues that minimalism encourages *realism* rather than literalism – and the two are opposites indeed – precisely by focusing our attention on the "least possible" and "least necessary" in every situation.[12] In any case, the present book is not the place to reach a final verdict on Minimalist art and architecture. My concern here is with literalism and theatricality, which I have argued are different things despite Fried's view that the two are so intertwined as to be more or less indistinguishable.

Looking back in 1996 on all the criticisms made of "Art and

Objecthood" over the years, Fried remarks that "no one of all those who have written against [the article] has contended that literalist art was not theatrical; instead, they have tried to reverse my negative assessment of theatricality itself . . ." (AO 52). The present book will be an exception to that rule, since it treats literalism and theatricality as opposites, and embraces theatricality for that very reason. The theatrical is essential to aesthetics because it alone is what saves us from the literal: namely, by having the beholder RO step in and replace the sensual object SO, as we saw in the case of metaphor. Literalism remains a common pariah for Fried and OOO because of the artwork's need for a depth autonomous from its situation, though at times Fried backpedals from his anti-situational views. This happens at least twice in connection with the sculptures of Caro, always among his favorite artists. The milder example is Caro's tabletop sculptures, which are not simply normal sculptures scaled down to fit on a table, but are tabletop-sized in a *qualitative* way: by always having an element that extends below tabletop-level, guaranteeing that they can never sit flat on the ground. It is on this basis that Fried responds to critics that "it is sometimes assumed that because . . . I criticized Minimalism's foregrounding of what might be called situationality or exhibitionality, I believed and perhaps still believe that modernist works of art exist or aspire to exist in a void. But I didn't and I don't" (AO 32). Yet the case of Caro's tabletop sculptures is a special one, if not altogether rare. For with these sculptures there is no rampant relation to the situation as a whole, no wild-eyed holism, but simply an internal relation of the sculpture to *one* element of its environment: an abstract tabletop, standing in for any particular table on which it might be placed. Properly speaking, the artwork in this case is not just the sculpture but the sculpture *plus* the abstract tabletop (both then combined with the beholder), as in the case of hydrogen and oxygen both being ingredients of water.

The more alarming example occurs when Fried links his compelling syntactic interpretation of Caro's sculptures to the linguistic structuralism of Ferdinand de Saussure. As concerns syntax, Fried tells us, "what I *saw* was that the entire expressive weight of Caro's art was carried by the relations among the girders, I- and T-beam segments, and similar elements out of which his sculptures were made, not . . . by the shapes of individual parts, nor by anything that could be called imagery, nor by what was then sometimes taken to be the industrial, modern-world connotations of his materials" (AO 29). So far, so good. This is not only a powerful reading of Caro's sculptures, but even – despite the fact that Caro is a sculptor rather than a painter, and despite Greenberg's praise of Fried's "syntactic" interpretation – an important break with the Greenbergian conceptual arsenal. Greenberg, after all, is more concerned with the vertical relationship between foreground and background than with horizontal relationships among elements in the foreground of a work. Yet there is cause for worry when Fried recollectively links his syntactic interpretation of Caro with "Saussure's theory of linguistic meaning as a function of purely differential relations among inherently meaningless elements" (*AO* 29).[13] For it is quite possible – even desirable – to interpret Caro and other artists syntactically, as creating higher unities from the relations between elements, without going further and concluding that these elements are themselves "inherently meaningless." To take this step is to fall into the sort of holism that has always haunted formalist theories in spite of themselves. A better term than syntactic might be "paratactic," referring to the side-by-side existence of aesthetic elements rather than their mutual reference. For even though the elements of Caro's sculptures do refer to one another in just the way Fried says, they by no means exhaustively define each other in the manner that Saussure's theory would suggest. Caro's elements are not inherently meaningless, but still have an aesthetic life of their own when taken individually. This is demonstrated by one of Fried's own favorite Caro pieces: the brilliant *Park Avenue* series, originally intended as a massive interconnected sculpture on Park Avenue in New York, but skillfully sliced by the sculptor into individual works once the funding for the larger piece fell through. If the Saussurean interpretation were correct, we would now experience the smaller works as meaningless mutilated stumps of a more natural whole, which is not at all what happens.

Yet despite his mixed message on the relation of elements to their total situations, we can safely describe Fried as someone who – if not as clearly as Greenberg – belongs to the Kantian formalist lineage in which an artwork is autonomous from most if not all of its surroundings, and in principle is autonomous from its beholder. The first to explore Fried's relationship with OOO in print – though before OOO took an openly pro-theatrical turn – was Robert Jackson of Lancaster University, in a pair of fine articles published three years apart (2011, 2014) in the journal *Speculations*.[14] As Jackson puts it: "Fried has made no apologies [about arguing] for the continuation of the Greenbergian paradigm that supports the formalist, autonomous and independent artwork; the elusive artwork that retains independence, despite changes in the surrounding historical or political context; the elusive artwork which continues the idealised, dedicated commitment

[to] critical aesthetic progress" (AOA 139). This obviously makes Fried a good candidate for intellectual alliance with OOO, which is exactly what Jackson proposes; indeed, it was Jackson himself who first reminded me to re-engage with the writings of Fried. The post-formalist argues that "artworks, artists and viewers are woven into deep relations; that of curatorial networks, exhibition history, canonised textbooks, critical tutors, and idealised myths of conflicted artists that intersect with tortured existential quandaries and religious hegemony" (AOA 140). By contrast, Fried's attack on literalism amounts to "a destructive account of [how literalism forgets] the unity of artworks, in favour of bonding the beholder and object together into a *contextual system*" (AOA 145), an account that makes sense only if we assume that the bond between beholder and object is in fact a contextual system rather than a new hybrid object. Although my own inclination is simply to reverse Fried on this point and embrace the theatricality of the bond, Jackson takes a more diplomatic route. Dipping into Fried's historical works, Jackson evokes the Diderot/ Fried concept of "absorption" (meant as the opposite of "theatricality"), referring to what happens when the figures in a painting are paying attention to what they are doing rather than to the beholder. In this way the beholder is "neutralized" despite being there anyway, an argument that Fried's longtime friend and ally Stanley Cavell presses hard in the case of film.[15] Jackson now gives an ontological twist to the theme of absorption:

> How can the beholder not be taken into account and yet circumstance dictates that they have a relation towards the work? For the same reason that the *thing in itself exists but can never be made present*. The beholder views a fiction, even if it is a sincere one or a representational scene of activity... It is the impossible glimpse of something 'not-present' that causes the beholder to be absorbed [in]to the work. (AOA 161)

This is why Jackson sees a close link between Fried's "absorption" and OOO's "allure": both terms refer to a way of making the thing-in-itself present without making it *directly* present. The same issue leads Jackson to the following claim: "note that the beholder does not instantly fuse into *The House of Cards* canvas [by Jean-Baptiste-Siméon Chardin] any more than a broom head does with the broom. They are absorbed, but not fused" (AOA 161). I would say instead that both absorption and fusion occur. There is a sense in which the broom head and the broom obviously do not splice together completely, since they remain as distinct and detachable as do the beholder and the artwork. If we accept Jackson's usage of "absorbed" as meaning the opposite of "fused" no less than of "theatrical," then absorption is a good term to cover the relation of the beholder and the artwork as separate entities, just as Fried uses it to cover the absorption of figures *within* the painting. Yet this relation can only exist as the interior of a larger object, constituted *theatrically*, in which beholder and artwork do fuse together – as we saw in the case of metaphor.

In any event, the importance of theatricality for OOO aesthetics is most easily seen if we recall the discussion of metaphor in Chapter 1. A successful metaphor creates a new object, though a *strange* one of the rare type RO-SQ. It follows from the insights of phenomenology that for every object there is always a tension between that object and its own qualities: "tension" meaning that the object both has and does not have those qualities, since within certain vaguely defined limits the object can exchange its current qualities for others. In the normal case of sensual objects, a tree can have countless different properties depending on how and from what angle and distance we confront it, and both the sensual tree and its sensual qualities are confronted directly in experience. Metaphor, and with it all other aesthetic experience, is strange in the sense that the object it creates is real rather than sensual. The Homeric sea, when described as "wine-dark," is so out of joint with wine that it is no longer the sensual sea of everyday experience and literal language. The sea is now withdrawn and mysterious, orbited by sensuous wine-qualities. This is what the diagonal paradox of RO-SQ means, and the impossibility of reducing it to a literal description is what makes it aesthetic: by which I mean the target of allusion rather than of direct propositional prose.

Yet there is a problem here. For insofar as the metaphorical sea of Homer withdraws from all literal access, it is no longer accessible, even though its wine-dark qualities remain so. This is a problem because it openly flouts the valid phenomenological principle that objects and qualities always come as a pair, even if a partly detachable one. In other words, we cannot simply have wine-dark qualities detachedly orbiting a hidden void. There must be an object *directly* involved in the metaphor "wine-dark sea." We have seen that it cannot be the sea, which is withdrawn from access. Neither can it be wine, which enters the metaphor only to provide qualities for the sea and not as an object in its own right; in that case, the metaphor would have to be reversed into "sea-dark wine." We have seen that there is only one alternative, one other real object on the scene: that other real object is *I, the beholder of the metaphor*. It is I who am forced to play the sea playing dark wine. Metaphor turns out to be a variant of performance art. So does every other kind of art, for that matter, since there is no art without the beholder's involvement: even at initial production stage when the artist is usually the only beholder, or one of very few. Such performance does not occur in cases of literal knowledge, since here the object does not disappear from the scene and thus has no need of replacement. What distinguishes aesthetic phenomena from other experience is that the beholder is called upon – assuming we hear the call, that we are at least somewhat convinced by the artwork – to stand in for the missing object and support the qualities that were only half-plausibly assigned to it. A completely plausible assignment would result in literal rather than aesthetic comparison: "a cornet is like a trumpet," "a moth is like a butterfly."

This recalls an issue raised earlier. It might be complained that with this step, OOO aesthetics has relapsed into what we Speculative Realists (following Meillassoux) call "corelationism."[16] The correlationist position, originating in Hume and Kant, claims that we cannot speak of thought without world or of world without thought, but only of the two in mutual correlation. That position is an obvious affront to philosophical realism, yet I – who claim to be a realist – now seem to have reduced the artwork to a correlation between artwork and beholder. But to think this way is to follow Kant's taxonomical mistake in assuming that thought and world alone must not be mixed. After all, no one would call it "correlationism" if we said that a flower is made from the combination of all its parts, or that present-day Germany is made up of a number of different *Länder* or states. No, the correlationist alarm is sounded only when someone mixes a person with a thing, and that is precisely what we do when we say that the beholder must take on the role of the missing object in any artwork. It is ironic that Kant, rightly depicted by Meillassoux as the textbook example of a correlationist, would probably be the first to pull the alarm, since the whole of his *Critique of Judgment* is based on the need to purify the judging human from whatever artwork or sublime experience is in question. By contrast, what we say here is that the artwork exists only as a hybrid of work and beholder. Yet there is a simple but important twist that differentiates this claim from correlationism. Namely, the correlationist thinks that the two terms of the thought-world correlate exist only in relation to each other, and that the correlation of thought and world is radically different in kind from any other combination of things. Yet for OOO, each of the terms has an autonomous reality not exhausted by its relation to the other, and the thought-world combination is no different in ontological kind from that between hydrogen and oxygen or wheels and a cart, however offensive this may be to the anthropocentric foundations of modern philosophy.

Even more importantly, thought and world are not just correlated, any more than all the parts of a flower or all the atoms in water are simply correlated. Instead, they also give rise to a new object, one on whose interior they exist, enabling them to make contact in flower-fashion or water-fashion. To give an example, I as the beholder of the Homeric metaphor "wine-dark sea" am one component of the metaphor as a whole, along with the wine-dark qualities I perform in sea-fashion. I am an object, the missing sea is an object, and the metaphor as a whole is an object. Given that aesthetic formalism demands mutual autonomy for both work and beholder, while OOO insists that the most important autonomy is that of beholder *plus* work as a newly combined hybrid, it should be clear how OOO escapes the taxonomical formalism that only cares about cleanly segregating two specific *types* of entities (human and world) while allowing everything else in the cosmos to combine freely.

As with most good ideas, this one is not lacking in partial precedents. Literary scholars, for instance, have long been familiar with the trend known as Reader-response criticism. This school is not committed like OOO to an ontology in which all relations are objects in their own right, and is generally *too* committed to the idea of texts as produced by situations, yet it brushes directly against the phenomenon of reading as a hybrid object. The German critic Wolfgang Iser, for instance, says some things that would not be out of place in the critique we have just made of Fried. In Iser's own words:

> meaning must clearly be the product of an interaction between the textual signals and the reader's acts of comprehension. And, equally clearly, the reader cannot detach himself from such an interaction; on the contrary, the activity stimulated in him will link him up to the text and induce him to create the conditions necessary for the effectiveness of that text. As text and reader thus merge into a single situation, the division between subject and object no longer applies, and it therefore follows that meaning is no longer an object to be defined, but is an effect to be experienced.[17]

The merging of text and reader into a single situation is precisely what we meant when contesting Fried's opposition to theatricality in the visual arts. Where Iser goes wrong is in claiming that the situation must be understood as an "effect" rather than an "object," in this way heeding too closely the obsession of recent decades with replacing all nouns by verbs and all substances by dynamic events. For if we call the merged situation of text–reader an effect or event rather than an object, this entails that the text–reader hybrid will be known by *what it does* rather than by *what it is*. Yet the problem with defining a thing in terms of what it does ("overmining") can be seen clearly in the shortcomings of actor-network-theory (ANT), which tells us that a thing is nothing more than whatever it "modifies, transforms, perturbs, or creates," thereby leaving no surplus in the thing that would enable it to modify, transform, perturb, or create differently in the future.[18] It is better to call the text–reader hybrid an *object*, since here as with every object, we have a unified reality that is not exhausted by any particular understanding of it, and not even by the reader's experience of it – after all, we can always misunderstand our own experiences and try to rectify this later.

But since we are speaking of the theatrical roots of aesthetics, it may be better to take an example directly from theater. Fried cites Antonin Artaud and Bertolt Brecht as key figures who problematize the theatrical in theater itself. However, it seems to me that both could be used more readily for *anti*-Friedian arguments, given that these authors make theater more exaggeratedly theatrical than ever before, if in opposite ways: Brecht asking the beholder to think, Artaud giving the beholder an experience more primal than thought. But here I prefer to mention a slightly older figure, the great Russian dramatist Konstantin Stanislavski. His system of acting – or "the method" as it is known in the United States, where it has been followed by numerous Hollywood stars – involves identifying with the inner motivations of a character, with some actors going so far as to live the rather miserable lifestyles of characters they currently portray. A characteristic passage from Stanislavski's classes helps to illuminate the stakes:

> "Look," [Xenia] Sonova said to us, "there's a drop of mercury in my hand and now carefully, very carefully, I pour it, see, onto the second, index finger of my right hand. Right on the very tip." So saying she pretended to put the imaginary drop on the inside of her fingertip on the motor muscles. "Let it run all over your body," she ordered. "Don't rush it! Gradually! Very gradually!"[19]

Though the beholder of artworks is rarely put through training quite this rigorous, we are called upon to do the same whenever we must stand in for the real object that withdraws from our grasp. This means that there is a primordial theatricality to all the arts, since without this theatrical participation of the beholder, the arts would consist of nothing but literal-looking statements and objects. In fact, it seems so clear that theater lies at the root of every art that I am convinced the *mask* was the first artwork in human history. For there is no clearer case of one object disappearing behind the qualities of another: giving rise sometimes to delight, but more often to raw terror. And compared with the mask, there is no form of art that works its dark magic more deeply on children and even animals: a further index of its primordial character.

The analogies of reader-response theory and method acting are useful for explaining the fusion of human and non-human into a new sort of hybrid object. Yet fusion is not the only point of importance here. There is also the fact – as Jackson noted with the broom and its handle – that the terms still remain separate, confronting each other on the *interior* of the larger object created by the fusion. The isolated interior of an object, the scene of a confrontation between its separate elements – whose origin lies in phenomenology – is a theme explored by recent authors outside the arts in order to yield insights in biology, sociology, and philosophy. In biology, there is the *autopoietic* model of the cell made famous by the Chilean immunologists Humberto Maturana and Francisco Varela, in which the cell is treated as a homeostatic and self-replicating system cut off from the outside world.[20] In sociology, there is the formidable German theorist Niklas Luhmann, for whom communication between any system and its environment is profoundly difficult: the very opposite of the communicative free-for-all found in Latour.[21] And in philosophy we have another German, Peter Sloterdijk, whose *Spheres* trilogy is devoted to a consideration of the environing bubbles within which anything takes place.[22] As luck would have it, we find a similar insight in a direct commentary on Fried's work, when the Leipzig philosopher Andrea Kern remarks: "The work of art can first become a work of art that depicts a world for the spectator when nothing external to the canvas exists, and when the canvas has become the entirety of space perceived to exist. That which the absorbed spectator beholds, according to Diderot, is a *totality which has no outside.*"[23] I would merely add to Kern's point that the absorbed spectator is not just an observer of the whole, but also joins it to form a new hybrid object.

Not unlike Iser and Stanislavski, OOO aesthetics points to the fusion of the beholder or performer with some other object in the name of creating a third, more encompassing entity, however short-lived it may be. And not unlike Maturana/Varela, Luhmann, and Sloterdijk, OOO is not just concerned with what is withdrawn from access, but about the way in which *what is* accessible occupies the interior of some larger object. Another largely forgotten philosopher of aesthetics, Theodor Lipps, spoke about the crucial role of *empathy* in art, and he too brings us to the edge of the theatrical model of aesthetics for which this book argues – despite Ortega's critique of his method.[24] As noted earlier, we feel close to Fried's denunciation of the literal, but opposed to his negative view of the theatrical. One of the implications is that we cannot accept his blanket dismissal of the theatricality he saw as swamping the visual arts in the 1970s and 1980s. This is not because all of it is good – much of it is pretentious garbage – but because we should not exclude the possibility that some of it is important. For example, I do not share the usual formalist coldness toward Joseph Beuys, one of whose works graces the cover of this book.

Adventures of Absorption

So far we have spoken mainly of Fried's "Art and Objecthood," in which the notion of theatricality figures as the chief enemy, and indeed as the death of all art. Although it is not unfair to present Fried's attitude toward the theatrical in this way – it continues to be his adjective of choice for art that is not to his liking – it would be an oversimplification. For what is most interesting in thinkers of Fried's stature are those moments when they run up against the limits of their own initial principle and feel the need to account for its opposite as well. This happens when the later Heidegger turns his attention from Being back to individual beings; in Latour, it occurs when this master thinker of networks turns his attention to the unformatted "plasma" that exceeds every network.[25] We will soon see that Greenberg, the most vehement apostle of flatness in painting, eventually concedes that "the first mark made on a surface destroys its virtual flatness," which entails that painting is inherently a matter of *anti*-flatness. We will also encounter something similar in his treatment of collage.

In Fried's work, too, we find something along these lines. His historical turn takes him initially to eighteenth-century France, where he finds a powerful anti-theatrical ally in the person of Diderot. Nonetheless, the development of French painting in that period leads Fried to note that it can be rather difficult to determine whether a given painting succeeds or fails in suspending theatricality. As he works his way through his trilogy, Fried eventually concludes that while anti-theatrical painting begins with the "supreme fiction" of pretending that the beholder of the painting does not exist, in Manet this ultimately flips into the opposite tendency of an unapologetic "facingness" in which the central pictorial figure directly challenges the beholder's gaze. A brief summary of Fried's claims in this direction will help show the fine line between the purported opposites of absorption and theatricality.

The young Fried of the 1960s was an art critic and not yet a famed historian of art, though he would soon butt heads with the established Manet specialists of his day. We have seen that his early critical work makes prominent use of "theatricality" as the primary term for what is wrong with Minimalism. Fried tells us he turned from criticism to history because he had already championed those contemporary artists who seemed most worth defending, and because art was beginning to take such a theatrical turn that he had no interest in remaining on the scene as a permanent scold. But while Fried's turn to art history marked a change of career that was in some respects drastic, his concern with the theatrical never abated. The first question to ask is whether "theatrical" is meant in the same sense in the criticism of the 1960s and in the later historical trilogy. Here Fried sends mixed messages. On the last page of his Introduction to *Absorption and Theatricality*, published in 1980, Fried emphasizes the continuity between his critical and historical work:

> In several essays on recent abstract painting and sculpture published in the second half of the 1960s I argued that much seemingly difficult and advanced but actually ingratiating and mediocre work of those years sought to establish what I called a *theatrical* relation to the beholder, whereas the very best recent work – the paintings of Louis, Noland, Olitski, and Stella and the sculptures of [David] Smith and Caro – were in essence *anti*-theatrical, which is to say that they treated the beholder as if he were not there . . . [T]he concept of theatricality is crucial to my interpretation of French painting and criticism in the age of Diderot, and in general the reader who is familiar with my essays on abstract art will be struck by certain parallels between ideas developed in those essays and in this book. Here too I want to assure the reader that I am aware of those parallels, which have their justification in the fact that the issue of the relationship between painting (or sculpture) and beholder has remained a matter of vital if often submerged importance to the present day. (*AT* 5)

But in 1996, Fried changes tack completely and blames those readers who have been too quick to assimilate his critical concept of theatricality to his historical one. In the long opening section of the book *Art and Objecthood*, entitled "An Introduction to My Art Criticism," Fried preaches the opposite lesson from 1980: "Another assumption I sometimes meet is that I think there exists not just a certain parallel but an actual continuity between the anti-theatrical tradition from the 1750s to the advent of Manet and the struggle against theatricality in abstract painting and sculpture in the 1960s. But of course I don't" (AO 52). Although Fried frames this as the result of a misunderstanding by sloppy readers, it actually points to a fruitful conflict internal to his own conception of theatricality. After correctly noting that "absorption" and "drama" – the key anti-theatrical terms of his historical work – have no parallel in his 1967 critique of the Minimalists, Fried shifts to the real crux of the problem:

> My work on eighteenth and nineteenth-century French painting has from the first been governed by the belief that the antitheatrical tradition reached a stage of absolute crisis, indeed was liquidated *as* a tradition in and by Manet's revolutionary canvases of the first half of the 1860s, and that at least as regards the issue of beholding whatever took place after that crisis was in an important sense discontinuous with what came before. (AO 52-53)

He adds that Manet's "repudiation of absorption in favor of facing-ness and strikingness . . . [breaks] fundamentally with the Diderotian tradition as a whole" (AO 53).

Beyond this, it is Fried himself who teaches us that the problems with Diderotian anti-theatricality began well before Manet. Much of the interest of *Absorption and Theatricality* stems from Fried's explicit recognition that eighteenth-century anti-theatrical painting was always filled with ambiguities and counter-tendencies. I will briefly summarize the most important of these, but first it is useful to recall the wider philosophical stakes of the question. Although the term "formalism" seems to have such a wide range of meanings as to be either confusing or useless, I argued in Chapter 2 that it has a very precise sense in the philosophy of Kant, whose *Critique of Judgment* remains the Bible of aesthetic Modernism. For Kant, in his ethics and metaphysics no less than his aesthetic theory, "formalism" refers above all to autonomy: the autonomy of human understanding and the thing-in-itself from each other, the autonomy of ethical action from its consequences, and the autonomy of beauty from what is personally agreeable. From a OOO standpoint such autonomy is admirable, since no zone of reality can be understood adequately in relational terms. Yet we have seen repeatedly that Kant also adopts another, less-than-admirable prejudice, assuming that autonomy should always be the *specific* separation of human thought from the world.

Earlier, I invoked Scheler as the most important critic of Kantian ethics due to his tacit understanding that the ethical unit is neither the individual human considered apart from the world, or the reverse, but rather the hybrid formed by person-plus-loved-object. On this note, I would venture a Schelerian reading of Fried's career-long interest in theatricality. In one sense, Fried invokes "absorption" as the eighteenth-century trend that defeats theatricality by portraying the figures in a painting as entirely absorbed in what they are doing, using a variety of techniques to exclude all awareness of the beholder. Diderot is convincingly presented as the theoretical master of this trend. Fried's appreciation of Caro's modern sculptures can also be seen as anti-theatrical in spirit, given that the syntactic relations among the parts of his sculptures can also be read as absorption in inanimate form. Yet chapter 2 of *Absorption and Theatricality* is entitled "Toward a Supreme Fiction," and the fiction in question is the idea that painting can exist in the absence of a beholder, which is nothing less than the central aspiration of the anti-theatrical tradition that Fried admires. He recognizes that already in the eighteenth century, especially in the paintings of David, it can be hard to decide whether a given painting is anti-theatrical or theatrical to the extreme. On the one hand, Fried is compelled to admit that theatricality inevitably arises even where we least expect it; on the other, he continues to treat it as the ruin of all art, and to use it as an ever-ready expletive for critiquing whatever art he deems unsuccessful. This discrepancy cannot be explained away by differentiating between the separate roles of art historian and art critic, as Fried suggests in 1996 (*AO* 49-50). Rather, it stems from his ultimately Kantian assumption that there is a vast gulf between absorption (relation of the parts of an artwork to each other) and theatricality (relation of the artwork to a beholder).

The standpoint of this book is different: namely, from a OOO perspective, the theatrical relation between artwork and beholder is simply absorption by other means. This makes it impossible to read theatricality as being *ipso facto* the death of art, just as our theatrical interpretation of metaphor suggested. Interesting pictorial effects can be obtained through the "supreme fiction" that the beholder does not count, but in the end, the beholder is no less an essential part of an artwork than hydrogen is of water – which is precisely why Fried admits that anti-theatricality is a fiction. This does not damage the autonomy of the artwork, because the Schelerian or Latourian side of OOO compels us to treat *all* entities as compounds, with the added twist – contra Latour – that a human *need not* be part of the compound. It so happens that artworks are a kind of object that requires a human ingredient, no less than politics, chess, or gourmet cooking. But even an object with a human ingredient is autonomous from all that does not belong to it, including the secondary attempt of the beholder to interpret the very compound object to which they belong. This has important consequences not just for aesthetics, but for philosophy as a whole; Fried must count as the pioneer of the aesthetic dimension of this question, like Scheler in ethics and Latour in metaphysics. Stated differently, we can say that Fried "Schelerizes" art just as Latour "Schelerizes" metaphysics, with the difference that of these three figures, Fried is the only one who seems to have drawn his conclusions reluctantly rather than triumphantly. It would have been much easier for his work if the history of art showed a clean division between obviously absorptive paintings on one side and obviously theatrical ones on the other, and if Manet had simply extended the Diderotian anti-theatrical tradition to the cusp of modernity. Yet Fried's intellectual honesty led him to discover a more complicated predicament.

But how exactly does Fried, the critic of Minimalist theatricality and supporter of Diderot, become – in spite of himself – someone who re-injects the beholder into the artwork? This is what makes his historical trilogy so fascinating, and I can only summarize it briefly here. Although a painting without someone to look at it would be nonsensical, a certain current of French painting in the eighteenth century – to Diderot's applause – did everything in its power to produce the supreme fiction that figures and objects in some paintings are so absorbed in their own reality as to exclude the beholder altogether. Chardin depicts a boy so absorbed in blowing a soap bubble that neither he nor his companion have any attention to spare for our presence. In another of Chardin's paintings, a boy is engrossed in building a house of cards, and his indifference to us is further accentuated by a desk drawer opened in our direction, as if to push us away from the picture. Jean-Baptiste Greuze paints a young redhead completely absorbed in study and reflection, and a family whose members mostly pay rapt attention to the father's Bible reading, except for a few young brats whose distraction merely emphasizes the absorption of the others. Carle Van Loo favors scenes of brilliant oratory by St. Augustine, baptism in the presence of bishops, or the countryside reading of a Spanish romance, in all of which the figures are so invested in what they are doing that we as beholders never feel taken into account. These plainly anti-theatrical examples fit perfectly with what we know both of Fried as a critic of Minimalism and as a reader of Diderot.

77

Soon enough, however, Fried signals a growing awareness of the limits of the anti-theatrical standpoint. Already in *Absorption and Theatricality*, he admits to difficulty in interpreting the works of David, the pivotal French painter of the eighteenth century. His celebrated pre-Revolutionary canvas *Oath of the Horatii* (1784) was apparently intended in anti-theatrical terms, as can be seen from the total absorption of the oath-swearing men at left and the weeping women at the right of the canvas. But viewed differently, their poses are all so unnatural as to scream almost melodramatically at the beholder. David himself later grew uncomfortable with what he increasingly saw as the inadvertent theatricality of this painting, and thus he took a different approach when attempting an anti-theatrical battle scene in *The Sabine Women* (1799), yielding what looks like a moment absorptively frozen in time. Yet this painting, too, comes to look very theatrical. More generally, one gets the sense that it is becoming harder to read any particular painting as either theatrical or anti-theatrical, at least for any prolonged period of time. This observation about David serves as a bridge to the next book of Fried's trilogy, *Courbet's Realism*. The painter Jean-François Millet excelled at depicting peasants absorbed in their labor. Or rather, some critics thought so, while others claimed the exact opposite: that Millet was trying so hard to make his peasants look absorbed that they actually seem to be posing theatrically (*CR* 237). In Courbet's own paintings, this increasingly ambiguous status of absorption and theatricality is addressed – Fried argues – by rejecting the *closure* of the painting found in such earlier artists as Chardin and Greuze (*CR* 234). As Fried notes, Chardin's aforementioned painting of a house of cards is the most un-Courbetian work we can imagine (*CR* 225). Rather than closure, Courbet aims at a "merger" of painting with beholder, or at least with the primal beholder of Courbet's paintings: namely, Courbet himself (*CR* 277). He projects himself physically into his paintings in such a way that painting and painter are no longer opposed, but are part of an "absorptive continuum" (*CR* 228), which Fried links with the metaphysics of Courbet's contemporary, the philosopher Félix Ravaisson (*CR* 247). On a personal note, this physical projection of Courbet into his own paintings was the subject of Fried's lecture in Annapolis that so engrossed me as a student, though I no longer recall whether Ravaisson was mentioned that night.

We now come to the final topic of Fried's trilogy: Manet, whose achievement is already foreshadowed at the close of the Courbet book. For Greenberg, Manet is the first modern painter because of his purported turn from illusionism to flatness, but we already know that for Fried, flatness is not the key to Modernism. As Fried sees it, Manet is responding instead to the breakdown of anti-theatricality, as signaled by Courbet's projection of himself as painter/beholder into the paintings. Manet does this through a radical "facingness" in which the central figure of each of his major paintings seems to inspect the beholder assertively, rather than pretending that we are absent. Beyond this attitude of his central figures, the reason Manet's paintings look flat is because every portion of the surface confronts the beholder in radical facingness like never before: a brilliant twist that enables Fried to subordinate Greenberg's central concern to his own (CR 286-287). In the third book of the trilogy, Fried elaborates on his rejection of Greenberg's version of Manet, noting that critics of Manet's own time did not take much note of the flat look of his paintings. In fact, this seems to have been an Impressionist concern projected backward onto Manet, who was more concerned with a novel solution to the problem of theatricality (MM 17). To summarize:

> Manet sought to acknowledge, not negate or neutralize, the presence of the beholder . . . [The] act of acknowledgment holds the key to Manet's pictures' notorious "flatness": as though what has always been taken as flatness is more importantly the product of an attempt to make the painting in its entirety . . . *face* the beholder as never before. (MM 266)

This new way of grappling with the problem of theatricality, in Fried's view, does not pertain to Manet alone, but is characteristic of his main generational comrades of the 1860s: especially the closely knit trio of Henri Fantin-Latour, Alphonse Legros, and the American transplant James McNeill Whistler. In Fried's words: "Something . . . tortuous and ambiguous took place in the 1860s, and . . . it seems likely that that something was intimately connected with the emergence of a double or divided sensibility with respect to issues of absorption and closure" (MM 279-280). Yet Manet differs from his peers by turning his back more decisively on the absorptive tradition: "in no Manet canvas of the 1860s is absorption positively stressed as in the works by Legros and Fantin . . ." (MM 281). He explains Manet's double bind as follows: "To the extent that the viewer nevertheless feels summoned by Manet's figures in the name of the painting . . . [his] most characteristic paintings insist both on the model's nonpresence and on the painting's presence to the beholder" (MM 344).

Yet in speaking of Manet's ambitious late paintings *The Execution of Maximilian*, Fried steps back from his qualified defense of the double bind, and appeals once more to the eighteenth-century Diderotian tradition:

79

the violence that since David or even Greuze had been part of the central French tradition and that surfaced once last time in [Manet's] *Execution* as that tradition reached its point of absolute crisis becomes readable as the violence of a conflict *between painting and beholder* – very much as if the Diderotian imperative to negate or neutralize the beholder, to establish the fiction of his nonexistence, had all along entailed relations of deadly mutual hostility between the two. (*MM* 357-358)

A profound sense of this hostility is, in fact, the most Friedian aspect of Fried, shaping his early criticism as decisively as his later historical work. Yet what he presents is less a conflict between painting and beholder than between *absorption* (which yields a pictorial closure that excludes the beholder) and *theatricality* (in which the beholder is supposed to become directly involved in the painting). Yet to see this conflict as decisive is, I hold, to cave in to formalism in the taxonomical sense of the term: in which the absorption of Chardin's boys in their soap bubbles and card castles, or of Caro's sculptural elements with each other, is treated as different *in kind* from our own absorption with the gaze of Olympia or with the New Jersey turnpike. While finishing this book, I was pleased to find Magdalena Ostas expressing the same view in her interpretation of Fried: "It is exactly this sense of [the] utter self-inclosure [of figures in a non-theatrical painting] that arrests and enthralls us, or that generates and sustains our enthusiasm, so that the painting comes to absorb us *in the same way* that the world around the figures fully absorbs them."[26]

One can still make aesthetic objections to Tony Smith's turnpike adventure, but not merely by objecting to the theatrical element of it. Stated differently, absorption and theatricality are just two different forms of a broader phenomenon we might call *sincerity*, a term taken from Emmanuel Levinas.[27] It should not really matter, ontologically speaking, whether the boy blowing the bubble is aware of the beholder or not. If the boy were openly posing for us, Fried would of course be free to call this "theatrical." But at the end of the day, theater is just another form of absorption: or rather, just another form of sincerity. Against Kantian formalism, there is no utterly radical difference between painting and beholder such that to cross the boundary from one to the other is to enter the kingdom of non-art. To see this is to see a possible way in which Fried and Greenberg – whatever their differences – were systematically unfair to art that incorporated living humans in a way that traditional painting and sculpture did not.

An excessive allegiance to Kant's absolute rift between thought and world can also be detected in Fried's recently published article on Søren Kierkegaard: a piece that strikes me as fascinating but wrong. Entitled

"Constantin Constantius Goes to the Theater," it provides a careful and enthusiastic reading of a passage in Kierkegaard's *Repetition*, published in 1843 under the name of Constantin Constantius: one of that philosopher's many pseudonyms. We have already seen an ambiguity in Fried's own career-long treatment of theatricality. In the simplest sense, he is an advocate of classic Diderotian anti-theatricality, in which absorptions internal to a painting achieve closure and thereby exclude the beholder. This principle also seems to govern his views on contemporary artworks, in which bad art is generally deemed to be bad due to its theatricality. Yet in a more nuanced sense, under the pressure of his historical work, Fried expands his initial critique to account both for the ambiguity of David and Millet and the explicit double bind of Manet. In which of these two senses does he interpret Kierkegaard as anti-theatrical? Unfortunately, it seems to be in the simpler sense. Attending a performance of a farce in Berlin, Constantius finds it unconvincing until he sees *someone else* absorbed in it: "In the third row of a box across from me sat a young girl, half hidden by an older gentleman and lady sitting in the front row."[28] Fried notes perceptively that "the crucial point, it quickly becomes clear, is that she had no awareness of being observed."[29] The farce itself does not work for Constantius, yet is somehow made convincing by the addition of a figure whose childlike wonder or absorption in the play makes the entire thing bearable. Though the farce itself is theatrical in Fried's bad sense, the young girl's naïve absorption creates a more intricate compound that counts, on the whole, as non-theatrical.

Yet the mere fact that the girl does not notice Constantius should not be taken as a sufficient criterion of closure, as if he were somehow outside the circle of absorption that links the girl with the farce. For if she is absorbed in watching the farce, Constantius is just as absorbed in her absorption with it. Even if this were somehow treated as a more sophisticated second-order observation, his position is no less sincere or naïve than the girl's. She expends her energy in taking the farce seriously, while Constantius expends his energy in being sincerely involved with her sincerity. In other words, his Beholder$_2$ position is not radically different in kind from the girl's Beholder$_1$, and things would not change all that much if she were to turn, notice him, and smile: in that case she would simply become sincere about something other than the farce itself. This is why I disagree with Fried's wonderfully impassioned reading of Kierkegaard: for its apparent attempt to place Constantius alone as a beholder outside the circle of absorption. And ultimately, for all his dithering and self-absorbed expressions of doubt, who is a greater philosopher of choice, commitment, and participation than Kierkegaard himself? If Kant is the supreme formalist philosopher who separates phenomenal thought and real world, Kierkegaard – following Dante – is the thinker for whom the commitments of thought and the heart generate new realities every bit as real as inanimate stones in empty space. For this reason, although Kierkegaard is usually contrasted with his avowed enemy Hegel, the contrast with Kant may be even more instructive. Whichever way the issue is turned, I for one find it impossible to read Kierkegaard as anything but the theatrical philosopher *par excellence*.

4

The Canvas is the Message

When responding to friends in the art world who question my continued interest in Greenberg, I simply refer to the intensity of my personal experience in reading him. To fall back on passion in this way is never enough to guarantee that we are right, but it does ensure that we are not merely blowing smoke – and this already dispels a good part of the problem with intellectual life. Most everyone can recall a handful of beautiful summers of reading, devoted to the works of a single author or related group of authors, during which something irreversible happened to one's brain. In my own case, there are two such summers – more than twenty years apart – that stand out for having no obvious connection with my professional specialty of metaphysics, but which drew their energy solely from the inexplicable pleasure of reading. One was spent devouring the works of Freud, while the other was devoted to reading every last word of Greenberg.[1] The least we can say is that these are two of the finest prose writers of their century – and contrary to widespread opinion, there is no way to write good prose without being on the scent of something real that exceeds literal description. Both authors take frank positions on issues of some controversy, and both are often portrayed as dated, despite having established the very frameworks in which they would later be negatively judged. Freud and Greenberg speak with candor and authority. However aggressive they may sometimes have been in their personal dealings, *as writers* they do not strike me as condescending: as if, in principle, they expected each of us to be capable of approaching their own respective degrees of mastery.

Even so, many still think of Greenberg primarily as an archaic figure refuted by the past half century of artistic practice, as in the email from my friend Veseli cited earlier. There is no question that

Greenberg was not a sympathetic critic of the chief figures in the art world since the 1960s, treating nearly all as sad departures from the Modernist cutting edge. Duchamp (an earlier figure whose dominant influence began in the 1960s) was simply "not a good artist," and the same for Andy Warhol (*LW* 221). Beuys was boring, and Gerhard Richter not so good. This in itself is no reason for concern, even for those who find these particular assessments wrong: the most difficult thing in any field is to detect and appreciate talent in generations younger than one's own. If Kant had lived a biblical lifespan and was able to read the mature philosophical works of Hegel, along with twentieth-century phenomenology, French Postmodernism, and the collected works of Deleuze, we could expect him to view all these authors with scorching derision; he was already headed down that path by dismissing his first important heir, Fichte. The same would no doubt be true of the authors of *The Federalist Papers* if they were restored to the flesh and asked to reflect on the various ensuing Presidents of the United States, including some of the best of them – not to mention the worst. It was Greenberg's misfortune that his career overlapped with the rise of the post-formalist artists he rejected as tasteless backsliders. For this reason, he is not just a safely revered classic as he might have been, but comes off as more of a boorish uncle who stomped on the dreams of the young and was never forgiven.

He is, nonetheless, a classic. The last seventy years of American art have been either Greenbergian or – more often – flamboyantly anti-Greenbergian, just as the last two centuries of philosophy can be defined in relation to Kant. But it is not only Greenberg's status as an enduring author that should insulate him somewhat from the revulsion of three generations of artists. Another factor is that he belongs to a wider intellectual trend crossing several different fields, and which makes his thinking a bigger phenomenon than the art world alone. We will discuss this topic shortly.

Fried contra Greenberg

Before proceeding further with Greenberg's ideas, we should speak briefly of some key differences between him and his estranged admirer Fried. We have seen that Fried takes pride in his 1966 essay on Stella as the place where he first found his original critical voice, free from Greenberg's overbearing influence, which by many accounts could be demoralizing. Fried does this by expanding, to the point of challenging, Greenberg's most famous thesis about modernist painting: that it is always an issue of the flatness of the canvas. This insight was foreshadowed in a remark by Ortega that did not appear in English until 1949: "[With impressionism,] Velásquez' background has been brought forward, and so of course ceases to be background since it cannot be compared with a foreground. Painting tends to become planimetric, like the canvas on which one paints."[2] The idea, apparently, was to make as little compromise as possible with the three-dimensional illusionism that dominated Western painting from the Italian Renaissance through Manet, and which in the nineteenth century – Greenberg held – had degenerated into a mere academic or *kitsch* technique.

Already in 1966, Fried plausibly contends that the development of flatness has more or less run its course in avant-garde painting, and that developmental pressure was now placed on *shape* instead. Even Greenberg admits that pure flatness is not just unattainable, but is directly flouted by Pollock, Newman, and Louis, all of them "opening up the painting from the rear" and thus giving it new depth by way of optical illusionism. Yet Greenberg did not take the critical turn from flatness to shape to the same degree as Fried himself; his indifference to the shape-obsessed art of Stella is evidence of this. For the most part, Greenberg was fixated on insisting that content in avant-garde painting must signal awareness of the chief feature of its medium: flatness. This is why Greenberg spoke so highly of Impressionism, Cézanne, Analytic Cubism, Mondrian, and other artists and movements that were so attentive to this principle, while dismissing other celebrated painters for falling into either explicit (Dalí) or implicit (Kandinsky) forms of three-dimensional illusionism. What does Fried do differently? He asks us to view Noland, Olitski, and Stella as the most advanced artists in the mid 1960s because they too remain aware of a (different) chief feature of their medium: namely, its shape.

Everything hinges on the interplay between content and its ground, which links Greenberg and Fried not only with Gestalt psychology, but more directly with Heidegger and Marshall McLuhan.[3] The key drama underway in painting, for both Greenberg and Fried, plays out between the content of a painting and the nature of its medium, though for the former this pertains to flatness and for the latter to shape. While it is fine to call the shapes within a painting *depicted* shapes, it seems like a strange choice when Fried calls the shape of the support a *literal* one, even when he adds the qualification that he is not speaking "merely [of] the silhouette of the support." For we have seen that the primary meaning of "literal" is not "physical," but "relational."

THE CANVAS IS THE MESSAGE

The fact that Greenberg emphasizes the flatness of the canvas does not mean that he – unlike Fried – is speaking of the canvas as a piece of literal physical material, as if he were somehow unwittingly setting the table for the Minimalists, though that is exactly what Fried contends (*AO* 36). I think he is wrong in interpreting Greenberg's flat canvas as a step toward literalism, though I am aware of how committed he remains to this thesis. In fact, there is nothing at all literal about the two-dimensional backdrop of a painting, since the canvas withdraws into the background for as long as we pay attention to the painting, and Greenberg strikes me as perfectly aware of this. The strange thing is that Fried is perfectly aware of it as well, as seen in his 1966 essay on Stella: "By *shape as such* I mean not merely the silhouette of the support (which I shall call literal shape), not merely that of the outlines of elements in a given picture (which I shall call depicted shape), but shape as a medium within which choices about both literal and depicted shape are made, and made mutually responsive" (*AO* 77). But just a few pages later, he seems to forget this third option and phrases everything in terms of a simple opposition between literal and depicted shape: "the development of modernist painting during the past six years [1960-1966] can be described as having involved the progressive assumption by literal shape of a greater – more active, more explicit – importance than ever before, and the consequent subordination of depicted shape" (*AO* 81). Given that depicted shape plays vanishingly little role in Greenberg's content-free art criticism, he is supposedly left with nothing but the literal shape, though this runs counter to his and McLuhan's emphasis on the unseen background character of the medium.

In any case, Fried does not just replace Greenberg's focus on flatness with his own on shape as the new key to Modernism. Just as importantly, he also uses this shift to claim that Greenberg is stuck in an *essentialist* vision of art, one that is insufficiently aware of the historical changes each genre undergoes. As Fried tells us in a footnote to "Art and Objecthood": "flatness and the delimitation of flatness ought not to be thought of as the 'irreducible essence of pictorial art,' but rather as something like *the minimal conditions for something's being seen as a painting.*" But to meet such conditions, Fried rightly adds, is not very interesting. Of greater interest is the question of "what, at a given moment, is capable of compelling conviction, of succeeding as a painting" (*AO* 169, n. 6). This brings us to his more sweeping claim against Greenberg:

> This is not to say that painting *has no* essence; it is to claim that that essence – i.e. that which compels conviction – is largely determined

by, and therefore continually changes in response to, the vital work of the recent past. The essence of painting is not something irreducible. Rather, the task of the modernist painter is to discover those conventions that, at a given moment, *alone* are capable of establishing his work's identity as painting. (*AO* 169, note 6)

Elsewhere, Fried uses the term "dialectic" for this process. This allows him to take a certain distance from Kant, whose views are the most common target of appeals to dialectical method. The possible stakes of this plea for dialectic are whether we adopt an "essentialist" or "anti-essentialist" view of art, with the latter being the supposedly dialectical approach. The point is expressed with especial enthusiasm by the Hegelian Pippin, who oddly considers both Fried *and* T.J. Clark – something of a "frenemy" of Fried – as "left-Hegelian" (*AB* 70). More specifically, Pippin sees Fried and Clark as united against the philosopher Arthur Danto, linked in his supposed essentialism with Greenberg himself – though we should note that Greenberg never much cared for Danto's work (*AEA* xxii), and that Danto explicitly preferred Hegel's philosophy of art to Kant's (*AEA* 194). In Pippin's words: "Danto's account turns a bit Greenbergian, as he narrates an attempt to find the 'essence' of painting as such, seeking subtraction and erasure as ways of eliminating what was merely borrowed from other media" (*AB* 71). By contrast, Fried and Clark are linked by Pippin with his favorite philosopher: "There is a great deal more at stake for Hegel [than 'essence'] and, accordingly, a great deal more at stake in the accounts of Clark and Fried, something tied to the historical, civilizational project definitive of the world in which such art was made" (*AB* 71). In short, Pippin is making what we could call an anti-formalist argument in which the artwork is not fundamentally cut off from its surroundings so as to obtain an autonomous existence. He is aware of the dangers of such an approach: "of course, the worry about any such sociohistorical account is reductionism, not doing justice to the art as art; treating it as instances or examples or in other ways tied to, perhaps 'caused' by, developments other than artistic [ones] – essentially epiphenomenal" (*AB* 72). Pippin nonetheless insists that there must be a link between the work and the historical horizon in which it was produced. Yet he shies away from Clark's effort to do so in Marxist terms by explaining all human culture as derived from the "accumulation of capital" (*AB* 72). Thus it seems as if Fried were more Pippin's man, since he avoids sweeping Marxist or other historical explanations of art while also steering clear of Greenberg's purported essentialism.

Among other things, we might ask whether Pippin gets Fried right when he calls him a "left-Hegelian," a view at odds with my own treatment of both Fried and Greenberg as Kantian formalists. One way in which Fried might be considered a Hegelian is through his opposition to "essentialism" in art, as ascribed by Pippin to both Greenberg and Danto. Yet there are three separate points, and important ones, on which I find Fried unfair to Greenberg. The first concerns Greenberg's supposed view that there is a "timeless and unchanging essence to the art of painting" (*AO* 35). Fried admits that "Greenberg didn't use either of the last two adjectives," but nonetheless asserts that "both are implicit in his argument" (*AO* 35). Pippin is supportive here: as a Hegelian he is naturally opposed to timeless and unchanging essences, and wants to follow everything in its emergence from the course of wider historical experience. Fried tells us that, having been decisively influenced at an early age by Greenberg's impressive critical writings, he initially did not question his mentor's account of modern art, an account he summarizes accurately enough. Toward the mid nineteenth century, the arts were all threatened with dissolution into a vast sea of *kitsch* (I 5-22). In order to avoid this, each art began trying to provide the kind of experience which it alone could offer. For example, instead of painting and music trying to tell stories – which ought to be the province of literature – they began to focus on the essential conditions of their medium and do work that reflected those conditions directly. In the case of painting, Greenberg argued, the medium is essentially *flat*; he added later that is also *framed* or *delimited*, an expansion capitalized upon by Fried in his interpretation of Stella. In Greenberg's eyes, this spelled the end for the traditional pictorial illusionism of European painting, thereby leading from Manet through the Impressionists and Cézanne to a veritable climax of flatness: the Analytic Cubism of Pablo Picasso and Georges Braque, treated by Greenberg as the most important art movement of the twentieth century. Even so, additional high points of flatness were to come, whether in the works of Mondrian, Joan Miró, and eventually Pollock. Though modern painting continued after Pollock, we have seen that Greenberg thought the limits of flatness had already been reached in the *optical* illusionism of Pollock's work, decades after the death of pictorial illusionism. And soon enough, we will encounter Greenberg's admission that flatness had already hit the wall several decades before Pollock, namely in Cubist collage.

Against this apparent conception of Modernism as trying to find the essence of all painting, Fried argued as early as his 1966 article on Stella that "what the modernist painter can be said to discover in his work – what can be said to be revealed to him in it – is not the irreducible essence of *all* painting but rather that which, at the present moment in painting's history, is capable of convincing him that it can stand comparison with the painting of both the modernist and the premodernist past whose quality seems to him beyond question" (*AO* 36). Three decades later, he describes this as an "attempt to historicize the essence of painting" (AO 38). For good measure, he adds that by historicizing our sense of what can "compel conviction" at any given point in time, he is able to

> [undo] the artificial separation that Greenberg was compelled to posit between two distinct yet somehow continuous phases in the modernist dynamic: a first phase, lasting from Manet through Abstract Expressionism, directed toward the discovery of the irreducible working essence of pictorial art, and a second phase, beginning with Newman, Rothko, and Still, directed toward the discovery of what irreducibly constitutes "good" art . . . (*AO* 38)

Though one is hesitant to challenge Fried on any point concerning Greenberg, whom he knew and grappled with in a way that is simply not true for most of us, it seems to me that the essentialist reading of Greenberg is inaccurate. First, nowhere does Greenberg say that attention to flatness is binding on all painters at all times as the very essence of their craft. He carefully restricts this imperative to Modernist painting, which he dates – like Fried himself, though for different reasons – as running from Manet through some not yet attained future point. It is even common, when reading Greenberg, to run across statements of the following sort: "The classic avant-garde's emphasis on 'purity' of medium is a time-bound one and no more binding on art than any other time-bound emphasis" (*LW* 16). An even smokier gun can be found in his 1945 critique of some newly translated theoretical writings by Mondrian, who "committed the *unforgivable error* of asserting that one mode of art, that of pure, abstract relations, would be absolutely superior to all others in the future" (II 16; emph. added). Greenberg's problem is obviously not with "pure, abstract relations," since he yields to few other critics in his high estimation of Mondrian. Rather, the error to which he refers is the claim that "one mode of art," whatever mode it might be, will be the true and essential path of art from here on out. The worst we can say of Greenberg is that his principles do not give us much traction in considering the pre-Manet history of art, nor do they empower fruitful speculation as to what future paths art might take once Modernism has run its course. Nonetheless, Greenberg always insists that his claim that painting must primarily be attentive to the conditions of its medium is historically limited to the Modernist period, which for him remained not yet completed.

Second, and somewhat strangely, the principle that Fried offers as his alternative to Greenbergianism is a principle forged by Greenberg himself. To cite Fried's words once more: "that which, at the present moment in painting's history, is capable of convincing [the painter] that it can stand comparison with the painting of both the modernist and the premodernist past whose quality seems to him beyond question." The notion that any artist needs to be able to stand comparison with the highest quality works of the distant or recent past appears often enough in Greenberg, and thus is hardly suited to be used as a weapon against him. See for instance his 1949 praise for Thomas Cole, whose "draftsmanship has a sensitive precision and an instinct for the unity of the page that enables it to stand comparison with Claude [Lorrain's]" (II 281), or his expressed conviction in 1965 that Caro "is the only new sculptor whose sustained quality can bear comparison with [David] Smith's" (IV 205). Indeed, Greenberg treats the search for a level of quality comparable to that of the Old Masters as the most powerful justification for the Modernist avant-garde in the first place.

Third and finally, there is nothing inherently artificial about Greenberg positing a split between two phases of Modernism: one running from Manet through Pollock and concerned to discover the essence of painting as such, the other beginning with Newman and focused on what inherently makes for quality in art. Rather, this is exactly how we should expect a long historical movement to work. After reaching a point of exhaustion from pushing a basic idea to its limit, that movement will begin to explore an incipient new principle that arises from the ruins of the previous one. The worst we can say here is that Greenberg never gives as clear an account of the Newman/Rothko/Still phase of Modernism as of his thoroughly studied Manet-to-Pollock era. But one could hardly demand a fully developed analysis of something that had just begun.

I would make a more general challenge to Fried's complaint about Greenberg's purported commitment to a "timeless and unchanging essence" in the latter's writings. The problem is the ambiguous status of the adjectives "timeless" and "unchanging." Are they qualifiers, or emphasizers? That is to say, does Fried think that a search for essence is fine as long as that essence is not timeless and unchanging? Or does he think that all essence is, necessarily, timeless and unchanging, and to be rejected for that very reason? It seems to me that Fried assumes the latter, although that is clearly not what Greenberg is up to. There is no need for an essence to be eternal. Although easel painting has to be done on a flat canvas, with flatness therefore an essential feature of that medium, this does not entail that focused attention on the flat medium will always be what is at stake in advanced painting from now on. There are long historical periods in which the notion of flatness sheds little light on what is going on in art (as Fried knows better than anyone), and thus it is no wonder that Greenberg spent vanishingly little time discussing pre-Manet art, for which he simply never fashioned the appropriate conceptual tools to the degree that Fried did. I should note that there is a more widespread confusion in intellectual life – though Fried does not seem guilty of this – between the claim that each thing *has* an essence and the related but very different claim that this essence can be *known*. That is to say, the key features of advanced art inevitably change due to the need for artists to respond to the best work of the previous generation, as well as the normal human tendency to become fatigued with what has already been accomplished. We can also deduce that there is a limit that cannot be crossed without the purported art no longer being art. No doubt there have been numerous critics – always looking benighted in hindsight – who have wrongly claimed that certain new paintings were "non-art," though many examples of such non-art now look like masterpieces: Picasso's proto-cubist *Les demoiselles d'Avignon*, initially ridiculed even by friends and friendly collectors, is perhaps the most famous example. Nonetheless, it does not follow that what counts as art is infinitely mutable, able to transgress *any* limit. What this limit might be is a matter on which each individual theorist must place a bet. For Fried it is primarily the theatrical that teeters on the brink of non-art; for my own part, I do not see how any *literal* object (SO-SQ) can possibly count as art, though a debate can always be had as to whether any particular work should be counted as merely literal.

I now wish to return to another point where I think Fried is not quite right about Greenberg. This concerns the latter's remark, in the essay "After Abstract Expressionism," that "a stretched or tacked-up canvas already exists as a picture – though not necessarily as a *successful* one" (IV 131-132). Fried quotes this remark at least four times in his 1996 Introduction to *Art and Objecthood*, making it clear that he still considers it a crucial *lapsus* on the part of his former mentor. The importance of the point for Fried is that it allows him to link Greenberg, rather implausibly in my view, with the Minimalists. In Fried's words:

91

> with respect to his understanding of modernism Greenberg had no truer followers than the literalists [i.e., the Minimalists]. For if, as Greenberg held, the "testing" of modernism led to the discovery that the irreducible essence of pictorial art was nothing other than the literal properties of the support, that is, flatness and the delimitation of flatness and the delimiting of flatness, it's easy to see how a cohort of artists might come to feel that that discovery did not go far enough, in particular that it stopped short of recognizing that what mattered all along was not those particular properties but rather literalness as such . . . (AO 36)

To repeat, I am not signing on to Fried's interpretation of Minimalism just yet. If Minimalism turns out to be nothing more than a form of literalism, then I agree it would not be very interesting, whether in art or in architecture. It is simply questionable whether that is what is really going on with this style. But let's assume for the moment that Fried is right in calling the Minimalists "literalists." Even if this were the case, there would be no grounds for calling Greenberg a literalist as well. Fried's mistake can be found in his assumption that Greenberg's "stretched or tacked-up canvas" is identical to the canvas as a literal object, and this is not so. Greenberg's point is that if the two sole irreducible conventions of painting are that it be flat and have a shape, then even a canvas with no marks on it would meet this description. Although Fried treats this as an impossible and fateful conclusion, it is basically harmless. Greenberg is not saying that a *literal* piece of canvas and a *literal* frame, qua physical objects, are enough to make a work of art. Instead, he is saying that once the conventions of painting as a genre have been met, then we have an artwork – albeit an unsuccessful one – that is something over and above the literal physical materials involved. Stated differently: if we were to look at a blank canvas inside a frame, we would not be seeing literal pieces of physical frame and physical canvas, but a boring piece of art.

An analogy from McLuhan may be of assistance here. For the great Canadian media theorist, television as a medium is more important than the content of any particular television show; here McLuhan and Greenberg resemble both each other and Heidegger, another author who shows fiery contempt for content (beings) as opposed to its unnoticed background (Being). But when McLuhan speaks of television as a medium, he is definitely not referring to the literal, physical features of the medium: cathode ray tubes, dials, glass screen, broadcast towers. Instead, these literal features are simply the physical components that assemble a basically non-physical medium: television itself. The same holds, I contend, for Greenberg's flat background canvas, which has nothing to do with canvas as a literal piece of physical stuff. If the technology had existed in Greenberg's time to project paintings immaterially into empty two-dimensional space, and if artists had worked regularly in such a medium, the essentials of his point about flatness would still hold good.

Having just discussed Fried's apparent rejection of essence, we turn to a second possibly "Hegelian" feature in his thinking: the dialectic. This theme arises in particular in "Three American Painters" (AO 213-265), the catalog essay for the show he curated at Harvard, featuring works by Noland, Olitski, and Stella. Looking back at this essay in 1996, Fried recalls that "I further suggest[ed] that the best model for the evolution of modernist painting is that of the dialectic understood as an unceasing process of perpetual radical self-criticism or, as I also put it, 'perpetual revolution'" (AO 17). While use of the word "dialectic" and the reference to "perpetual revolution" may strike Hegelian chords in Pippin's ears, there is no direct link here with Hegel. For there is nothing inherently "dialectical" about the notion of perpetual radical self-criticism, which is equally compatible with Kant's model of unattainable regulative ideas, or Heidegger's asymptotic unveiling of a truth that can never be made directly present. Fried is simply using "dialectic" in a much looser sense than Hegel or Pippin. In any case, the Fried of 1996 casts shade on his own earlier references to both the "dialectic" and to "radical self-criticism." As he puts it: "What excited me at the time was the seeming theoretical sophistication of such a model, which in effect gave dramatic form to certain Hegelian assumptions behind Greenberg's avowedly Kantian reading of as self-criticism . . . But the sophistication, such as it was, came at too high a price" (AO 18). What is at stake in separating Fried from the notion of dialectic? This is not just a tedious professorial dispute over whether Fried is more of a Kantian or more of a Hegelian. Instead, it is a question of whether Fried accepts two of the anti-formalist pillars of the dialectic: (1) the assumption that there is no reality-in-itself in opposition to thought and hence no artwork-in-itself, and (2) the assumption that nothing – including art – is in any way self-contained, since art belongs to a broader movement that includes history, culture, and society. Based on what we have seen, it is safe to say that Fried is not dialectical in senses (1) or (2), and that he is much more of a formalist than Pippin thinks: especially in Fried's anti-theatrical views, the basis of all his intellectual work.

That brings us directly to theatricality, the third point of disagreement between Fried and Greenberg, and the one most relevant to us. This term is obviously Fried's key opponent in "Art and

Objecthood" and even in his famous trilogy of art-historical works. As for Greenberg's own views on theatricality, there are important excerpts from interviews in the last year of his life in which he disagrees sharply with his former protégé on this topic. The first comes on April 5, 1994, just over a month before his death, in conversation with Karlheinz Lüdeking of the German periodical *Kunstforum*:

> Lüdeking: *Aren't [Anselm] Kiefer's paintings too theatrical for you?*
> Greenberg: What's wrong with theatrical?
>
> Lüdeking: *I thought you would find that repulsive.*
> Greenberg: Why? Aren't you confusing me with Michael Fried?
>
> Lüdeking: *You would contradict Michal Fried on this point?*
> Greenberg: Yes. I believe that the theatrical is not necessarily bad. (*LW* 226-227)

The second took place with Saul Ostrow of *World Art* on an unspecified date, but since it is entitled "The Last Interview," we surmise that it took place sometime between the discussion with Lüdeking on April 5 and Greenberg's death on May 7. If anything, the elderly critic is even harsher about Fried in this later interview:

> Ostrow: *Michael Fried tries to build part of his argument against theatricality on just such a distinction [as you just made between sensuous and aesthetic pleasure]. For him, theatricality forces self-consciousness onto the viewer.*
> Greenberg: He's picked up on something that's beneath him. He goes on about the importance of whether the subject is facing you, or whether the subject is absorbed in some activity. I don't think he sees that well anymore. God knows, [the opera singer Luciano] Pavarotti's theatrical in the best way, without being too show-offy, but an Italian tenor is supposed to be theatrical. And there's Pavarotti doing it without any effort, no effort at all. That's what is of importance. (*LW* 240)

Here Greenberg drastically underestimates the importance of what Fried is up to with facingness and absorption. Nonetheless, it is worth noting his rejection of Fried's polemical use of theatricality as a supposed turning point in modernist criticism. We need to push the matter beyond the limited question of how Italian tenors ought to behave on stage. From a OOO standpoint, the need for theatricality in art spells doom not just for the Kantian approach to aesthetics, but to the long Kantian era of philosophy as a whole.

Background and Foreground

Greenberg's most famous piece of writing is also one of his earliest and least typical: "Avant-Garde and Kitsch" (I 5-22). When we think of kitsch, we think primarily of tasteless low-brow or middle-brow products, coveted by tacky upstarts who hoard tourist souvenirs and consume second-rate popular culture. This need not be at the level of Norman Rockwell, Disney, and below: *The New Yorker* is dismissed by Greenberg as a kitsch publication no less than *The Saturday Evening Post* (I 13). His essay makes the case for why this is a danger to high culture, and for how the avant-garde should be regarded as an attempt to protect high-quality art from kitsch. Yet it is striking how seldom the theme of kitsch recurs in the remaining decades of Greenberg's career. As he shifts from general cultural critic to a more focused theorist of Modernist art, his primary target is no longer kitsch, but what he calls *academic* art. The clearest definition of the term he ever gave can be found in a late-career lecture in Sydney:

> Academicization isn't a matter of academies – there were academies long before academicization and before the nineteenth century. Academicism consists in *the tendency to take the medium of an art too much for granted*. It results in blurring: words become imprecise, color gets muffled, the physical sources of sound become too much dissembled. (*LW* 28; emph. added)

This passage is extraordinary for several reasons. On an obvious level, it gives us a lucid account of what Greenberg means by academicism, one that says more than it openly states. Academicism occurs when the conditions of the medium in which one is working are ignored; that much is plainly stated. But Greenberg also indicates what academic artists are paying attention to when they ignore the medium: namely, the *content* of art. We can infer from this that the proper role of the avant-garde is to pay attention to the medium rather than content. But since every art has some sort of content, however minimal, the goal cannot be to *erase* content from art. Instead, the aim of the avant-garde should be that content somehow refers or alludes to its medium. This is consistent with everything we know about Greenberg. He is always hostile to what he calls "literary anecdote" in painting, and though he did not love abstraction for abstraction's sake – as we will see in his harsh obituary remarks on Kandinsksy – he conceded in late career that abstraction does have the merit of removing everyday associations from painting, thereby focusing our attention on medium rather than content. The way to come to grips with the inherent flatness of the canvas medium of easel painting is not to display a blank canvas in a frame, but to utilize content that is somehow appropriate to that flatness. Analytic Cubism was always his favorite example of success in doing so.

More generally, Greenberg claimed that "Picasso, Braque, Mondrian, Miró, Kandinsky, Brancusi, even Klee, Matisse, and Cézanne derive their chief inspiration from the medium they work in," before adding sarcastically in a footnote that "the chief concern of a painter like Dalí is to represent the processes and concepts of his consciousness, not the processes of his medium" (I 9). Greenberg never warmed to Surrealism, which he saw as merely preserving the tired conventions of nineteenth-century academic illusionistic oil painting: by focusing solely on strange content that today we might call "psychedelic," Dalí and his confederates missed the real thrust of modernism by paying no attention to the background conditions of their canvas medium. In the case of Dalí's painting, filled as it is with realistic-looking three-dimensional space – even if populated with utterly bizarre figures and objects, and named with equally bizarre titles – the presence of traditional illusionism seems fairly clear-cut. Perhaps more surprising is that Greenberg advances a subtler version of this same critique against Kandinsky. Though Kandinsky is praised in the passage above in the same breath as permanent Greenberg idols such as Cézanne, Matisse, and Picasso, within a few years he had become rather harsh in his view of the great Russian abstractionist. In a somewhat cruel obituary not long after Kandinsky's death, Greenberg does not bluntly call him an "academic" artist, but does call him a "provincial" one. While provincialism in art is normally associated with Sunday amateurs daubing in cultural backwaters, Greenberg asserts that there is a second, more insidious kind of provincial:

> The other sort of provincialism is that of the artist – generally from an outlying country – who in all earnest and admiration devotes himself to the style being currently developed in the metropolitan center, yet fails in one way or another really to understand what it is about ... The Russian, Wassily Kandinsky, [was a provincial of this latter sort]. (II 3-4)

Greenberg does not deny Kandinsky's general sophistication as an artist, conceding he was right to grasp that Cubism had freed painting from the obligation to paint images of familiar everyday things. Yet in doing so, Greenberg holds, he had failed to understand what Cubism was really after: not abstraction per se, but rather "its recapture of the literal realization of the physical limitations and conditions of the medium and of the positive advantages to be gained from the exploitation of these very limitations" (II 5). As for the consequences of this failure for Kandinsky's art, Greenberg is explicit:

> he came to conceive of the picture ... as an aggregate of discrete shapes; the color, size, and spacing of these he related so insensitively to the space surrounding them ... that this [space] remained inactive and meaningless; the sense of a continuous surface was lost, and the space became pocked with "holes" ... [H]aving begun by accepting the absolute flatness of the picture surface, Kandinsky would go on to allude to illusionistic depth by a use of color, line, and perspective that were plastically irrelevant... Academic reminiscences crept into [Kandinsky's paintings] at almost every point other than that of what they "represented." (II 5)

He ends this cold notice by concluding that, on the whole, Kandinsky is a dangerous example for younger painters (II 6).

We see that at this point in his career, Greenberg had passed damning judgments on painters as different as Dalí and Kandinsky for precisely the same reason. By falling into the trap of illusionistic depth, Dalí (explicitly) and Kandinsky (tacitly) had missed the central imperative of avant-garde painting. Picasso and Braque in their High Analytic Cubist phase did not venture into full-blown abstraction, but had stuck with recognizable if highly distorted everyday objects (candlesticks, violins, art dealers). Yet they used various profiles of these objects, simultaneously available on the same flat picture plane, to signal their awareness that flatness was the real point of Cubism. We will see that Greenberg eventually reached a more nuanced view of Cubist flatness, realizing that it also had to be countered rather than simply affirmed.

Before exploring the point further, I want to recall once more that Greenberg was not alone in stressing the importance of flatness, though in other fields this was done with different terminology. The most obvious example is Heidegger, whom I regard as the most binding influence in twentieth-century philosophy: by which I mean that the future of philosophy hinges more on the proper assimilation and overcoming of Heidegger than of any other figure. If we compare Heidegger with Greenberg – the twentieth century's greatest philosopher with its greatest art critic – an important similarity jumps out immediately. Namely, both share a lasting hostility to content. That is not Heidegger's own word for the topic we are discussing. Greenberg might speak of the flat medium versus the content of a painting, but in Heidegger's case the dichotomy was between *Being* and *beings*. In Heideggerese, this is known as the "ontological difference," probably the most important concept of his career.[4] Whereas beings are always present, Being always hides: incapable of coming fully to presence and withdrawing behind whatever confronts us directly. As of 2019, I have written hundreds if not thousands of pages on Heidegger, and my reading has found enthusiasts almost everywhere but among mainstream Heidegger scholars.[5] Nonetheless, I am confident in my interpretation of his ontological difference between Being and beings. Among other difficulties, it is not widely recognized that this concept has two distinct faces that should not be collapsed into one. Let's speak only of the first face here, though the second will soon become even more important for our ultimate reservations about Greenberg. The first aspect of the ontological difference, as already mentioned, is the opposition between that which is present and that which with-draws. In later years Heidegger describes this with a number of basi-cally synonymous pairs such as veiling/unveiling, sheltering/clearing, and the like. The problem with presence as opposed to withdrawal, though Heidegger does not put it this way, is that presence is *rela-tional*. It does not give us the thing itself, but only the thing as it relates to something else: namely human being, or *Dasein*.

Nothing is more worrisome to Heidegger than the spread of global technology, in which he sees the United States and the Soviet Union as equally complicit, for all the noisy surface differences of their political systems. Technology is the reign of pure presence, reduc-ing everything in the world to a stockpile of manipulable material, stripping away its concealment and its mystery.[6] One explanation of Heidegger's long-term allegiance to Nazism is that he felt – wrongly, of course – that Adolf Hitler was the man to confront the growing wasteland of global technology. What, then, was Heidegger's alter-native to *Technik*? This is always left somewhat vague, though it seems bound up with kitsch Romanticism about peasants and appeals to the supposed similarity between modern Germans and ancient Greeks. All of this runs the gamut, in Heidegger, from nationalism to outright anti-Semitism.[7] Yet we gain a more definite sense of what Heidegger hoped for from a brief passage in a famous if overrated work of his middle years, *Contributions to Philosophy*. There we read as follows: "The age of [philosophical] 'systems' has passed. The age that would elaborate the essential form of beings from out of the truth of Being has not yet come."[8] To elaborate the essential form of beings from out of the truth of Being: this might sound like gibberish to a Heidegger novice, but for our purposes its meaning is clear enough. Individual beings will always be with us; they obviously cannot be abolished. Yet instead of conceiving of beings as immediately and obviously present, known through their measurable and manipulable qualities in the manner of technology, we might rebuild beings in such a way as to reflect an awareness of the elusive Being that is forever concealed behind them. Since we have just been speaking about Greenberg and flatness, Heidegger's formulation should immediately ring a bell. Greenberg never thought that content could be eliminated from painting; even abstraction in art is still a form of content, however unfamiliar from everyday life. But Heidegger and Greenberg both search for a way in which explicit surface content can somehow signal its awareness of the medium in which it operates. In other words, Heidegger's history of metaphysics as "ontotheology" (the false assumption that Being itself can be made directly present) is a direct parallel to Greenberg's notion of "academic art" as that which takes no account of its medium.

Another obvious parallel is McLuhan, who despises surface content every bit as much as the two authors just discussed. The meaning of McLuhan's most famous slogan, "the medium is the message," is precisely this: it makes no difference whether we make "good" or "bad" use of television, fingerprinting, or nuclear weapons. In each case, it is the medium itself that is decisive.[9] This idea is the foundation of all of McLuhan's work, which in my view remains underutilized. When Greenberg told his audience in Sydney that "academicism consists in *the tendency to take the medium of an art too much for granted*," one could imagine McLuhan ghostwriting these words, if not that he suffered a career-ending stroke at just about the same time. Seen through McLuhan's eyes, the mission of the artist looks a lot like that of the philosopher in Heidegger's *Contributions*. Where Heidegger writes in the 1930s of rebuilding the form of beings from out of the truth of Being, McLuhan argues in 1970 that the artist's role is to transform *clichés* into *archetypes*.[10] In other words, the mere visible "beings" known as dead media that have outlived their usefulness (such as yesterday's newspaper) should be reworked into new media, new archetypes. Joyce was among those figures most admired by McLuhan for having purportedly done so. The archetype organizes our experience but is never directly visible in it, much like Being for Heidegger or the flat background medium for Greenberg. It is not clear that any of these authors succeeded in clearly establishing the relationship between surface figure and hidden background: a concept pioneered by Gestalt psychology at an earlier date. But simply stating the problem in these terms was a monumental event in twentieth-century intellectual life, and it is not yet clear that we have lived up to it.

Yet there is a sense in which McLuhan avoided a crucial error that plagues both Heidegger and Greenberg. Here we return to the second face of Heidegger's ontological difference, alluded to above. The first face, we saw, was the difference between the tacit and the explicit, the veiled and the unveiled, the medium and the message. I fully endorse this distinction, which alone is capable of combating literalism and relationism in philosophy, the arts, or anywhere else. Being displays the autonomy and self-containment that individual beings can never provide – in Heidegger's view, not OOO's – much like the concept of "medium" in both Greenberg and McLuhan. The second face of his ontological difference, however, is less plausible and more constricting. This comes from Heidegger's tendency to identify individual beings as more superficial than Being not just because they are present, but because they are *many*. This is true not only of his numerous invocations of Being, but of his discussions in an arts context of the concealed "earth," which is described not just as concealed, but as a unified rather than pluralized force.[11] Only rarely, most often in his later reflections on "the thing," does Heidegger show much sympathy for the life of discrete individual objects. And though he sometimes speaks of the Being of individual beings, especially in his accounts of how scientific revolutions occur, for the most part he seems to hold that all individual beings partake of a single Being rather than assigning a private withdrawn reality to each of them.[12]

McLuhan manages to escape this particular trap. Media for him are individual, appear and die in the course of time, and also tend to reverse into their opposites through a process he calls "overheating."[13] It seems to me that Greenberg escapes the monistic trap no better than Heidegger, though he was able to explore the possible mechanics of an escape in a way that the philosopher was not. One of the paradoxical defects of formalism in the arts is that, while it jealously guards the autonomy of individual works from all external relations to biography, socio-political conditions, and "situations" more generally, it is nonetheless strangely holistic in its treatment of all elements internal to a work. We caught a glimpse of this when Fried's magnificent syntactic interpretation of Caro's sculpture was unfortunately read by way of Saussure's linguistic structuralism, in which elements have no meaning on their own but are thoroughly deployed in a total system of differences. In a 2012 article I made the same point about the formalism of the New Critics in literature, citing the case of Cleanth Brooks.[14] When reading Brooks, one often has the sense that the slightest alterations inside a poem are enough to generate a completely different poem, since each element is treated as a mirror reflecting all the rest. But we know this is an exaggeration. There are often variant texts of classic pieces of literature, and only in rare cases do these variants result in anything like different works; most involve trivialities of punctuation or spelling.

One often has the same sense of an underlying holism when reading Greenberg as well. To give one such instance, Greenberg claims in 1954 that "how much any part [of an artwork] is worth aesthetically is decided solely by its relation to every other part or aspect of the given work" (III 187), which sounds like something the New Critics would say about literature. Another comes in his Bennington College seminars of 1971, in which he repeatedly uses the word "relational" as a positive term about art – though he means nothing like Bourriaud does – and dismisses "non-relational" as a "camp" term produced by recent avant-gardist hipsters (HE 97-99). But even more decisively, it is clear that Greenberg thinks of the flat canvas medium as a unified medium embracing all of the content in a painting, thus entailing that all aspects of a painting are holistically intertwined through the same background, even if not mirroring each other directly. Even more than this: for Greenberg, all paintings share the flat canvas background as their single medium. Ignoring the question of shape for the moment, all canvases are flat in the same way, and that means the flatness is the same flatness for every painting. This is where Greenberg and Heidegger begin to look like blood brothers, though Heidegger is far more extreme: for whereas Greenberg only says that flatness is the medium of all *painting*, Heidegger makes Being the medium for everything. Despite this difference in scope, they end up in exactly the same predicament: content is individuated, pluralized, and superficial, while the medium is always deep and one. What this means is that content is always paralyzed from the start, since it has no role for either of these authors than to signal its awareness of a deeper hidden background medium. In an infamous example, Heidegger proclaims the disasters of Hiroshima and Auschwitz to be unimportant surface incidents, because the real catastrophe happened long ago with the forgetting of Being in ancient Greece.[15] Nothing in Greenberg sounds this sinister or obtuse, but for him too, there is a sense in which all modern art worthy of the name is "syntactic" in Fried's Saussurean sense, with the elements exhausting themselves in mutual differentiation and achieving a single total effect. Stated differently, individual elements in an artwork are not allowed to have their own, independent, concealed backgrounds.

So far, we have identified two separate problems associated with the differing formalisms of Fried and Greenberg. In Fried's case, we were led to defend theatricality as the fusion of beholder and work – no doubt against Fried's wishes, but as a direct result of his own historical insights. In the case of Greenberg, the issue is different: the individual elements of an artwork's content are treated as lowly surfaces without private depths of their own. What are the implications of these problems for the present and future of art and criticism? We will begin to work out an answer in Chapters 6 and 7 below. But for the sake of fairness to Greenberg, we should take a closer look at his evident awareness that flatness can only be pushed so far before encountering an aesthetic counterthrust. This happens most ingeniously in his 1958 article on collage, "The Pasted Paper Revolution" (IV 61-66).

The Limits of Flatness

We have seen that in the 1940s, Greenberg was still so committed to flatness as the core feature of Modernist painting that he was willing to discard the achievements of as prominent a Modernist as Kandinsky. By the time of his article "Modernist Painting" in 1966, he had come around to seeing abstraction as an important gateway to flatness, rather than as a "provincial" distraction from the true stakes of Cubism. After seeming to hold the line by stating that abstraction is less important than Kandinsky and Mondrian think, he goes on to more or less concede their point:

> All recognizable entities . . . exist in three-dimensional space, and the barest suggestion of a recognizable entity suffices to call up associations of that kind of space. The fragmentary silhouette of a human figure, or of a teacup, will do so, and by doing so alienate pictorial space from the two-dimensionality which is the guarantee of painting's independence as an art. (IV 88)

In other words, Greenberg no longer sees how any trace of a recognizable entity in a painting can escape the sort of illusionism he distrusts in a Modernist context. At this stage, therefore, he can no longer imagine a convincing Modernist painting that would be anything but abstract. Yet in the same article, he also makes an important concession about flatness: "The flatness toward which Modernist painting orients itself can never be an utter flatness. The heightened sensitivity of the picture plane may no longer permit sculptural illusion, or *trompe-l'oeil*, but it does and must permit optical illusion. The first mark made on a surface destroys its virtual flatness . . ." (IV 90). But whenever Greenberg may have come to a personal realization that flatness has its limits, he eventually dated this breakthrough to a far earlier point in art history than Pollock:

> *The Old Masters* had sensed that it was necessary to preserve what is called the integrity of the picture plane: that is, to signify the enduring presence of flatness underneath and above the most vivid illusion of three-dimensional space. The apparent contradiction involved was essential to the success of their art, *as it is indeed to the success of all pictorial art*. The Modernists have neither avoided nor resolved this contradiction; rather, they have reversed its terms. One is made aware of the flatness before, instead of after, being made aware of what the flatness contains. (IV 87; emph. added)

The change from his earlier views should be obvious. My point is not to catch Greenberg in some hypocritical inconsistency, but the opposite: to show how he continued to develop his understanding of the historical implications of flatness after his early dismissal of Kandinsky's abstraction. When reading the Greenberg of the 1940s, one has the sense that flatness is a tool for understanding art from Manet onward; I recall no effort on his part in early career to apply his favorite concept to pre-modern art history. But by 1966 he is edging toward the view that the tension between flatness and surface is inherent in painting itself, rather than being the concern of painters in a delimited Modernist period, and thereby runs the risk of deserving the charge of "essentialism" lodged against him by Fried and later Pippin. Yet Greenberg never quite reaches that point, as seen from his failure to do more than hint at the possibility of rewriting all of Western art history on the basis of flatness. And furthermore, in the 1960s he seems to have entered a new phase in which he ties innovation in painting less to the struggle for flatness than to an awareness of the dangers of an *excessive* focus on the two-dimensional plane. As we will soon see, the most important example is his discussion of how Picasso and Braque ran up against the limits of Analytic Cubism but still managed to keep things moving with their shift to collage. Whether or not Greenberg gets the Cubists right, we have seen that he follows a distinctly twentieth-century line of thought that also includes Heidegger and McLuhan. This way of thinking begins with a repression of the surface, the ontic, or content in favor of depth, but goes so far in its repression that the superficial is eventually resurgent. Elsewhere, I have called this process the revenge of the surface.[16]

Although "flatness" in everyday language suggests a superficial outer layer of something, the significance of flatness for Greenberg is always that it plays the role of deep background rather than surface: analogous to Heidegger's Being, rather than beings. And conversely, although three-dimensional illusionism suggests perceptual depth, it actually puts all depicted entities into a purely relational space, one in which things lack a depth of their own. But here is the question. Since the later Greenberg emphasizes the inevitable illusion that remains even after the best efforts to remove it, should this be read as a return to the *literal* in art? That seems to be Fried's view, since he reads the Minimalists as the logical outcome of Greenberg's own teaching, through their insistence on the literal physical materials of their basically content-free art. Or to the contrary, does Greenberg's turn embody a new if embryonic project, as OOO contends? The general thrust of that project would amount to a severing of Greenberg's – and Heidegger's – previous bond between content and surface. Rather than explicit content and even "marks on a canvas" being inherently superficial in comparison with their background medium, the medium would now be located in the heart of individual pictorial elements themselves. To rephrase it as a defense of Kandinsky, the "academic reminiscences" of empty space between his various abstract shapes would be beside the point. For the mission of content in avant-garde art would no longer be to hint slyly at a universal background medium lying behind all content, but rather to explore how each scrap of content already consists of both foreground and background in its own right. To give it a final alternate phrasing, it is no longer a question of erasing the autonomy of individual pictorial elements in favor of a background that looms over them all (Heidegger, Greenberg), or in favor of a syntactic disappearance of these elements into their mutual interactions (Fried's Saussurean reading of Caro's sculptures), but of isolating those elements to the point that each is seen to have its own background. This is, in fact, my view. One of the immediate implications would be to give Kandinsky a much higher status in the history of Modernism than Greenberg is willing to entertain, with Dalí perhaps an even bigger winner. There is the further irony that, just as Fried's vehement opposition to theatricality brought him in the end to the quasi-theatrical notion of "facingness," Greenberg's obsession with flatness brought him to see that background flatness is not just the saving power, but also the danger.

Greenberg is on record as admiring the Cubism of Picasso and Braque above all other art movements of the twentieth century, primarily for their having achieved an art that broke with five centuries of pictorial illusionism and helped lead us to "the flattest pictorial art we have ever seen in the West" (III 118), or at least since Byzantine times. But this achievement entailed an inherent risk. As Greenberg puts it: "By the end of 1911 both [Picasso and Braque] had pretty well turned traditional illusionistic paintings inside out. The fictive depths of the picture had been drained to a level very close to the actual paint surface" (IV 62). To Greenberg's credit, he acknowledges that in the very moment when Picasso and Braque reached his own critical ideal of what Modernism ought to be, they approached a point of crisis. He continues: "It had become necessary to discriminate more explicitly between the resistant reality of the flat surface and the forms shown upon it in yielding ideated depth. *Otherwise they would become too immediately one with the surface and survive solely as surface pattern*" (IV 62; emph. added). Hence the turn toward collage. For Greenberg, the strategic significance of collage as a way to beat back the encroachment of apocalyptic flatness is so obvious that he "wonders why those who write on collage continue to find its origin in nothing more than the Cubists' need for renewed contact with reality" (IV 61).

Though the full-blown story of collage begins in 1912, when Braque "[glued] a piece of imitation wood-grain paper to a drawing," Greenberg notes some provisional steps in this direction starting two years earlier (IV 62). In his 1910 *Still Life with Violin and Palette*, Braque painted a nail casting a shadow near the top of the picture, which seems to be the only shadow depicted anywhere on the canvas. In Greenberg's reading, this imposed "a kind of photographic space between the surface and the dimmer, fragile illusoriness of the Cubist space which the still-life . . . inhabited" (IV 62). In this way, the nail divides the flat pictorial surface from the literal canvas by hinting at a separation between the two. Through its very success in eliminating illusionistic depth, Cubism courted the danger of collapsing into surface decoration, but with this 1910 painting it is now a matter of two separate planes rather than just one, and of a certain distance between them. Greenberg notes that something similar happened in Braque's 1911 *Man with a Guitar*. Though it can be somewhat difficult to see in reproductions, there is a painted loop of rope at the edge of the canvas – at roughly ten o'clock – whose "sculptural delineation" again serves to distance the cubist painting proper from the literal surface with which it was otherwise in danger of merging (IV 62). This paved the way for an even more decisive gesture:

In the same year Braque introduced capital letters and numbers stenciled in *trompe-l'oeil* in paintings whose motifs offered no realistic

excuse for their presence. These intrusions, by their self-evident extraneous and abrupt flatness, stopped the eye at the literal, physical surface of
the canvas in the same way that the artist's signature did; here it was no
longer a question of interposing a more vivid illusion of depth between
surface and Cubist space, but one of specifying the very real depth of
flatness of the picture plane so that everything else shown on it would be
pushed into illusioned space by force of contrast. The surface was now
explicitly instead of implicitly indicated as a tangible but transparent
plane. (IV 62)

Even more than previously, we are now dealing with two planes
rather than one, and hence the cubists have secured the minimal
degree of illusion needed to prevent their painting from becoming
decorative wallpaper.

But 1912 proved to be the decisive year. In a further innovation,
Picasso and Braque began "to mix sand and other foreign substances
with their paint; the granular surface achieved thereby called direct
attention to the tactile reality of the picture" (IV 62). Braque, after
first adding marbleized surfaces and rectangles painted like wood
grain to some of his paintings, then took the final step with his first
collage, *Fruit Bowl*. From a Greenbergian standpoint, this seems to
be one of the most important artworks of all time. What Braque did
sounds simple enough: he pasted "three strips of imitation wood-grain
wallpaper to a sheet of drawing paper on which he then charcoaled
a rather simplified Cubist still-life and some *trompe-l'oeil* letters"
(IV 63). But the result was revolutionary. Under normal conditions,
lettering will always seem to be located on the literal canvas surface.
In this case, however, it seems to belong to illusionistic depth by
contrast with the pasted wood-grain wallpaper, which by definition
adheres even more to the literal surface than does anything else. And
yet, "the *trompe-l'oeil* lettering, simply because it was inconceivable
on anything but a flat plane, continued to suggest and return to it"
(IV 63). Greenberg adds that Braque heightened these complex effects
both by placing the letters in such a way as to maximize pictorial
illusion, and by drawing and shading directly on the pasted wood-
grain strips. This leads *Fruit Bowl* to an astonishing achievement
beyond all triumphs of avant-garde flatness: "The strips, the lettering,
the charcoaled lines and the white paper begin to change places in
depth with one another, and a process is set up in which every part
of the picture takes its turn at occupying every plane, whether real or
imagined, in it" (IV 63).

That is the essential claim of Greenberg's article. The final few
pages turn to the High Cubist manner of pushing collage even further,

concluding with his assessment that the celebrated collages of Juan Gris are overrated and miss the mark. But as concerns the first point, Picasso and Braque began adding different varieties of paper and cloth, meaning in this way to "expedite the shuffling and shuttling between surface and depth" (IV 63). Among other tricks, "depicted surfaces [are] shown as parallel with the picture plane and at the same time cutting through it, as if to establish the assumption of an illusion of depth far greater than that actually indicated" (IV 64). Eventually, "there seemed no direction left in which to escape from the literal flatness of the surface – except into the non-pictorial, real space in front of the picture" (IV 64). One result was Picasso's pathbreaking *Guitar* of 1912: "he cut out and folded a piece of paper in the shape of a guitar and glued and fitted other pieces of paper and four taut strings to it. A sequence of flat surfaces on different planes in actual space was created to which there adhered only the hint of a pictorial surface . . . and it founded a new genre of sculpture" (IV 64). As for Gris, his collages achieved much less dynamism between the various planes: "He used his pasted papers and *trompe-l'oeil* textures and lettering to assert flatness all right; but he almost always sealed the flatness inside the illusion of depth by placing images rendered with sculptural vividness on the nearest plane of the picture, and often on the rearmost plane too." As a result, his collages "have about them something of the closed-off presence of the traditional easel picture" (IV 65). This brings Greenberg to deliver a final blow: "Instead of that seamless fusion of the decorative with the spatial structure of the illusion which we get in the collages of [Picasso and Braque], there is [in Gris] an alternation, a collocation, of the decorative and the illusional" (IV 66).

With his impressive reading of Cubist collage, Greenberg shows what we have seen to be an important trait of great thinkers in every field: the ability to recognize that one's central doctrine always reaches a limit, and must eventually find a way to incorporate its opposite. We saw the same trait in Fried, when he managed to finesse Manet's anti-absorptive art into what is otherwise an uncompromising history of absorption as the core of modern painting. In Greenberg, we find a recognition that his treasured flatness starts to become an outright liability as early as 1911. By dissecting the motivation of Cubist collage as a way to create an ambiguous and alternating multitude of picture planes, Greenberg emerges from an unspoken crisis of his own, adding flexibility to what might have begun to look like a monotonous story of painterly awareness of a unified canvas ground. What makes this one of Greenberg's most important articles is the palpable sense that it is trying to teach us something new: something not just unknown in Greenberg's previous writing, but in some way directly at odds with it.

Nonetheless, it should be asked whether Greenberg's solution – to say nothing of Picasso and Braque's – is adequate to the crisis it addresses. In effect, Greenberg claims that the excessive overlap between pictorial and literal surface can be countered by "a process ... in which every part of the picture takes its turn at occupying every plane [in it], whether real or imagined . . ." In a complex collage such as *Fruit Bowl*, let's say that this amounts to a total of four or five separate planes in alternation and collision with each other. Even so, this would really just be a pluralized version of Greenberg's earlier model, with its basic flaw still intact. The facet of a piece of fruit, or an affixed strip of imitation wood-grain wallpaper, can now occupy any of four or five different planes in a kind of grand optical illusion, rather than being restricted to just one. Yet here as in Greenberg's earlier model, depth is still to be found nowhere else but in a *plane*. Individual elements of pictorial content might shift freely from one plane to another, but their sole function is still to hint knowingly at the specific planar backgrounds in which they happen to be lodged. Flatness is still the guiding principle, even if a given collage now has multiple dimensions of flatness rather than just one.

This does add renewed drama to a Cubism that had become dangerously flat by 1911, as Greenberg beautifully describes. Yet he still allows content to be enriched, freed from the aesthetic hell of "literary anecdote," only through its activating our sense of a deeper flat plane that it inhabits. From a OOO standpoint, what this misses is that objects – including those that inhabit paintings – always have a depth *internal* to themselves, not just in an encompassing spatial plane that they share with numerous other entities. You, I, a fruit bowl, a teapot, and a monkey are more than the surface content we emit to others: not because we are projected into multiple flat planes simultaneously, but because our surface content already hints at a depth that belongs to us alone. The analogy between Greenberg and Heidegger again proves helpful. What these thinkers share is a profound sense of the inadequacy of surface content, which Heidegger calls *Vorhandenheit* or presence-at-hand, and which he undercuts by appeal to the Being that lies much deeper than all tangible beings. Greenberg's appeal to painting's medium – the flat canvas – against all surface content is an analogous maneuver. Yet there is also a common shortcoming in their respective solutions. For Heidegger, Being is not just deeper than beings: it is also *one*, while individual beings are superficially plural.

Greenberg's reading of Cubist collage shows him to be entrapped in the same presumption. Unlike Heidegger, he does find an ingenious way to multiply the number of background planes, but there is still an unfortunate opposition between the many things on the surface and the unified planes underneath. It is a trap McLuhan alone manages to avoid, given his built-in professional need to focus on the effects of numerous *specific* media in reshaping human existence.

The way of addressing the problem is the same in the different cases of Heidegger and Greenberg. The only path beyond Heidegger is to abandon the idea of Being as a single unified plane at a distance from all specific entities, and to unlock the private depth found in each and every individual thing, a path he treads gingerly beginning in 1949.[17] Already in the much earlier *Being and Time*, Heidegger's hammer does not really vanish into a holistic background system of tools – despite his claim that it does so – but remains an autonomous nucleus that is sometimes able to rupture the smoothly functioning whole in which it participates. Likewise, the path beyond superficial pictorial content is not to appeal to a single flat plane, four planes, six of them, nine of them, or however many the audacious innovations of Picasso and Braque might be able to produce. Instead, the individual entities or figures contained in painting, or any other genre, each have their own medium: their own withdrawn selves, as signaled imperfectly by their surface properties.

5

After High Modernism

The reader will probably have gathered by now that OOO's critique of formalism does not change its basic sympathy for the formalists by comparison with those who have rejected them since the 1960s. By virtue of accepting the autonomy of artworks (as of all other objects) and agreeing that unparaphraseable taste – rather than discursive conceptuality – is the relevant faculty in aesthetics, we have taken a distance from those who try to leave Kant, Greenberg, and Fried somewhere along the roadside. Furthermore, we continue to assert the bond between aesthetics and art, in the face of post-1960s movements that assert a division between the two. Though my artist friend Veseli has suggested that this leaves me in a somewhat old-fashioned predicament, that risk is already consciously run by my wider philosophical position, which insists that Husserl and Heidegger remain the high-water mark of recent philosophy, unsurpassed by the popular wave of post-war French thinkers. Wrong turns do occur in intellectual life, and can take decades to overcome, though we may learn many new things in the meantime. In the interest of such learning, this chapter will briefly consider some of the more prominent figures who might be thought to refute or supersede the formalist position. We may find insights here worth incorporating, and even certain points on which the formalists end up holding the short straw, but my general view is that the only way forward is to pass all the way through the formalist tunnel. We begin with two critics of Greenberg from his own generation.

The Other "Bergs"

In the Epilogue to his 1975 book *The Painted Word*, Tom Wolfe famously predicted that in the year 2000, "the three artists who will be featured, the three seminal figures of the era, will be not Pollock, [Willem] de Kooning, and [Jasper] Johns – but Greenberg, [Harold] Rosenberg, and [Leo] Steinberg."[1] Since the three critics just mentioned were roughly the same age, and devoted their careers to writing about many of the same artists, they do make for a plausible triad of comparison, quite apart from Wolfe's edgy and tasteless jest with their typically Jewish surnames. The key point of dispute between Greenberg and Rosenberg is well known. Greenberg was a personal friend of Pollock and an early champion of his work, to such an extent that we can hardly view their careers in any but symbiotic terms. Greenberg before Pollock was a rising but grumbling New York art critic distressed by the parochial condition of American art in the shadow of Paris; Pollock before Greenberg lacked a systematic champion of his work. What is crucial is that Greenberg always defended Pollock's paintings *as paintings*, in aesthetic terms no different in kind from those used to interpret all previous masters. By contrast, Rosenberg could only make sense of Pollock's productions in a way that Greenberg viewed with contempt: as "action paintings" or "events" in which Pollock's *performance* was more important than the resulting work itself.

In 1952, Rosenberg published an article with the title "The American Action Painters," later included in his collection *The Tradition of the New*. Oddly enough, not a single painter is mentioned by name in this piece, though Pollock is so obviously meant that Rosenberg's later denial cannot be taken at face value. Let's consider some of the choicest passages from the fifteen or so pages of this brief article: "At a certain moment the canvas began to appear to one American painter after another as an arena in which to act . . . What was to go on the canvas was not a picture but an event" (*TN* 25). The painter's final product is not just unimportant, but is something to be actively negated: "Call this painting 'abstract' or 'Expressionist' or 'Abstract-Expressionist,' what counts is its special motive for *extinguishing the object* . . ." (*TN* 26; emph. added). Or rather, what is to be extinguished is the art object as a purported autonomous whole, since the painting that results will still have importance as a documentary record of the act that gave rise to it: "It is to be taken for granted that in the final effect, the image, whatever be or be not in it, will be a *tension*" (*TN* 27). With this word, Rosenberg means nothing like the OOO tension between objects and their qualities, nor even some sort of tense equilibrium between artist and work, but simply a tension internal to the artist's own "psychic state" (*TN* 27).[2] This turn to the psychology of the artist spurs Rosenberg to an all-fronts assault on formalist autonomy. Painting is said to be inseparable from the artist's biography (*TN* 28). Action painting has "broken down every distinction between art and life," and incorporates "anything that has to do with action – psychology, philosophy, history, mythology, hero-worship. Anything but art criticism" (*TN* 28). It is all about "the way the artist organizes his emotional and intellectual energy as if he were in a living situation" (*TN* 29). Rosenberg adds, with a Surrealist-sounding slap at Kant: "An action is not a matter of taste. You don't let taste decide the firing of a pistol or the building of a maze" (*TN* 38).

The harshness of Greenberg's written response, a full decade later, is already telegraphed in the title: "How Art Writing Earns its Bad Name" (IV 135-144).[3] Greenberg finds it unfortunate that Rosenberg wrote his "action painting" essay as a supposed *advocate* of the painters in question, since it really just provides cover for philistine dismissal of Pollock and his circle. He laments that, in Rosenberg's eyes, "the painted 'picture,' having been painted, became an indifferent matter. Everything lay in the doing, nothing in the making" (IV 136). As a result: "The covered canvas was left over as an 'event,' the solipsistic record of purely personal 'gestures,' and belonging therefore to the same reality that breathing and thumbprints, love affairs and wars belonged to, but not works of art" (IV 136). Restated in the terms of this book, Rosenberg gives us Pollock *literalized*, since the latter's works lose all autonomy and find their exhaustive meaning not only in the artist's life history, but in "psychology, philosophy, history, mythology, hero-worship." Oddly enough, only art criticism is excluded from this carpetbag of professional relations, for the reason that the existing field of art is what "action painting" explicitly aims to negate (*TN* 28). By reducing action painting to biography and numerous other disciplines, Rosenberg also strips us of the critical ability to distinguish between higher- and lower-quality versions of it (IV 140). Even so, the notion of "action painting" did catch on with the public, which Greenberg sarcastically guesses is because it "had something racy and demotic about it – like the name of a new dance step . . ." (IV 137).

Now, there is an obvious sense in which Rosenberg's interpretation of Pollock is absurd. Anyone can go online and find footage of Pollock at work on his paintings, and this footage is admittedly of compelling interest. But by no means does it back up Rosenberg's theory. Pollock appears to be concentrating intensely while painting: but he is clearly *painting*, not acting out some personal trance that would be accessible to "psychology" and "hero-worship" but not to the art critic. If "action painting" were really what Pollock was up to, then why is it not primarily this footage that one finds for sale in auction houses or on display at museums? Surely this would be a better documentary record of the purported art-action than any mere canvas? The only reason such a bizarre interpretation as Rosenberg's could even occur to a critic is if they were so dumbfounded by Pollock's canvases themselves that grounds for interpretation could be sought nowhere else than outside the walls of the work. It is easy to understand why the first appearance of the Pollock drip paintings might have had such an effect on critics. But with practice one does learn to distinguish the more from the less successful among Pollock's works, and for reasons having nothing to do with mastery of his life story.

And yet, however failed it may be as an interpretation of Pollock, we in the twenty-first century can see that Rosenberg's theory anticipates later developments rather well. Though Pollock was surely no action-artist, this description might indeed hold for such later figures as Beuys, Bruce Nauman, or Cindy Sherman, many of whose works employ the artist's presence as the very core of the work. We know that Greenberg despised this later turn, just as Fried would reject it as "theatrical" in the worst sense of the term. Here I would repeat the classic formalist lesson that autonomy is crucial if we are to prevent everything from melting indistinguishably into everything else, in the confusing sort of free-for-all holism that already worried Kant when he walled off ethics and aesthetics from everything that did not directly belong to them. Pollock's canvases do have a reality apart from his life and actions, despite Rosenberg's disqualification of this reality. The same is not true of a work such as Beuys' *I Like America and America Likes Me*, which can only be understood as an experience or a performance; after all, someone had to witness it, even if it were only Beuys himself. Just as it would be absurd to replace Pollock's canvases in the Museum of Modern Art with films of their being made, it would be absurd for the opposite reason to replace the whole of Beuys' performance piece with, say, the felt blanket torn by the coyote during its tug-of-war with the artist. What Rosenberg misses – like most contemporary philosophers – is the fact that "event" is not really an alternative to "object," but is immediately converted into an object in its own right. Like any other object, an art object need not be physical, solid, durable, or devoid of human interaction: it need only be more than its components and deeper than its current effects. It thereby resists both undermining and overmining, which means that it resists being exhausted by any form of knowledge, or by any relation at all. Performance pieces are also objects, but simply include the artists within the works than classical art objects ever did, including those in which Courbet projected himself into his paintings.

Greenberg had much less to say about the third "Berg," Leo Steinberg, though my remarks here will be of greater length. As far as I can determine, his only reference to Steinberg came in a 1954 defense of abstract art in *Art Digest*. Here he complains that Steinberg's defense of abstraction is merely half-hearted, since he contends that abstraction "is never as non-representational as we think," as if to defend the movement only by softening its radical edge (III 186-187). Let's begin by recalling Greenberg's reason for coming to favor abstraction, despite his early critique of Kandinsky for overemphasizing it. We cite again the following passage from the article "Modernist Painting":

> All recognizable entities . . . exist in three-dimensional space, and the barest suggestion of a recognizable entity suffices to call up associations of that kind of space. The fragmentary silhouette of a human figure, or of a teacup, will do so, and by doing so alienate pictorial space from the two-dimensionality which is the guarantee of painting's independence as an art. (IV 88)

By no means does this negate Greenberg's equally firm conviction that neither abstract nor representational art is inherently superior to the other. As we read in 1954: "What counts first and last in art is whether it is good or bad. Everything else is secondary. No one has yet been able to show that the representational as such either adds or takes away anything from the aesthetic value of a picture or statue" (III 187). And yet, "my experience . . . tells me nonetheless that the best art of our day tends, increasingly, to be abstract. And most attempts to reverse this tendency seem to result in second-hand, second-rate painting or . . . *pastiche*, pseudo-archaic sculpture" (III 189). In short, Greenberg holds that representational art may rule one period of art and abstraction another, with the present moment – meaning 1954 – being one in which abstraction happens to be thriving. We can infer that this is due to the close link between abstraction and Greenberg's own pet theme, flatness. What Greenberg never does is question the very distinction between abstract and representational

114

art. Steinberg himself takes precisely this step, to Greenberg's visible annoyance.

In fact, if we take the flatness of the canvas medium to be Greenberg's primary concern, and the role of abstraction in augmenting flatness to be his secondary one, it is remarkable how Steinberg lunges straight for the jugular on both points. Let's begin with the secondary theme, abstraction. Steinberg effectively declares that there is *no such thing* as abstraction: that even the most austere geometrical shapes and fields of disembodied color arise ultimately from the human experience of nature. In Steinberg's 1953 essay "The Eye is a Part of the Mind," we read as follows: "representation is still an essential condition, not an expendable freight ... a central esthetic function in all art; and ... the formalist esthetic, designed to champion the new abstract trend, was largely based on a misunderstanding and an underestimation of the art it set out to defend" (OC 291). In short order, he adds the strange qualification that "about half" of the great art produced in human history can be considered representational: a stunningly small figure, given the broad scope Steinberg grants to representation, which he seems to find pretty much everywhere in art (OC 291). He reminds us that even such proto-abstractionists as Monet and Cézanne repeatedly swore allegiance to nature (OC 292, 296). Oddly enough, he also adds a point that might easily have been made by Greenberg himself: "The mechanical, the uncreative element lies not ... in imitating nature, but in academicism, which is the passionless employment of preformed devices" (OC 293). Steinberg continues the thought on the following page: "Almost anyone with a modicum of talent and sufficient application can appropriate another man's mode of representation. But he cannot discover it" (OC 294). And even more beautifully: "The mannerist ... he who displays Michelangelo's musculature over again, is not at all repeating Michelangelo, since what he arranges on the canvas lies already in the domesticated state" (OC 295).

In fact, Steinberg claims not just that the imitation of nature is equal to abstract art in avoiding the academic and the mannered, but that it is *superior* to this end: "In the formalistic system of ideas [i.e., Greenberg's] the recurrent coincidence of significant form with deepened observation [of nature] remains unexplained ... The most that can be said [against nature-imitation] is that we of this century happen to have turned our interest elsewhere" (OC 297). But Steinberg's argument now takes another strange turn. He began by subordinating mental abstraction to the imitation of nature, but now seems to reverse this gesture, emphasizing that what counts as natural is determined by the mind: "natural fact can be purely apprehended only where the human mind has first endowed it with the status of reality. Only then is the act of seeing backed by a passion, being focused on ultimate truth" (OC 297). And further: "art seeks the pure apprehension of natural fact wherever natural fact, as registered by the senses, is regarded as meaningful reality. Where it is not so interpreted we shall find some form of anti-humanist distortion, of hieratic stylization or abstraction" (OC 297). And yet, he unconvincingly concludes, "such abstraction will continue to apprehend and to express reality . . . Only the matter that now calls for representation is drawn from a new order of reality," by which he means that of the mind (OC 297). In Steinberg's defense, he does go on to give a wonderful account of how the apparent anti-realism of medieval art was in fact guided by the neo-Platonic view that ideas are more real than base material beings. But note that his slogan has thus stealthily shifted from "imitation of nature" to "imitation of what is most real," and it is far from clear that the latter has any inherent connection with nature, given Steinberg's astonishing tendency to conflate the natural with the mental. It is the same sleight of hand found among philosophers who claim that Berkeley – the most idealist philosopher of the West, who holds that nothing exists unless it is perceived by some mind – is nonetheless a realist, since after all he is "a realist about ideas."[4] By the same token, we could easily say (and Steinberg would) that Mondrian's abstract paintings too are imitations of nature, as long as we add the qualification that Mondrian has a very different conception of "nature" from nearly everyone else. The motive for such inflationary maneuvers is generally a wish to devalue the inflated term: such as "realism," in the case of philosophers who want to call everyone under the sun a realist in order to remove realist objections as a threat to their own position. Steinberg proceeds in opposite fashion, inflating the scope of the "imitation of nature" so that it covers the world as a whole, with no space left over for abstraction even to exist.

Steinberg is more persuasive when he focuses on the earthly root of all ideas, as in the following critique of Ortega's reading of contemporary art as idealism: "we are forced to ask: by what faculty of mind or eye does the artist discover and distill the forms of his private irreality? Whence come the plastic symbols of his unconditioned subjectivity? Surely no amount of introspection will yield shapes to put on canvas" (OC 303-304).[5] Yet this tendency to see traces of nature everywhere leads Steinberg to mix a basically literal discipline with an emphatically non-literal one, when he adds that "an awareness of nature in its latest undisguise seems to be held in common by science and art" (OC 304). He also sounds Rosenbergian tones when he calls for depicting nature as an *event*: "the dissolution of the solid in contemporary art [means that] the substantial object has been activated into a continuing event" (OC 305-306).

Only in the article's final paragraph do we catch sight of Steinberg's motive for insisting that all painting is imitative. Namely, what he most wishes to eliminate is the formalist notion of art as something *self-contained*. To speak of paintings "as though they had no referent outside themselves, is to miss both their meaning and their continuity with the art of the past. If my suggestion is valid, then even non-objective art continues to pursue art's *social role* of fixating thought in esthetic form . . ." (OC 306; emph. added). There is no doubt that art will always have some kind of social role; what can be doubted is whether the discernment of this role will ever tell us enough about art as art. For to place anything in a social relation – or any relation – is to *literalize* it: and while – contra Fried – the theatrical is not the death of the art, the literal does indeed bring about that death. Steinberg initially claims to show that there is no art that is not a representation of nature, but ends up with the much weaker theses that (a) we could not paint at all if we never had any sense-experience, and (b) all art exists in relation to something else. Both are mere truisms that become something worse when Steinberg uses them to derive the sweeping doctrines that everything is nature and everything is relational.

Abstraction became important to Greenberg because likenesses of everyday objects inevitably suggest three dimensions, and this subverts the flatness he prizes above everything else in modern art. Steinberg rejects the very existence of abstraction for the reason that, while representational art explicitly imitates nature, abstract art does so *implicitly* anyway, and hence both exist in relation to the world. On this point, OOO differs from both critics. The flat canvas medium does not matter to us, since the background of objects is to be found not primarily in the medium as a whole, but in every discernible element in the painting: whether it be a realistic-looking Louis XVI, or an unsettling bacterial profile glimpsed in some midnight work of Kandinsky. This was our previously stated difference from Greenberg. Our difference from Steinberg is that the formal self-containment of an artwork cannot be abandoned. However many causal entanglements – biographical, psychological, social, political, natural – went into producing an artwork or even into sustaining it, the work itself (like any object) is something over and above these supports. As such, it admits portions of its environment in a highly selective manner.

We turn now to the title essay of Steinberg's *Other Criteria*, where he takes issue with Greenberg's criterion of flatness, the deeper basis for his endorsement of abstraction. Steinberg laments that "Greenberg wants all Old Master and Modernist painters to reduce their differences to a single criterion ... either illusionistic or flat. But what significant art is that simple?" (OC 74). We have seen that Steinberg's strategy for combatting the claims of abstraction was to argue that even full-blown abstraction is just representation by other means. In the present essay, he follows an analogous line of argument: there is no important difference between "illusionistic" and "flat" art, because great artists of every era have *always* operated with a tension between surface and depth rather than an endorsement of one over the other. As usual, Steinberg makes his case in vigorous prose that is sometimes quite moving:

> The more realistic the art of the Old Masters became, the more they raised internal safeguards against illusion, ensuring at every point that attention would remain focused upon the art. They did it by radical color economies, or by eerie proportional attenuation; by multiplication of detail, or by preternatural beauty ... They did it by abrupt internal changes of scale; or by shifting reality levels – as when Raphael's *Expulsion of Heliodorus* inserts a group of contemporaries in modern dress as observers of the biblical scene; or by overlapping reality levels, as when a frescoed battle scene on a Venetian wall curls up at the edges to become a fake tapestry ... (OC 72)

In the wake of Greenberg's belated concession that the Old Masters did take the inherent flatness of their paintings into account, Steinberg charges through the half-open door: "They do not merely 'take account' of the tension between surface and depth, as if for the sake of decorative coherence, while reserving their thrust for the appearance of depth. Rather, they maintain an explicit, controlled, and ever-visible dualism" (OC 74). Steinberg goes so far as to claim that the Old Masters already achieved what Greenberg saw as unique to Cubist collage: the oscillation of pictorial elements between multiple flat planes. Referring to a "not untypical" manuscript page of the early fifteenth century entitled *Missus est Gabriel angelus*, Steinberg tells us that "three reality levels oscillate in and compete for [the] capital M [on the manuscript page] ... All three at once. The eye is puzzled; instead of seeing objects in space it sees a picture" (OC 75).

Moreover, while Greenberg held that it was a modern, post-Kantian innovation for art to take account of the conditions of its medium, Steinberg contends that "all important art, at least since the Trecento, is preoccupied with self-criticism. Whatever else it may be about, all art is about art" (OC 76). Yet Steinberg draws different lessons from this theme than Greenberg. For he is annoyed at, not heartened by, "how often recent Abstract American painting is defined and described almost exclusively in terms of internal problem-solving" (OC 77), or as "an evolving technology wherein at any one moment specific tasks require solution – tasks set for the artist set for the artist as problems are set for researchers in the big corporations" (OC 77-78). Recourse to internal problem-solving is indeed a classic formalist maneuver in every field, meant to block an extraneous outside world from any invasion of the interior. There are obvious limits to the formalist approach, given that no artwork exists entirely in a vacuum. But to give an artwork *provisional* autonomy at least prevents hasty recourse to political innuendo, such as Steinberg's pointless attempt to link Greenbergian formalism with the "corporate technocracy" of the Detroit automobile industry: as if attention to internal problems were merely the nightmarish consequence of capitalism run amok, rather than a theoretical decision with merits and drawbacks like any other (OC 78, 79). In any case, Steinberg cries out for painting to be put in relation with anything but itself: in Greenberg's criticism he misses any "hint of expressive purpose, or recognition that pictures function in human experience. The painter's industry is a closed loop" (OC 79).

Since we already considered Steinberg's relationist proclivities when discussing his views on the imitation of nature, let's close with a few additional words on his apparent rejection of the difference between illusion and flatness. When Cubist collage addresses the growing threat of excessive flatness by creating an oscillation between multiple background planes, Greenberg hails this as a major advance. Steinberg retorts that this was always already being done by the Old Masters, and thus is hardly worth all the excitement. Yet there is a twofold danger to Steinberg's tactic. The first is that no one before Greenberg seems to have spoken of the Old Masters in such terms, or at least Steinberg does not quote anyone who did – as he surely would have if precedents were available. If no critic actually beat Greenberg to the punch on the theory of oscillation between different planes, then to claim that the Old Masters were already painting that way seems to ratify Greenberg's central idea while merely pushing it further back in time. It is a backhanded way of granting that the idea is important enough that someone else must have thought of it first: hardly a recipe for devastating critique.

But there is a second danger for Steinberg as well. Namely, by appropriating and extending Greenberg's notion of figure/ground oscillation, Steinberg automatically signs up for any weaknesses belonging to that conception as well. As argued above when discussing the collages of Braque and Picasso, the chief weakness is that despite multiplying the flat background planes, Greenberg's theory of collage still views depth only as something belonging to a plane, rather than allowing that each pictorial element has its own hidden reservoir. Earlier I criticized this conception on philosophical grounds, as having too much resemblance to a familiar philosophical model – dating to pre-Socratic times, but often repeated since – in which a single hidden Being exists in tension with a pluralized surface of beings, with the implication that multiplicity is always superficial. Steinberg's proposed solution is holism, an oddly formalist gesture for someone who wants to oppose formalism as badly as he does: "The eye is puzzled; instead of seeing objects in space it sees a picture" (OC 75). If Steinberg really wants to revive our attention to content in paintings, as he claims, then eliminating "objects in space" is not the way to do it.

T.J. Clark vs. The Petty Bourgeoisie

The British art historian T.J. Clark, who taught for many years at the University of California at Berkeley, is worth discussing here because of his overt intellectual friction with Fried. Clark is one of the leading social historians of art, and may well have been the prime target of Fried's previously cited admonition from *Absorption and Theatricality*: "I should also say that I am skeptical in advance of any attempt to represent [the] relationship [between painting and beholder] and [the 'internal' development of the art of painting] as essentially the products of social, economic, and political forces defined from the outset as fundamental in ways that the exigencies of painting are not." This would be a perfectly fair description of Clark's way of thinking. For instance, in a book chapter entitled "In Defense of Abstract Expressionism" – which is not much of a defense – Clark defines the movement as follows: "Abstract Expressionism, I want to say, is the style of a certain petty bourgeoisie's aspiration to aristocracy, to a totalizing cultural power" (FI 389). Along with Pollock, Clyfford Still is bluntly diagnosed as *petit bourgeois*; as evidence, we are reminded that Still supported the anti-communist persecutions of Senator Joseph McCarthy. Clark also proposes that we "[conceive] of Abstract Expressionism as vulgar," and he does not hesitate in acting on this conception (*FI* 391). Adolph Gottlieb is termed, against critical consensus, "the great and implacable maestro of Abstract Expressionism," but is also immediately linked with Lawrence Welk and Charlie Parker, who we are apparently meant to take for vulgar, *petit bourgeois* musicians (*FI* 392). Even European transplant Hans Hofmann, in many ways the godfather of New York's emergence as a world art capital, is tarred with the same brush as his adopted homeland: "a good Hofmann is tasteless to the core, tasteless in its invocations of Europe, tasteless in its mock religiosity, tasteless in its Color-by-Technicolor, its winks and nudges toward landscape format . . . and the cloying demonstrativeness of its handling" (*FI* 397). Suddenly pouring too much Derrida sauce on the sandwich, Clark reports that in the best works of Mark Rothko, "a hectoring absolute of self-presence is maintained in face of the void" (*FI* 387). In summation, Clark opines that "Abstract Expressionist painting is best when it is most vulgar, because it is then that it grasps most fully the conditions of representation – the technical and social conditions – of its historical moment" (*FI* 401).

That historical moment, of course, was post-war America. And we soon discover that Clark's purported revolutionary agenda serves as thin cover for class and national snobbery. Which is not to say that his snobbery never yields insights. The following passage, for instance, looks all the more prescient following the loathsome political rise of Donald Trump: "It is not that the petty bourgeoisie in America *has* power, but that its voice has become, in the years after 1945, the only one in which power can be spoken . . ." (*FI* 388) And as a corollary, "vulgarity . . . is the necessary form of that individuality allowed the petty bourgeoisie" (*FI* 389). We will never be able to dispense with a social understanding of the conditions under which culture arises. Yet Clark is frequently guilty of what logicians call the "genetic fallacy," assuming as he does that everything is inherently stamped with the conditions of its origin. For even if we accept Clark's rather shrill pronouncement that post-war America is a veritable *Imperium* of *petit-bourgeois* vulgarity, this would only solve half of his problem. The other half would require establishing that artists such as Pollock – who did not attain a lasting mass audience, despite Clark's delighted reproduction of *Vogue* magazine photos of his work – were so awash in the petit-bourgeois vulgarity of their time and place as to be unable to offer anything more (*FI* 303). It is strange that Clark, who usually goes to such lengths to define artistic Modernism as a *negation* of its surroundings, is unwilling to grant any such negative prowess to an artist of Pollock's caliber.

Another problem with Clark is that in confronting his formalist opponents, he never really assumes the responsibility of answering them systematically. For instance, what could have been a smoking-hot debate between Clark and Fried ultimately fizzles when Clark is either unwilling or unable – it is hard to be sure – to provide the examples Fried quite reasonably demands.[6] It is hardly surprising that Clark views the early, Marxist-leaning Greenberg as the "good" Greenberg (CGTA 72). But while anyone reading Greenberg's collected works will find that the Marxist period does not last for very long, Clark insists on blaming this change on the much later Cold War and McCarthyism, rather than considering the evolutionary path of Greenberg's own thought, in which content-focused academic art replaces bourgeois kitsch as his true aesthetic enemy well before McCarthy emerged (AAM 106). As mentioned, Clark insists that modernity involves "practices of negation" (CGTA 78). One wishes – as does Fried in his debate response – that Clark would be clearer as to what exactly is entailed by this term. What we do know is that Clark reads the significance of the artistic medium in terms of "negation and estrangement" rather than in Greenbergian terms (CGTA 81). Among other things, flatness might have "appeared as a barrier to the ordinary bourgeois' wish to enter a picture and dream, to have it be a space apart from life in which the mind would be free to make its own connections" (CGTA 81). This at least helps explain Clark's disagreement with Greenberg's view that "art can substitute *itself* for the values capitalism has made valueless" (CGTA 83).

To catch the gist of Fried's response to Clark, it is enough to quote the first two sentences: "At the center of Clark's essay is the claim that practices of in the arts are fundamentally practices of negation. This claim is false" (HMW 87). The one surprising twist in Fried's objection is his argument that Clark is more like Greenberg than he knows, since both are concerned with stripping away the inessential features of art to reach an essential, or at least un-negated core (HMW 89). Though there is some truth to this comparison, I stand by my earlier objection to Fried and Pippin's characterization of Greenberg as an essentialist in the way they mean. But the core of Fried's riposte turns on a more surprising point of detail: "it is a curious feature of Clark's essay that he provides no specific examples for his central argument." As Fried continues a paragraph later:

> How are we to understand this refusal to discuss specific cases? In an obvious sense, it makes Clark's position difficult to rebut: one is continually tempted to imagine what he would say about particular works

of art . . . and then to argue against those invented descriptions. I found myself doing this again and again in preliminary drafts of this response until I realized that it was pointless. For the burden of proof is Clark's . . . (HMW 88)

Clark's response, which ends the exchange, never does get around to offering a good example. This is not to say that his response is useless, since it does convey further information about his views, as well as what I take to be one interesting point: "I still find it striking that modernist writers so confidently outlaw the real impulse of Dada and early Surrealism from their account of twentieth-century art, while giving such weight to artists – like Arp or Miró or Pollock – who were so affected by it" (AAM 104). We will consider Dada and Surrealism in the next chapter of this book.

I am less interested in the remainder of Clark's response, which displays the spectacle – too common in his writings – of theoretical focus dissolving amidst scattershot socio-historical claims. He describes Duchamp as a "commodity entrepreneur," always a cheap tactic in the anti-capitalist mood of our time, in which to associate anyone with commodities is now widely assumed to be a kill-shot (AAM 104). It is not long before Clark airs the related cliché that autonomy is a "bourgeois myth" (AAM 107) used to promote the world-view of this apparently execrable social class, though one might just as easily say – with no less merit – that relational aesthetics is a "proletarian myth" or perhaps even an "aristocratic myth." Clark also reports that he finds the work of high modernist heroes Caro and Olitski to be "boring"; since no reasons are given, this may simply have been an attempt to get under Fried's skin (AAM 107). Finally, Clark takes the following unexpected shot at Fried's philosophical underpinnings: "when it comes to Fried's ontology, all the nods to Merleau-Ponty cannot save Fried's prose from sounding like old-time religion" (AAM 107). While I have expressed some reservations about Merleau-Ponty as a philosopher, what Clark is objecting to in this passage is the simple notion that a thing is what it is and not everything else.[7] Any sweeping philosophical rebellion against such a classical principle of logic and metaphysics requires an argument – which Clark never provides – rather than the mere innuendo that committing oneself to autonomous or independent beings is "old-time" or "bourgeois." Clark's numerous sly remarks on the political and demographic failings of others never really condense into a memorable case for the contextual embeddedness of art.

Krauss: Background as Simulacrum

Rosalind Krauss is University Professor at Columbia, and the driving force behind the prominent journal *October*. She was at one time the personal friend and intellectual comrade of Greenberg and Fried before taking a rather different path. The most obvious difference for readers is that Krauss is heavily invested in post-war French theory in a way that Greenberg and Fried simply are not, even if Fried sometimes crosses paths with the thought of Jacques Derrida. This alone gives Krauss a very different list of natural allies and enemies from her former associates. Beyond this, we might add that Krauss has her structuralist moments and her poststructuralist moments, with the two currents intersecting less in her writing than might be expected. On the whole, I am less interested in the poststructuralist Krauss, who tends to repeat familiar deconstructive tropes such as challenging the distinction between originals and copies.[8] The structuralist Krauss is something very different: an ambitious risk-taker who can startle us with her boldness even at moments when we do not yet feel convinced. It is easy to recognize this bolder version of Krauss, since she usually pulls from her briefcase a sketch of the Klein Group, an important fourfold mathematical structure that lies at the basis of semiotics. For our present purposes, however, it is more illuminating to examine her understanding of collage in order to contrast it with Greenberg's rather different interpretation of the genre.

Before getting to that, we should note that Krauss is neither an admirer of aesthetic autonomy, nor a philosophical realist, nor an adherent of the notion that art must primarily be aware of its medium in order to avoid academicism. This positions her as the opposite of OOO in all three respects, and as more compatible with the still basically Postmodernist spirit of our age. Krauss' thinking on art, like her general outlook on the world, has a strongly relational cast that leaves no room for the existence of anything outside the interplay of a field of differences. In a 1980 discussion of Picasso, for instance, she admiringly cites Saussure's view that language consists of no positive terms but only of differences.[9] Though I already disagreed when Fried endorsed a Saussurean reading of Caro's sculptural syntax, Krauss is much more emphatic in these leanings than Fried ever was. For example, in *The Optical Unconscious* she appears to endorse the verdict of "the social historians" that modernist autonomy is a myth, since it is actually nothing more than the ideological construction of "a discursive field" (*OU* 12). I have disputed this idea elsewhere

124

in a critique of Michel Foucault, in many ways the patron saint of discursive fields, and there is no reason to repeat the exercise here.[10] But the basic problem with denying autonomy to the various elements that occupy a field is that it amounts to a form of overmining, and all such strategies fail in the same way: through their inability to explain how a determinate holistic field could ever undergo change, given its exclusion of any surplus that might make change possible.

We turn to the theme of collage, making use of two writings by Krauss in particular. The first is her intensely personal 1993 book *The Optical Unconscious*. It is by any standard an unusual work: part theory, part literature, part personal reminiscence, and part edgy picture-book. Amidst the stylistic charms of this work, we also find the unpleasant *curio* of an unflattering physical description of Greenberg, repeated verbatim no less than five times (*OU* 243, 248, 266, 290, 309). Whether mitigated or not by previous cruelties in the other direction – by many accounts, the man could be hurtful – these passages signal the continuing presence of Greenberg's ghost in her work. We know that what haunts both admirers and detractors of Greenberg – and Krauss has played both roles at different stages of her life – is his concern with the central importance of the medium in art. In her own words: "[The] drive to perform a relay back to the base of the artistic medium, back to the support, back to the objective conditions of the enterprise, is a modernist obsession" (*OU* 48).

We saw in the previous chapter that Greenberg treats collage as a response to the unbearable pressures of flatness generated by Analytic Cubism, with pictorial space more or less collapsing onto the literal flat canvas medium. Greenberg's interpretation was that collage sets up a multitude of background planes in place of the usual single one, thereby creating ambiguity as to which collage element occupies which plane at any given moment. The reader will also recall the OOO critique of this theory: Greenberg seems committed to allowing no depth to anything other than a plane, and challenges flatness only by positing a multitude of flatnesses in one and the same work, leaving individual pictorial elements in a role of permanent superficiality along multiple superficies. Krauss' own departure from Greenbergian collage theory has different motives, which are of interest despite an occasional overreliance on Derridean terminology that muffles her independent voice in a way that her structuralist forays do not. Most interesting of all is the following sentiment, expressed in *The Optical Unconscious*: "The ground is not behind; the ground is what . . . vision . . . is" (*OU* 15; emph. removed). Stated differently, Krauss aims to haul the background from Greenberg's canvas basement up to the floor inhabited by the beholder. This has obvious resonance with OOO's understanding of metaphor, according to which the reader participates in constructing a new depth atop the old one. But the full meaning of Krauss' statement is best understood by returning to an earlier piece, "In the Name of Picasso" (*OAG* 23-41).

Midway through her interpretation of the great Spanish artist, Krauss reminds us of the two chief aspects of the sign according to Saussure: (1) the sign is a material proxy for an absent referent, since if the referent were present we would not need to signify it; (2) the sign belongs to a play of differences without positive terms (*OAG* 33-37). She gives intriguing examples of both factors at play in Picasso's collages. For instance, there is "the appearance of the two *f*-shaped violin soundholes that are inscribed on the surface of work after work from 1912-14" (*OAG* 33). Krauss notes that these holes are rarely identical in shape or size, meaning that they are signs "not of violin, but of foreshortening: of the differential size within a single surface due to its rotation into depth" (*OAG* 33). Drawing a general lesson from this, she concludes that "because the inscription of the *f*s takes place within the collage assembly and thus on the most rigidly flattened and frontalized of planes, 'depth' is thus written on the very place from which it is – within the presence of the collage – most absent" (*OAG* 33). The other example Krauss chooses, from among what she terms myriad possibilities, is "the application of newsprint to construct the sign of space as penetrable or transparent . . . In so doing, [Picasso] inscribes transparency on the very element of the collage's fabric that is most reified and opaque: its planes of newspaper" (*OAG* 33). These are intriguing observations even if, for philosophical reasons, OOO cannot agree with their premise. For what Krauss is aiming at here is the elimination of any *real* depth, in favor of a simulated inscription of depth on the surface of the work itself. As she puts it a few pages later: "We are standing now on the threshold of a postmodernist art . . . in which to name (represent) an object may not necessarily be to call it forth, for there may be no (original) object. For this postmodernist notion of the originless play of the signifier we could use the term *simulacrum*" (*OAG* 38-39). Krauss cites Baudrillard here, along with Guy Debord, and I find that this strengthens her case. For if in her Derridean moments she seems most concerned to eliminate any referent of the sign, and thus suspend any philosophical realism, it is Baudrillard who converts simulacra into a new sort of reality by speaking of our *seduction* by them.[11] That is to say, Baudrillard does not just try to demolish any genuine reality lying beneath appearances, but also turns our active engagement with images into a new layer of reality, much in the way OOO contends that the theatrical performance of metaphor creates a new object in its own right. This is the side of Baudrillard that makes him more than just another Postmodern anti-realist, and it may help explain why his work is aging better than many expected. There is some of this in Krauss as well, given her defense of an *optical* unconscious that differs both from the hidden real background (which she, unlike OOO, deems non-existent) and from conscious awareness, as we will see in connection with her use of Jacques Lacan.

But first, we should also consider Krauss' examples of how Saussure's second main feature of signs – the pure play of difference without positive terms – functions in Picasso's collages. In speaking of the artist's 1913 work *Violin and Fruit*, Krauss gives us two such instances. The first is that "a piece of newsprint, its fine type yielding the experience of tone, reads [either] as 'transparency' or 'luminosity'" (*OAG* 35). At the same time, "the single patch of wood-grained paper ambiguously allocated to table and/or musical instrument composes the sign for open, as opposed to closed form. Yet the piece of wood graining terminates in a complex contour that produces the closed silhouette of a neighboring form" (*OAG* 35-37). The technical term to describe when this happens, when "each signifier thus yields a matched pair of formal signifieds," is "diacritical" (*OAG* 37). Objects are supposedly no longer at issue, since we are focused instead on an interplay of signs that Krauss calls "the very system of form" (*OAG* 37). In the collage, we have a collage-plane set down on top of a background plane that it obscures, yielding a sort of "literalization of depth." What makes it a "literal" depth is that in it, "the supporting ground that that is obscured by the affixed plane resurfaces in a miniaturized facsimile in the collage element itself" (*OAG* 37). Stated differently, "the collage element performs the occultation of one field in order to introject it *as* figure – a surface that is the image of eradicated surface" (*OAG* 37). It is not just any old simulacrum, then, but a simulacrum in particular of unsimulated genuine depth. In collage, the ground does not appear to us directly, but as "masked and riven. It enters our experience not as an object of perception, but as an object of discourse, of *re*presentation" (*OAG* 38).

There is much here to chew on, though again I find it unhelpful when Krauss invokes Derrida's agenda, asserting that "collage operates in direct opposition to modernism's search of perpetual plenitude and unimpeachable self-presence." That is to say, "modernism's goal is to objectify the formal constituents of a given medium, making these, beginning with the very ground that is the origin of their existence, the objects of vision" (*OAG* 38). But I for one find no "unimpeachable self-presence" in the sort of Modernist art championed by Greenberg. "Self-presence" is Derrida's *terme d'art* for what we usually call "identity," and his introduction of this term may be the most disastrous feature of his philosophy.[12] Initially, there is much to be said for Derrida's critique of *presence*, which builds on a similar enterprise launched by Heidegger. By "presence," Heidegger means the idea that the essence of a thing can be made directly visible to the conscious mind, overlooking the way that reality eludes human access. For Heidegger – as for Greenberg – this hidden background is really there, independent of the mind; it has an identity, for the simple reason that it is what it is and not something else. By contrast, Derrida pushes his luck by trying to refute identity in the same stroke as presence, by redefining the former as a "self-presence." That is to say, he claims that everything differs not just from everything else, but also from itself, and hence everything exists in the arena of the "play of signifiers" without positive terms. Elsewhere, I have defended Aristotle's concept of identity against what I consider to be Derrida's false innovation on this point.[13] The simplest way to put it is that the identity of any given thing is not "self-present," but is that which guarantees *absence* in the best sense of the term: an apple or horse are so much themselves that they withstand most relations in which they find themselves, as opposed to Derrida's version in which things are absent only because they are always slipping off elsewhere and are never anywhere in particular.

Returning now to Greenberg, who we have seen is very close to Heidegger and McLuhan (and not Derrida) on this point, the background is that which is always most absent. No matter how much we may talk about the background medium, such talk can never do the work of the medium itself. It is true that Greenberg wants pictorial content to signal awareness of its own superficiality by shaping itself in the image of its medium, with flat and ultimately abstract content favored over all other kinds. Yet this does not mean that any actual or even possible painting, in Greenberg's view, could possibly give us the "self-presence" of the background: as seen from his insistence that if a naked piece of white canvas might count as an artwork, it certainly would not count as a very good one (IV 131-132). Tension between foreground and background is always needed for Greenberg, just as Heidegger requires that Being manifest itself in individual beings while also hiding behind them. In fact, Greenberg and Krauss show a surprising degree of agreement that the background of a collage – or any artwork – never becomes present. The difference between them is

128

that while Greenberg multiplies the hidden background from one to several in his interpretation of collage, Krauss reduces them from one to zero: all the better to implode the background into a series of signs of absence inscribed on the very surface of the work.

Krauss is not alone in performing this gesture, of course. Along with Derrida, there is the rather different spirit of Lacan, who in Krauss' words "pictures the unconscious . . . not as something different from consciousness, something outside it. He pictures it as *inside* consciousness, undermining it from within, fouling its logic, eroding its structure, even while appearing to leave the terms of that logic and that structure in place" (*OU* 24; emph. added). This is, in fact, an accurate summary of Lacan's position. According to most contemporary readings, the Lacanian Real stands not for some sort of real world outside the mind, but for an immanent trauma in consciousness itself, one that has no reality apart from the explicitly human realms of his two other major terms: the symbolic and the imaginary. Krauss even gives us an epigraph from Lacan's famous essay on Poe's tale "The Purloined Letter," in which the stolen letter is not hidden at any secret depth but is sitting in plain sight (*OU* 32). She speaks shortly thereafter of "a foreground, then, that is also a background, a top that is clearly a bottom" (*OU* 36). The encounter with the Real is "the break in the field of vision or the break within the flow of language" (*OU* 87). Just as Hegel converted Kant's external thing-in-itself into an immanent moment of thought, Lacan dragged Freud's unconscious from a buried netherworld and redefined it as a flaw in the jewel of consciousness.

In short, Krauss has signed up for a form of philosophical idealism. She tries to finesse herself out of this jam just like Hegel and Lacan, not to mention such contemporary admirers of these figures as Žižek. Among other things, Krauss cites Lacan's famous example of a tin sardine can looking back at him, as if to suggest a novel equality of subject and object (*OU* 165).[14] But no reciprocity of this kind is ever enough to escape idealism, since human and world are still the *only two terms* allowed in the picture; above all, there is no talk of objects looking at each other, meaning that a human subject must always be somewhere on the scene. Thus, we are still inside the Kantian formalism that was supposedly just overcome. Later, Krauss speaks of Jean-François Lyotard's view that "phenomenology's founding principle is not 'intentionality' but passivity" (*OU* 217). She might also have mentioned Jean-Luc Marion, who has built an entire philosophy out of this principle of passive givenness, even turning it into a theology.[15] But here once more, the inversion of the human being from an active conscious agent into a passive receiver of something from elsewhere does nothing to escape idealism, as long as humans and non-humans remain the only two pieces of the puzzle.

Having said all of this, there is still an important respect in which Krauss is a better match for OOO than Greenberg's own position. For although Krauss strips all depth from the cosmos and gives it the aspect of sign or simulacrum, and though it is impossible for a philosophy of withdrawn objects to agree with such a basically Postmodernist program, there is a sense in which Krauss empowers discrete pictorial elements in a way that Greenberg does not. For even if she holds that rotation in depth is flattened onto the surface of the collage, for her this does not happen thanks to the entirety of the surface plane. Instead, it is due to some rather discrete objects: the *f*-shaped soundholes on a violin. Despite Krauss' overt hostility to philosophical realism, this is a point on which alliance might well be possible.

Rancière: The Distribution of the Sensible

In recent years, the French philosopher Jacques Rancière has become one of the most influential thinkers among practicing artists. He is perhaps even better known as a political theorist, being a famous proponent of radical equality: an idea that has shaped the entire course of his life. Initially he was known as a leading disciple of the founder of Marxist structuralism, Louis Althusser; Rancière was in fact one of several co-authors of Althusser's major book, *Reading Capital*.[16] His break with his teacher came in the wake of the May 1968 student protests in Paris, which Althusser viewed with disdain. In Žižek's account of the break, Rancière responded by undertaking "a ferocious critical examination of Althusserian-structuralist Marxism with its rigid distinction between scientific theory and ideology and its distrust toward any form of spontaneous popular movement, [with such movements] immediately decried as a form of bourgeois humanism."[17] Rancière's itinerary, in short, is that of a radical anti-elitist, as seen in his anti-authoritarian philosophy of education no less than his theories of politics and aesthetics. But perhaps it is misleading to speak of his theories of politics *and* aesthetics, for there is a sense in which Rancière obliterates any distinction between the two. This is not because he thinks that art must always carry a political message – he is skeptical of this traditional Leftist view – but because he redefines the two domains in a more general sense that encompasses both.

130

Rancière often describes politics as a "distribution of the sensible," a phrase that hints at the close link he sees between politics and aesthetics (*PA* 3). He defines the matter as follows: "I call the distribution of the sensible the system of self-evident facts of sense perception that simultaneously discloses the existence of something in common and the delimitations that define the respective parts and positions within it" (*PA* 7). This distribution parcels out both that which is shared and that from which certain people are excluded. A favorite theme of Rancière is that "politics revolves around what is seen," and an important corollary is that politics revolves around who is regarded as having "the ability to see and the talent to speak" (*PA* 8). Much like Žižek and especially Badiou, Rancière's politics lays great stress on those situations in which those who were previously unrecognized suddenly lay claim to visibility. Rancière refers to these unrecognized ones as "the part of no part," while Badiou speaks of the excess of the parts of a situation over its elements, or of inclusion over belonging. For these thinkers, any situation is haunted by an excess beyond whatever it officially recognizes, with undocumented immigrants being an obvious example. In Rancière's own words: "Politics exists when the figure of a specific subject is constituted, a supernumerary subject in relation to the calculated number of groups, places, and functions in a society. This is summed up in the concept of the *demos*" (*PA* 47-48). Unsurprisingly, *demos* is also where Žižek locates the site of what he calls "politics proper," meaning that politics only happens when the previously unrecognized surges up and demands to be taken into account.[18]

What does art have in common with politics thus defined? Everything, according to Rancière: "The arts only ever lend to projects of domination or emancipation what they are able to lend to them ... quite simply, what they have in common with them: bodily positions and movements, functions of speech, the parceling out of the visible and the invisible" (*PA* 14). The context of this statement is Rancière's dissatisfaction with "politically engaged" art, in the sense of art with an overtly political message. Instead of this tired and often self-congratulatory genre, Rancière wants to raise the question of aesthetics and politics at "the level of the sensible delimitation of what is common to the community, the forms of its visibility and of its organization" (*PA* 13). This construction of a common space dominates Rancière's view of art no less than of politics, and he often describes it beautifully. For instance, a poem "dissipates in the very act of instituting a common space, similar to a national holiday fireworks display" (*AD* 34). Or even more sweepingly: "there is no

131

border separating the gesture of the painter devoted to high art from the performances of an acrobat devoted to amusing the people, none separating the musician who creates a purely musical language from the engineer devoted to rationalizing the Fordist assembly line" (*AD* 101). As such, there can be no question of a formalist artwork cut off from the beholder and the rest of the world: "An image never stands alone. It belongs to a system of visibility that governs the status of the bodies represented and the kind of attention they merit" (*ES* 99). Aesthetics is incapable of teaching concrete lessons about the political situation of the moment, but gives us instead "a shift from a given sensible world to another sensible world that defines different capacities and incapacities, different forms of tolerance and intolerance" (*ES* 75). In words reminiscent of Badiou's theory of the event, Rancière declares that "such breaks can happen anywhere and at any time. But they cannot be calculated" (*ES* 75).

The link Rancière draws between politics and aesthetics should now be clear. He is interested primarily in aesthetic acts as "configurations of experience that create new modes of sense perception and induce novel forms of political subjectivity" (*PA* 3). Novelty is the key, just as for Badiou, since it is "this 'newness' . . . that links the artist who abolishes figurative representation to the revolutionary who invents a new form of life" (*PA* 11-12). But again, the intersection of art and politics does not consist in the expression of some predictable Leftist content: "What aesthetic education and experience do not promise is to support the concept of political emancipation with forms of art" (*AD* 33). Rancière is interested instead in what he calls "metapolitics," defined as "the thinking which aims to overcome political dissensus by switching scene, by passing from the appearances of democracy and of the forms of the State to the infra-scene of underground movements and the concrete energies that comprise them" (*AD* 33). Unlike Danto, who sees Marxist aesthetics as hopelessly confined to literal content, Rancière credits Marxism with being "the ultimate form of metapolitics" due to its history of tunneling beneath political surfaces to focus instead on "the truth of the productive forces and relations of production" (*AD* 33). It is in this spirit that Rancière dismisses "the academic opposition between art for art's sake and engaged art" (*AD* 43). More broadly, there is "no longer any boundary separating what belongs to the realm of art from what belongs to the realm of everyday life" (*ES* 69).

Before going further, we should stress that "aesthetics" for Rancière means something inherently non-hierarchical; in this sense of the term, the "aesthetic regime" marks a historic break with the earlier "representative regime," even if the new form does not entirely erase the older one (*PA* 47). The representative regime, for its own part, replaced an even earlier "ethical regime" of images (*PA* 16). But as for the aesthetic regime, it not only breaks down hierarchies, but also points to a situation in which thought becomes foreign to itself, for which Rancière gives historical examples: "Vico's discovery of the 'true Homer' as a poet in spite of himself, Kantian 'genius' that is unaware of the law it produces, Schiller's 'aesthetic state' that suspends both the activity of the understanding and sensible passivity, Schelling's definition of art as the identity between a conscious process and an unconscious process, etc." (*PA* 18). But again, the main point for Rancière, who is a sort of present-day fanatic of egalitarianism, is that the aesthetic regime "is the implementation of [a] certain equality. It is based on the destruction of the hierarchical system of the fine arts" (*PA* 49). The representative regime, which Rancière also calls the "poetic" regime, "identifies the arts ... within a classification of ways of doing and making, and it consequently defines proper ways of doing and making as well as means of assessing imitations" (*PA* 18). This regime knows nothing of "art" as something that rises beyond all distinction between genres, which is first produced by the aesthetic regime. The latter "is the true name for what is designated by the incoherent label 'modernity'" (*PA* 19). In fact, Rancière sees this label less as incoherent than as a "simplistic" way of covering up the democracy of the aesthetic regime by misreading it in terms of a linear departure from figurative art (*PA* 19).

For Rancière, the heroic figure of the new regime is Friedrich Schiller, whose notion of the "*aesthetic state* ... is this regime's first manifesto (and remains, in a sense, unsurpassable)" (*PA* 19).[19] What Schiller calls "play," Rancière identifies with his own term "distribution" (*AD* 30). He even reads Schiller as an early champion of another of Rancière's key aesthetic and political concepts: *dissensus*. Even the casual reader will note that this term looks like the opposite of *consensus*, and indeed it is. We first consider the political sense of the term. For Rancière, "the people" is an ambiguous term in any society, since it refers simultaneously to those recognized by existing law, the people as embodied in the state, those left unrecognized by the status quo, and those who claim recognition under another law than that of the state. As he puts it, "consensus is the reduction of these various 'peoples' into a single people identical with the count of a population and its parts, of the interests of a global community and its parts" (*AD* 115). By contrast, politics is about asserting the alternative; furthermore, "art is a practice of dissensus" (*AD* 96). And "aesthetic common sense, for Schiller, is a dissensual common sense" (*AD* 98) Rancière gives us a lucid definition of his own concept of consensus, though it is one with a regrettably heavy dose of anti-realism: "What 'dissensus' means is an organization of the sensible where there is neither a reality concealed behind appearances nor a single regime of presentation and interpretation of the given imposing its obvious on all. It means that every situation can be cracked open from the inside, reconfigured in a different regime of perception and signification" (*ES* 48–49). And though we cannot agree with him here, we do salute his claim that such a model of politics is superior to "the endless task of unmasking fetishes or the endless demonstration of the omnipotence of the beast" (*ES* 49).

Whatever else Rancière might be, he is not a Postmodernist, though not because he thinks especially highly of Modernism. Postmodernism appeared as a celebration of various techniques that challenged Modernist presuppositions, techniques such as "the crossing-over and mixture between the arts that destroyed Lessing's conventional set of principles concerning the separation of the arts" and "the collapse of the paradigm of functionalist architecture and the return of the curved line and embellishment" (*PA* 23). But for Rancière this is somehow superfluous: for in a sense, Modernism was never really happening anyway. His alternative term, of course, is "the aesthetic regime," and "in this regime, art is art insofar as it is also non-art, or is something other than art . . . There is no postmodern rupture" (*AD* 36). And again, "there is no need to imagine that a 'postmodern' rupture emerged, blurring the boundaries between great art and the forms of popular culture. This blurring of boundaries is as old as 'modernity' itself" (*AD* 49). Thus, we should drop the Modern/ Postmodern divide for an analysis of "the politics founded on the play of exchanges and displacements between the art world and that of non-art" (*AD* 51).

Obviously enough, by working along these lines, Rancière has departed from the conception of Modernism in the arts that follows from Kant and more recent figures such as Greenberg and Fried. If we take Greenberg as an exemplary midpoint of aesthetic Modernism, and consider that two of his major concepts are the autonomy of art and its medium-specificity, we note that Rancière discounts both. Unsurprisingly, he dismisses what he calls "vain debates over the autonomy of art," and instructs us that "artistic practices are not 'exceptions' to other practices. They represent and reconfigure the distribution of these activities" (*PA* 13, 42). And finally, "the set of relations that constitutes the [artwork] operates *as if* it had a different ontological texture from the sensations that make up everyday experience. But there is neither a sensory difference nor an ontological difference" (ES 67). Rancière is even more skeptical about Greenberg's pet theme, the importance of the medium. Whereas Greenberg sees the disappearance of pictorial illusionism as linked to the need to purify painting of ulterior elements, Rancière historicizes painting differently: the growth of Renaissance illusionism came from the primacy of the *story* in art, while the downfall of the third dimension is linked to the increased stress on "the flatness of pages, posters, and tapestries" (PA 11). In conversation with Gabriel Rockhill of Villanova University, Rancière rejects the idea that the rise of abstract painting is linked to growing awareness of the flat canvas, and instead makes his usual Schillerian appeal to a more global sense of aesthetics: "[the] supposed dismissal of subject matter first presupposes the establishment of a regime of equality regarding subject matter" (PA 49-50). The autonomy of individual artworks, and of art as a specific region of endeavor, is dissolved into a soup containing all human activities, or at least all those that might be construed as "distributions of the sensible." Meanwhile, the changes in the history of art are stripped of any important link with the characteristics of the medium, and are historicized more broadly in the manner of Foucault-inspired literary critics.

We are now in a position to examine some of the most important features of what we might call Rancière's ontology, even if he never uses this term. Returning to his conversation with Rockhill, we hear the French thinker helpfully declare: "I by no means think ... that there is no science but of the hidden. I always try to think in terms of horizontal distributions, combinations between systems of possibilities, not in terms of surface and substratum." He proceeds to give political reasons for this ontology: "Where one searches for the hidden beneath the apparent, a position of mastery is established" (PA 46). Yet one could also say the opposite, and in my view more accurately. For it is only when we think that knowledge of the world is directly attainable that we begin to set up accreditation processes for those who know how to attain it, whereas the Socratic profession of ignorance about genuine reality is what brings all technical specialists low. For obvious reasons, we also cannot accept Rancière's refusal of the distinction between autonomy and heteronomy – central to all three of Kant's *Critiques* – for the simple reason that without this distinction, everything will be mixed with everything else, with no remaining principle of discernment (PA 32). Yet Rancière makes two additional points with which we do agree. First, he rightly notes that

135

we need not follow the recent tendency to embrace Kant's sublime as a new path to art and ethics; the Kantian notion of beauty, apprehended only by taste, already marks a radical break with the intellectualism of most philosophers (*ES* 64). Second, despite his exclusive focus on the horizontal at the expense of the duality of depth and surface, Rancière observes in a marvelous phrase, that "reality is never entirely soluble in the visible" (*ES* 89).

Let's close with some isolated points that resonate with our earlier discussion. First, there is Rancière's close and positive attention to the theater, focusing on the early twentieth-century masters Artaud and Brecht (*ES* 4). Ironically, given his view that the distinction between autonomy and heteronomy is insignificant, what one gets from Rancière's interpretation of theater is the sense of a "formalist" attempt to refuse the reduction of theater to communal political life. As he rightly puts it: "it is high time that we examine [the] idea that the theater is, in and of itself, a community site" (*ES* 16). In place of this recent philosophical piety toward community, Rancière sees theater as the production of a "unique individual adventure" for each and every spectator (*ES* 17). Yet far from stimulating the growth of supposedly bourgeois individualism, Rancière envisages egalitarian results from this non-communal theater: "[The] shared power of the equality of intelligence links individuals, makes them exchange their intellectual adventures, in so far as it keeps them separate from one another" (*ES* 17). While Fried worried about theatricality as an active intermixing between beholder and work, Rancière seems to fear the opposite critique of excessive passivity, though he assures us this is not the case: "Being a spectator is not some passive condition that we should transform into activity. It is our normal situation" (*ES* 17). This realization even counts for Rancière as the heart of emancipation, and he applies it to theatre in a way that resembles Ostas' critique of the Friedian separation between internal absorption and external beholding. Namely: "Emancipation begins when we challenge the opposition between viewing and acting ... when we understand that viewing is also an action that confirms or transforms [the] distribution of positions. The spectator also acts, like the pupil or scholar" (*ES* 13). This makes Rancière – and here we agree – the polar opposite of Nietzsche and his defender Heidegger, who push hard for an aesthetics based on the active creator rather than on the passive "woman's aesthetics" that takes the spectator as its model.[20] On this point OOO endorses Rancière over Nietzsche, since the object-oriented account of metaphor also treats the "passive" reader or spectator of art as an active performer of the missing object.

Artists need not be viewed as uniquely heroic creators, but simply as the best-informed spectators of their own work; by the same token, critics must not be treated as inferior to the artists they analyze.

There is also Rancière's treatment of collage. We have seen what Greenberg and Krauss made of this genre: for Greenberg it multiplied the one background plane into many, while for Krauss it inscribed depth on the very surface that was supposed to forbid it. For Rancière, by contrast, collage is the embodiment of the constant exchange he sees between art and non-art: "Before combining paintings, newspapers, oilcloths or clock-making mechanisms, it combines the foreignness of aesthetic experience with the becoming-art of ordinary life. Collage can be realized as the pure encounter between heterogeneous elements, attesting *en bloc* to the incompatibility of two worlds" (*AD* 47). Rancière also criticizes so-called relational art for its "simplistic opposition between objects and situations," as OOO would do for the different reason that a situation is also an object, whereas Rancière would argue conversely that every object is embedded in a total situation (*AD* 56). But let's end with an important observation by Rancière that leads directly to our next chapter. If we imagine art in previous ages as providing a mood of somber awe, bordering on religious fascination, we immediately notice how rarely this happens in any contemporary gallery. In today's art exhibitions, except in those cases where we are asked to feel moral outrage in the face of depicted oppression and atrocity, our most likely experience is outright laughter. In Rancière's words: "Humour is the virtue to which artists nowadays most readily ascribe" (*AD* 54). On that note, we turn to two schools of twentieth-century art that seem unusually eager to amuse us: Dada and Surrealism.

6

Dada, Surrealism, and Literalism

The previous chapter considered the views of Rosenberg, Steinberg, Clark, Krauss, and Rancière, five influential art theorists of the post-war period who, while very different in orientation, all count as anti-formalists in this book's sense of the term. Their relationist consensus despite many divergences make it even more important to reassert OOO's commitment to the independence of artworks and of all other objects: not because nothing is ever affected by anything else, but because nothing is affected by *everything* else. Stated differently, influence between one field and another or one entity and another can never be taken for granted. It comes at a price, and needs to be seen as something that happens intermittently and selectively rather than constantly and automatically. How relations occur is a key philosophical problem, and not something that should be taken as a *fait accompli* simply because we know from experience that there are causal influences in the world. After all, we know equally well from experience that many things do not affect each other. The only way to do justice to both points is to recognize that relations are something to be explained rather than assumed.

Perhaps the best way to see this in an art context is through Danto's useful anecdote of the "chained cat," which he also calls a "metaphysical sandpit." At Columbia University, where he was long employed until his recent death, there was – and perhaps still is – a bronze statue of a cat, chained to a railing to prevent its being stolen. Danto wittily notes that he is "open to the suggestion that it is not a chained sculpture of a cat, but a sculpture of a chained cat" (*TC* 102). And in fact there is no reason, for us or for Danto, to exclude the possibility that the chain is also part of the artwork. Formalism in our sense does not mean that only traditional paintings and sculptures can count as visual art, as if security chains were to be excluded *a priori*. It is quite conceivable, even probable, that some sculptor would make an entire career of producing deliberately chained works. Note that this poses no problem at all for OOO's formalism of autonomous objects, which is happy to treat cat-*plus*-chain as a single autonomous artwork in cases where it seems appropriate, just as we can treat H_2-*plus*-O (more commonly known as water) as a single molecule and not only as a relational assemblage of three different atoms. Yet there is a serious problem here for our opponents the relationists and contextualists, for they cannot link the chain to the cat without also linking the rest of the universe to the cat. As Danto puts it: "Of course what we take to be a bit of reality [outside the artwork] can in fact be part of the work, which is now a sculpture of a cat-chained-to-an-iron-railing, though the moment we allow *it* [i.e. the iron railing] to be a part of the work, where does . . . the work end? It becomes a kind of metaphysical sandpit, swallowing the universe down into itself" (*TC* 102).

The point is that we cannot do without some autonomy some-where. Presumably, the attempt has already been made by some artist to claim that the entire universe, or even all possible universes, constitute a total holistic artwork, perhaps signed under the artist's own name. This would indeed be very clever, if not for the fact that someone *saying* they have done this does not prove they have actually pulled it off – Thierry de Duve's claim to the contrary notwithstand-ing (*KAD* 302-303). Beyond the mere decree of having accomplished such a cosmic work, it would be necessary to draw someone into a genuine aesthetic experience that covers the universe as a whole, and for various reasons I doubt this is possible. Of course, we as artists or beholders may decide not to stop at the cat, the chain, or the railing, and expand the artwork instead to include the room, the building, the whole Columbia campus, the entire neighborhood of Morningside Heights, all of Manhattan, or some even wider aesthetic field. But we will always come to a stop somewhere, and that somewhere will be the outer wall of our increasingly complex autonomous object. The only way to circumvent this is to remove art from the realm of aes-thetics altogether and make it the mere correlate of an act of *declaring* that something is art, as some post-1960s theorists have in fact held.

Nor is it helpful to call it "arbitrary" where we decide to build the wall between a given artwork and its exterior, since OOO does not dispute the point that in some cases it might not be clear where the work ends. We are not trying to govern the artworld by excluding certain entities *a priori* as possible elements of artworks, or to put the Dadaist genie back into its bottle. But even if anything *can* enter an artwork as one of its elements, it does not follow that everything *is* an element of an artwork. The conceptual artist Joseph Kosuth (AAP 80-81) joins de Duve (*KAD* 301) in claiming that the artist declares what counts as art. By contrast, the seemingly old-fashioned OOO position is that the existence of an artwork requires *beauty*. We do not consider "beauty" to be vague or ineffable, but have defined it in a very precise sense as the theatrical enactment of a rift between a real object and its sensual qualities. And this cannot be done simply by announcing that it has occurred. Either we encounter a mere object with literal qualities, in which case it is simply not something aesthetic, *or* we are made to perform the work of an absent object that we have been convinced is missing, in which case we do have an aesthetic experience. The literal cannot be converted into the aesthetic by fiat. The aim of this chapter is to consider why this is so.

Literalism and Modernism

In the first four chapters of this book we developed the basic features of a OOO theory of art, partly from our own resources and partly from a series of agreements and disagreements with Kant, Fried, and Greenberg, whose importance cannot be doubted even by those who reject their conclusions. What I want to do here is quickly summarize the basic lesson of each of those chapters, in order to refresh the reader's memory prior to the closing arguments of this book.

Chapter 1 gave a basic overview of OOO in my version, as distinguished from the related but separate efforts of Ian Bogost, Bryant, Morton, and others.[1] From an object-oriented perspective, aesthetics can be defined negatively as anti-literalism and positively as the tension between an object and its own qualities, which it both does and does not possess. This is pertinent to more than artworks, since aesthetics in the OOO sense also encompasses the experience of passing time, the theoretical understanding of any entity, and even the causal interaction between inanimate beings. In this book we are focused on art, which we take to be a sub-category of the beautiful. The word is still unpopular today, but we are happy to join Hickey and Scarry in defending it to the hilt. In OOO terminology, beauty arises from the specific tension between real objects (RO) and sensual qualities (SQ). Not all beautiful things are art, and the question remains as to what art is by contrast with the rest of the beautiful. But literalism is *never* beautiful, and is not even a form of aesthetics, precisely because it sees no distinction between objects and their qualities, for it holds that a thing is nothing more than a bundle of qualities in the manner of Hume.

Chapter 2 reviewed the basic discoveries of Kant's *Critique of Judgment*, which I and many others still take as the gold standard of philosophical aesthetics more than two centuries after its publication. Kant defends the autonomy of the work of art, since it does not consist in its subjective agreeableness for me or anyone else, nor in its functional usefulness, but must earn the label "beautiful" in its own right. Kant denies all literalism to the work of art, since it can neither be conceptually understood, nor produced according to known formulae, nor replaced by prose descriptions of its content. OOO staunchly agrees with these features of Kant's anti-literalism. What we cannot accept is what we might call Kant's *modernism*. I mean this term in a purely philosophical sense, and by no means imply that I dislike Modernist art of the sort admired by Greenberg and Fried, since I happen to admire it myself. By Modernism in the philosophical sense, I mean the taxonomical style of philosophy that carves up the universe into just two kinds of things: (1) human beings, and (2) everything else. This book is not the place to decide exactly where modern philosophy began and where it ended, if indeed it has ended. But Descartes is a good default answer, and Kant perhaps the greatest master of the modern tradition. OOO's response to Kant's aesthetic Modernism is that he is wrong to put beauty on the human side of the fence, though Greenberg and Fried are equally wrong to put it on the object side of the fence. Our non-modernism – to borrow another term from Latour – entails that every human–object interaction is itself a new and distinct object, just like every chemical compound is a new and unified thing separate from the elements that compose it.

In Chapter 3 we considered the anti-theatrical views of Fried. We noted that even though Fried basically agrees with Diderot's claim that the figures in a painting should seem absorbed with other entities internal to the painting, and that the beholder of the painting should thus be deliberately excluded from it, Fried admits that this is merely a "supreme fiction." For it is he himself who shows us that important French painters such as David and Millet have a hard time being cleanly theatrical or anti-theatrical, and that Manet launched Modernism in painting with a dose of deliberate theatricality, under the name of "facingness." The OOO response to Fried is that the real enemy is literalism, not theatricality. And while the young Fried of 1967's "Art and Objecthood" sees literalism and theatricality as strolling hand-in-hand in the Minimalist works he so dislikes, OOO sees theatricality as the very antidote to literalism. To perform or enact something is to *be* it, which means that any literal description of such performance is nothing better than a translation. Although "performativity" has long been a key *anti*-essentialist term in the hands of Judith Butler and kindred theorists, to perform something in the OOO sense means to be it in a hidden and essential sense that no outside understanding can ever exhaust.[2] In any case, by disagreeing with Fried's initial stricture against mixing work and beholder, this chapter took another anti-Modernist step.

In Chapter 4 we considered Greenberg's doctrine that the medium or background of an artwork is more important than its surface content. We saw that this was ultimately the same insight that drives the philosophy of Heidegger and the media theory of McLuhan, both of which OOO views favorably. Greenberg is famously contemptuous of the content of artworks, and in practice his criticism rarely sheds much light on that content. What OOO most rejects in Greenberg, as in Heidegger, is another aspect of their shared modernity. Namely, they not only oppose a deep medium to a superficial content, but further assume that this deep medium is a One, making all multiplicity automatically shallow by contrast. Greenberg's novel interpretation of collage as producing a multiplicity of planes simply gives us several conflicting Ones instead of the usual solitary and majestic One. The right way to deal with this problem is not the Postmodern trick of dispensing with the background and saluting the superficial immediacy of signs and simulacra, since this is merely a highway to literalism: for the fight against the literal always requires an element of depth, villainous though depth may sound to Derrideans, Foucauldians, and Lacanians. But OOO also argues – against Greenberg and Heidegger – for a fragmented depth, so that the medium of the artwork is not found in the unified canvas, but in each and every element of the work, some of them left in suppressed literal form while others are freed up by way of the object-quality tension we call beauty.

To summarize, there are two basic threads in the OOO theory of art: the first is an anti-literalist one, and the second a non-modernist one. On the first count, we are in substantial agreement with the formalist lineage of Kant, Greenberg, and Fried. But on the second we are largely alone, since the view that the human being and the objects of its attention combine to form an entirely new object has precursors but no fully professionalized guides, and its implications for art are by no means clear. The present book will conclude as follows. Here in Chapter 6, we will consider what seem to be the strongest possible counter-examples to anti-literalism in art: (1) Dada, which seems capable of turning even the most literal everyday objects into art, and (2) Surrealism, its purported cousin, scolded by Greenberg for an excessive focus on literal, if unsettling, surface content. In Chapter 7, we will step into the unknown by proposing a philosophically non-modern transformation of the formalism known so far.

Dada and Literalism

Gavin Parkinson has written something that strikes me as both true and astounding: "the reputation and work of Marcel Duchamp . . . [have] surpassed those of Picasso in the eyes of art historians, artists, and Duchamp's admirers alike" (*DB* 6). However familiar this situation may be with respect to today's art world, we should never forget its sheer improbability. In Picasso we have a child prodigy who did not disappoint in later life, growing up to become one of the great masters in the history of Western art. Greenberg risks no controversy when he asserts that "over the twenty-odd years from 1905, the beginning of his Pink Period, to 1926, when his Cubism ceased being High, Picasso turned out art of a stupendous greatness, stupendous alike in conception and execution, in the rightness and consistency of its realization" (IV 27). If anything, Greenberg courts the ire of Picasso fans who resent his belittling of *Guernica* and most of his other post-1926 work (*HE* 91). At any rate, few balanced observers would argue that Picasso was not one of the greatest figures in the recorded history of art. Duchamp, by contrast, was a painter of visibly mediocre gifts who first became famous for inserting such everyday objects as a urinal or a comb into art exhibitions, before seemingly quitting art to play chess full-time. And yet Parkinson is right that what guides art today is the spirit of Duchamp, not of Picasso. We should not forget what a bizarre outcome this is: enough so that analogies are difficult to find. Perhaps we can generate a hypothetical one by pairing up Albert Einstein and Alfred Jarry, the French absurdist writer who coined the humorous term "pataphysics" to refer to what he called a "physics of imaginary causes."[3] Bearing this in mind, imagine a present-day science writer seriously penning the following words: "the reputation and work of Alfred Jarry . . . [have] surpassed those of Einstein in the eyes of historians of science, scientists, and Jarry's admirers alike." If there is some parallel universe in which such things are being written, then the history of science in that universe must have taken a most unlikely turn.

It should also be recalled that Duchamp's peak influence was not contemporary with his most famous works, but dates to his old age in the 1960s, the same decade in which he eventually died. A good index of his late-blooming reputation can be found in the pattern of Greenberg's mentions of him. From the dawn of Greenberg's career in 1939 through early 1968, I count a total of 333 essays, articles, and reviews, along with the booklets on Miró (1948) and Matisse (1953).[4] During that nearly three-decade period of productivity and acclaim, I find only two mentions of Duchamp: a 1943 reference to some pieces in Peggy Guggenheim's new gallery (I 141), and a 1967 barb about how minimalism uses the third dimension because this is where art meets non-art, and Duchamp is sarcastically "credited" with this discovery (IV 253). That brings us to May 1968, the symbolic birth of the Postmodern era during which Greenberg's fortunes have fallen far indeed. As chance would have it, that was also the month in which he made his first serious criticism of Duchamp. Although the Duchamp revival was well underway by the early 1960s, Greenberg's 1968 Sydney lecture seems to be the point when he first felt the need to respond directly to the Dadaist's growing influence (IV 292-303). De Duve exaggerates when he reports that "from the late sixties on, hardly a single one of [Greenberg's] articles has not contained a violent attack on Duchamp, blaming him for all the woes of the art-world" (*KAD* 292). Greenberg's references to Duchamp do increase after 1968, but not to the extent de Duve suggests. What can be said is that Greenberg's discussions of Duchamp become more extensive and vitriolic whenever they do occur. Rather than quote these attacks individually, allow me to summarize the spirit of these assaults:

(1) Duchamp rejects quality as an aesthetic standard.
(2) He treats the shock value of advanced art not as an unfortunate side effect that wears off over time, but as the central purpose of art.
(3) He shocks established standards not by internal aesthetic means, but by transgressing everyday social decorum: displaying urinals, breasts, or the spread-out naked body of a murdered woman in a fine art context that will be predictably horrified by such gestures.
(4) He privileges thinking in art, turning artworks into transparent concepts to an excessive degree.
(5) He overestimates the radical break his work makes with the past.
(6) Though he thinks himself to be the pinnacle of artistic advance-ment, Duchamp is actually an academic artist who takes the medium of art too much for granted, despairs of being able to

innovate from within, and is thus led into a sort of juvenile sabotage through shocking affronts to the fine arts gallery context. (GD 259)

This list more or less covers the range of Greenberg's objections to the leader of Dada, though there is also the related complaint that Duchamp's works are somewhat like jokes or mathematical proofs: funny or interesting the first time, but not many times thereafter.

Now, what should we make of this list? The only item that strikes me as clearly wrong is the last one: the assertion that Duchamp is an "academic artist." We saw that in his late Sydney lecture Greenberg defined academic art, with admirable clarity, as art that takes its medium for granted – a definition that, in their own ways, Heidegger and McLuhan also uphold (LW 28). To take one's medium for granted, to focus thereby on content rather than background, is another way to say that one is a *literalist*. The interest of this point is that Greenberg regards both Surrealism and Dada as forms of academic art, and thus as kinds of literalism, though from a OOO standpoint this misreads both movements. But at least it is clear why Greenberg says this about Surrealism: for even Dalí's wildest tableaux continue the post-Renaissance tradition of illusionistic three-dimensional scenes, and therefore he does nothing to come to terms with what Greenberg takes to be the all-important medium of painting, the flat canvas. The same would hold, in Greenberg's eyes, for René Magritte and other Surrealists. In the next section I will challenge this interpretation of Surrealism as literalism. But to interpret Dada as being unaware of its medium seems a much harder case to make. For if anyone in the twentieth century challenged our sense of what counts as a valid artistic medium, it was surely Duchamp, whatever other problems we may find with his approach. From the famous industrial ready-mades, to the strange and amusing *The Large Glass*, to the wonderfully toy-like La-*boîte-en-valise* with its stash of miniature works by Duchamp, to the repellent butchered nude of *Étant donnés* in Philadelphia, it can hardly be claimed that the artist failed to explore a wide range of non-obvious media.

That much, I think, needs to be acknowledged. Nonetheless, I am among those who still rate Picasso above Duchamp, and even among those who have grown bored with the near ubiquity of Duchampian irreverence, in which chuckles fill many galleries and aesthetic experience almost none. Let's ask the following question: are the true limits of Duchamp as our guide to the future already found on Greenberg's list above, or do they remain unformulated there? It seems to me that the remaining complaints on the list can be sifted into two basic types. Objections 2 and 3 are a fairly clear application of formalist notions: Duchamp wishes merely to shock, and his shocks are social rather than aesthetic. The other three, Objections 1, 4, and 5, seem more diverse at first glance, but ultimately they refer to Duchamp's privileging of the intellect against what he often dismissed as "retinal art" (*DB* 6). Number 4 makes this point explicitly. Number 5 is linked closely with it, since Duchamp's claim to make a radical break with the past is associated with the claim that he has a radical new *idea* of art that no one has tried before. Number 1 is also connected with Duchamp's anti-Kantian primacy of thinking in art, since the quality Duchamp rejects is that of autonomous aesthetic taste, not the notion that some plans for artworks might be better than others. Duchamp's works are generally based on ideas, as Kosuth notes (AAP 84), and these ideas are supposed to startle viewers accustomed to more standard artistic genres.

In a critical though generous response to my article on Greenberg and Duchamp, Bettina Funcke takes issue with my six-point list; or rather, she finds something missing in Greenberg's own approach to Duchamp. Funcke begins by partly agreeing with Greenberg's frustration, if not with his sense of timing: "Greenberg was writing from what he saw as a point of exhaustion; in his view Duchamp was entirely played out and we needed to find a new direction" (NO 276). She continues: "That may not be something we can agree with now, but it may be that forty years later, we can finally sort of come to the same conclusion as Greenberg: OK, you were not right about the art of the 1970s, but *now* we have caught up with you, because now everything feels exhausted to us, too" (NO 276). But of course, "this feeling of exhaustion, that things have been overly exploited, is perennial" (NO 276).

Yet the main point of Funcke's article lies elsewhere, when she claims to find Duchamp's real contemporary importance elsewhere: "more so than the readymade ... [t]his is his play with information and documentation, with the very reception of his own work, through printed and editioned representations ... This is something that basically falls outside Greenberg's investigation, and is not really addressed by the 6-point critique that you mention" (NO 276). Funcke adds later that "these points of critique seem to make sense only as long as we focus on the readymades and other objects as *objects* per se, ignoring their context, their discourse, their perverse histories, and everything that Duchamp worked to put into place, a practice which is now much more common because of his work" (NO 277).

146

Her finely chosen example is *Fountain*, Duchamp's infamous urinal of 1917. For although it usually counts as the textbook ready-made, it turns out to be less a singular object than a series of documentary and historical traces. After all, few people saw the original *Fountain*, which was eventually lost. All that remains of that work are some photographs taken by Alfred Stieglitz, a critical commentary on the work that was probably written by Duchamp himself, and three other urinals that stood in for the missing original in the much later shows of 1950, 1963, and 1964. In Funcke's words: "the artwork does not occupy a single position in space and time; rather, it is a palimpsest of gestures, presentations, and positions . . . In short: it turned art into discourse . . . Had anyone previously done such work with copies and editions within the realm of high art?" (*AO* 279).

Nonetheless, Funcke concludes on an ambivalent note. In one respect, she seems highly supportive of this documentary trend. For while Greenberg's critique of Duchamp seems focused on the ready-mades, "there were a lot more powerful tools in Duchamp's toolbox: the way he made manuals for his own work, the status of the copy and the editioned object, the tweaked reproduction of one's own work, the way art can turn into discourse . . ." (NO 281). By contrast, even in the work of as celebrated a painter as Pollock, "there are not so many concrete strategies to take away and use in your own work" (NO 281). But even as Funcke praises these Duchampian developments, a note of fatigue slips into her voice: "I want to stop and point out that all these examples do not invalidate Greenberg's critiques. Obviously Greenberg would have seen all of this as a confirmation of his doubts about the direction in which Duchamp was taking art" (NO 281). And more importantly, we do have today an "over-exploited legacy of Duchamp," consisting in the very "work of documentation, information, altered photographs, forgeries, identities, narrativising, and transferrals" whose initial importance to the art world Funcke already proclaimed (NO 281).

My response is as follows. In the first place, we have seen that the OOO concept of "object" is broad enough that the shift from ready-made solo physical entities to tangled webs of documentation and commentary does not shift the underlying ontology. A series of manuals or practices is no less an object for us than is a solid ceramic urinal. The question for OOO is simply whether the painting, sculpture, ready-made, or web of documents in question is able to establish sufficient autonomy and depth to count as important art, since all of these things can be done well or poorly. Where Funcke has a point is that traditional formalism did not see any room for "documentation, information, altered photographs, forgeries, identities, narrativising, and transferrals" on the roster of legitimate works of art. It was, in this sense too, a fundamentally taxonomical operation which held that certain kinds of entities were always candidates to be artworks while certain other kinds could never be. In expanding our sense of what might count as art, Duchamp clearly did the future a service, as even Greenberg came to concede. Finally, Funcke disagrees with Greenberg's claim that the past half century of art can be called Duchampian. Her reasoning is that this view "leaves out the influence of Andy Warhol, whom [Greenberg] could not really deal with, and who shifted the terrain again" (NO 276). On this note we turn to Danto, the critic most closely associated with Warhol.

Danto tells us that his serious involvement with art came when "as a soldier in the Italian campaign [of the American Army in World War II], I came across a reproduction of Picasso's blue period masterpiece, La Vie" (AEA 179). In the years that followed, the record shows Danto studying both philosophy and art, and even pursuing an artistic career in the 1950s as a follower of Willem de Kooning (AEA 123). Yet Danto often relates that his "great experience" came later, in April 1964, when he saw Warhol's Brillo Box at the Stable Gallery in New York (AEA 123). Just months thereafter, he gave a lecture at the American Philosophical Association conference entitled "The Artworld," of which he proudly states that "[this] paper, not once so far as I know cited in the copious bibliographies on pop in later years, really did become the basis for philosophical aesthetics in the second half of [the twentieth] century" (AEA 124). While this is no doubt true, there is something confusing about Danto's chronology. For even if his collision with Brillo Box was Danto's great experience, there had already been an earlier encounter with pop – Roy Lichtenstein's The Kiss, in the pages of Art News – that was not without impact on his life: "I must say I was stunned . . . [I]n my own mind I understood immediately that if it was possible to paint something like this . . . then everything was possible" (AEA 123). But while the phrase "everything was possible" is the sort of liberating view later celebrated by the mature Danto, the Lichtenstein piece had a strange effect on his art career: "It also meant that I lost interest in doing art and pretty much stopped. From that point on, I was single-mindedly a philosopher . . ." (AEA 123). The significance of pop for Danto lay precisely in the fact that, as he saw it, it was no longer possible to distinguish art from non-art simply through a different visual appearance of the two. For all practical purposes, Warhol's Brillo Box was indistinguishable from any of the mass-produced Brillo boxes in supermarkets. Thus art really needed philosophy for the first time, though Kosuth would draw the opposite conclusion (AAP 76).

Danto is my favorite of the "Postmodernist" art critics, though this may be simply because I enjoy his familiar philosophical way of tackling topics. Among philosophers, it is Danto who elevated Warhol to a world-historic figure even bigger than Duchamp. Danto has a talent for clever examples, with one of the best coming at the beginning of his first and best-known art book, *The Transfiguration of the Commonplace*. I will speak primarily of that work here, along with some supplemental materials from another of his widely read books, *After the End of Art*, and to a lesser extent of his monograph *Andy Warhol*. We can focus on four of Danto's most central claims: (1) It is no longer possible to tell the difference between art and non-art by the mere visual look of an entity. (2) Since the visual look is no longer enough, the content of an artwork is not the key to determining its status. The effect here is ambivalent: on the one hand this turn away from content sounds like a Greenbergian move, but on the other, Danto critiques Greenberg by appealing to the importance of content in certain individual cases – as when he insists that we pay attention to the war motif of *Guernica*. (3) In order to oppose content, Danto makes a rather OOOish appeal to Aristotle's *Rhetoric*, and to metaphor as an especially important species of rhetoric. (4) Finally, Danto claims that Warhol rather than Duchamp is the real watershed in recent art history. On top of these four points, Danto adds some miscellaneous observations that are useful for our purposes, in particular his mixed signals about the term "essence."

The Transfiguration of the Commonplace begins with an imaginative riff on a passage from Kierkegaard, in which the philosopher describes a painting entitled *Red Sea* that was really nothing but a red square; he compares this painting to his own life for reasons that need not concern us here (*TC* 1). Danto expands on this story by imagining a whole series of other red squares identical, or nearly so, to the one recollected by Kierkegaard. The first can be called *Kierkegaard's Mood*, and though visually identical with *Red Sea*, the purported subject matter of the title sets it apart from its predecessor. Danto proceeds to imagine other works with the same outward look: a witty Moscow landscape called *Red Square*, a Minimalist work also called *Red Square* for more straightforward reasons, and a metaphysical painting entitled *Nirvana*. Next comes "a still-life executed by an embittered disciple of Matisse, called *Red Table Cloth*" (*TC* 1), which Danto allows for the sake of argument to use a thinner layer of paint. The following item, again a red square, is "merely a canvas grounded in red lead" (*TC* 1), though it clearly belongs to art history, since it had been readied for use by the Venetian Renaissance painter Giorgione prior to his early death. Next to this is another canvas grounded in red lead, but not an artwork at all: it is simply an object produced for some unknown everyday purpose. He closes the imaginary show by adding *Untitled*, a painting executed by an angry young artist named J who demands last-minute admission to the show of red squares. Here Danto adds the witty remark that J's work is lacking in richness (*TC* 2).

This extended example gives a useful presentation of Danto's primary claim as a philosopher of art: the insufficiency of an object's outward look in determining whether it should count as an artwork at all. He reminds us that a similar point was already made about literature, in a famous short story by Jorge Luis Borges entitled "Pierre Menard, Author of Don Quixote."[5] As is well known, it recounts the verbatim rewriting of *Don Quixote* by a fictional twentieth-century Frenchman. Though every word and punctuation mark is exactly the same as in Cervantes' original novel – making the books visually identical in Danto's sense – the narrator notes the vast differences between the two: whereas Cervantes wrote in a contemporary style in his native language, Menard wrote his own novel rather preciously in an archaic style of a foreign tongue, and so forth. In Danto's words: "Borges' contribution to the ontology of art is stupendous" (*TC* 36). He observes further that this lesson was missed by a rival critic: "Greenberg believed that art alone and unaided presents itself to the eye as art, when one of the great lessons of art in recent times is that this cannot be so . . ." (*AEA* 71) Later, he refers to this more harshly as Greenberg's "breathtaking obtuseness" (*AEA* 92). In any case, we cannot just open our eyes and look. With respect to Warhol's *Brillo Box*, "no one unfamiliar with history or with artistic theory could see these as art, and hence it was the history and theory of the object, more than anything palpably visible, that had to be appealed to in order to see them as art" (*AEA* 165). For Danto, this shift is enough to separate art from aesthetics, given that the latter is a term linked with perception rather than thought. Speaking in my hometown of Iowa City in 1994, he correctly notes that the ambitions of contemporary art "are not primarily aesthetic" (*AEA* 183).

Now, it is true that Danto's invocation of an old principle from the philosophy of science, to the effect that all observation is theory-laden (*TC* 124), could be read as another barb at Greenberg's supposed reliance on raw aesthetic perception. But strangely enough, Danto's distrust of the outward visual look of things turns into something that

150

Greenberg himself would endorse: a distrust of *content* in art, and a corresponding interest in its medium. Granted, Danto never goes as far as Greenberg in this direction, and even makes sure to argue – explicitly targeting the older critic – that when Picasso painted *Guernica*, he "was little concerned with the limits of the [canvas] medium: he was more concerned, by an inestimable degree, with the meaning of war and suffering" (*AEA* 73). Yet it remains striking that Danto opposes the theory of art as mimesis insofar as he links mimesis with content: "Taken as a theory of art, what the imitation theory amounts to is a reduction of the artwork to its content, everything else being supposedly invisible ..." (*TC* 151). He complains that Marxist theories of art have the general defect of being content-oriented, and likewise attacks the idealist philosophy of Berkeley for reducing the world to a set of sensory images (*TC* 151). Danto's imagined example of the numerous different paintings of the same red square seemed to propose the total *context* of an artwork as an alternative to its mere visual content. Yet I have argued that context literalizes objects no less than its visual properties do, since it merely treats the objects as a bundle of relations instead of a bundle of optical data. This entails that for art to function on a deeper level than the relational context or visual look of a work, it needs to accept a brand of philosophical realism, which is in fact what OOO holds. In any case, Danto is willing to defend medium over content even to those who regard the art medium itself as unimportant. For there is another medium on the scene whose presence cannot be denied: "There is also ... a philosophical analogue to the concept of medium. It is the concept of consciousness, which is at times described as a pure diaphanousness, never opaque enough to be an object for itself" (*TC* 152). It is interesting to note that, by contrast, Kosuth's own defense of conceptual art seems to amount to a *defense* of content (*AAP* 84). and in this way his distrust of traditional philosophy – which seems the result of a somewhat cocky youthful adherence to Ludwig Wittgenstein – is actually a distrust of the realism implied by Danto's suspicion of content (*AAP* 76, 96). In any case, Danto is surer than ever that not only does art need philosophy (*TC* viii), but even that contemporary art verges on becoming philosophy of art (*TC* 56).

In a further effort to explain how art goes beyond mere visible content, Danto too has recourse to an analysis of metaphor, which he rightly treats as a branch of rhetoric (*TC* 168). The central concept of Aristotle's *Rhetoric* is the enthymeme, meaning something the rhetorician leaves unstated rather than saying it explicitly. The classic example is that a speaker in Ancient Greece can say that a certain man has been crowned three times with laurel, without making explicit the fact – obvious to anyone living in that time and place – that this means he has thrice been a champion at the Olympic games. The point is that by leaving out information, and thus acting as a "truncated syllogism" (*TC* 170), an enthymeme communicates more than it openly states. This is why so many authors, from Plato onward, have viewed rhetoric as a form of manipulation even when it says nothing untrue. It involves "a complex interrelation between the framer and reader of the enthymeme. The latter must himself fill the gap deliberately left open by the former: he must supply what is missing and draw his own conclusions . . ." (*TC* 170). In the terms of McLuhan's media theory, rhetoric is thus a "cold" medium that withholds much detail and requires active participation, thereby ensuring in-depth involvement on the part of the auditor or beholder.[6] Where rhetoric is concerned, "explicitness is the enemy" (*TC* 170), since something stated will never be as powerful as something personally felt. Here Danto calls our attention to how little Iago actually says in Shakespeare's *Othello*; his manipulations are performed on the basis of innuendo rather than outright lies (TC 170).

Turning now to the branch of rhetoric called metaphor, which Aristotle handles most directly in his *Poetics*, Danto appreciates this topic in much the same way as OOO. He glosses Aristotle, reasonably well, as saying that we can explain metaphor as a way of suggesting "a middle term t so that if a is metaphorically b, there must be some t such that a is to t what t is to b" (*TC* 170). But in fact I think this gets it wrong, since it follows from our discussion in Chapter 1 that the point is not to find the middle term t between two objects, which will merely be one or more shared qualities: "darkness" as that which binds wine and the sea, for instance. Instead, the real trick is zeroing in on the inscrutable a after it has been granted the qualities of b. But more importantly, we agree with Danto's analysis of how metaphor works: namely that the missing term, whatever it may be, "has to be found, the gap has to be filled in, the mind moved to action" (*TC* 171). He further observes that metaphors "resist . . . substitutions and precisifications" (*TC* 177), meaning that they resist paraphrase of any sort. This is why texts, like anything else, cannot be translated without something being lost (*TC* 178). Danto concludes that "the structure of the metaphor has to do with some features of the representation other than the content" (*TC* 175), which is precisely the sort of mechanism he seeks. This rejection of visible content also accounts for Danto's own reason for linking art with philosophy: "It is my view that art, as art, as something that contrasts with reality, arose together with philosophy . . ." (*TC* 77). We simply note that by "reality," Danto means something more like "visible surface actuality." His thesis is that a contrast with such actuality is what is sought by both art and philosophy, with the latter in his view having arisen independently on just two occasions: in Greece and India, "civilizations both obsessed with a contrast between appearance and reality" (*TC* 79).

Returning to Danto's fascination with Warhol, it might be wondered why the American pop celebrity should count as more important than Duchamp, who is in a real sense the great-grandfather of contemporary art. Danto openly calls Pop "the most critical art movement of the [twentieth] century" (*AEA* 122). In the wake of *Brillo Box*, "a whole new theory of art was called for other than the theories of realism, abstraction, and modernism . . ." (*AEA* 124). And even more strongly, "Warhol, and the pop artists in general, rendered almost worthless everything written by philosophers on art, or at best rendered it of local significance" (*AEA* 125). Even so, why make such claims about Warhol rather than Duchamp, who might look to some like the originator of whom Warhol was merely the derivative follower? I admit to not being fully satisfied with Danto's answer, which not only takes a detour beyond the surface similarities of *Fountain* and *Brillo Box*, but goes outside art altogether to measure the overall historical impact of these pieces. As Danto puts it:

> In my view pop was not just a movement which followed one movement which followed one movement and was replaced by another. It was a cataclysmic moment which signaled profound social and political shifts, and which achieved profound philosophical transformations in the concept of art . . . Whatever he achieved, Duchamp was not celebrating the ordinary. He was, perhaps, [at most,] diminishing the aesthetic and testing the boundaries of art. (*AEA* 132)

While the difference is not hard to see, its importance is not immediately compelling. Nor is the difference clarified much in Danto's monograph on Warhol. There we read, citing from the Kindle edition, that "Warhol was not anti-aesthetic in quite the same way that Duchamp was. Duchamp was trying to liberate art from having to please the eye. He was interested in an intellectual art. Warhol's motives were more political" (*AW* 558). Or later: "Andy made his grocery boxes whereas Duchamp could not, in principle, have made his readymades" (*AW* 638). But even if Duchamp had produced his own urinal, we cannot imagine Danto calling him the first Pop artist, since for Danto it is ultimately a matter of Warhol's heralding a broader cultural movement in American life, a criterion that cannot be called aesthetic.

Before bidding farewell to Danto, we should note his ambivalent attitude toward "essence," one of the most vilified concepts in recent philosophy. If the essence of a thing means what a thing really is, beyond all the accidental features on its surface, and even beyond our ability to know it, we can immediately sense the two directions from which it will be attacked. From one side, by denying any such thing as a "depth" existing beneath a "surface" – as if depth were the patriarchal relic of a bygone era – Postmodern philosophers claim there is nowhere for an essence to hide: hence, a thing is nothing more than the sum total of its public actions and effects. From the other side, which rejects essence less in itself than in its supposed impermeability to knowledge, the Hegelian influence in present-day philosophy mocks the notion that what a thing really is could be permanently hidden from us. There are times when Danto seems fully allied with such objections. For example, he celebrates what he calls "the *ontological* success of Duchamp's work . . . [which] not merely put an end to the era of, but to the entire historical project . . . [of] seeking to distinguish the essential from the accidental qualities of art . . ." (*AEA* 112). Yet before long Danto declares himself "an essentialist in the philosophy of art, notwithstanding the fact that in the polemical order of the contemporary world, the term 'essentialist' has taken on the most negative of connotations" (*AEA* 193). It seems to me that Danto reaches the right position when he says that the problem in the previous history of aesthetics is not the view that there is an essence of art, but that the great figures, "from Plato through Heidegger . . . got the essence wrong" (*AEA* 193). This is not to say that Danto or anyone else can get it exactly right if they just try a bit harder than Plato and Heidegger. For we have seen that there is a problem with any attempt to grasp the essence of anything directly, as if a thing could be replaced by a paraphrase of itself.

Surrealism and Literalism

We saw that the problem with Greenberg's use of the pejorative term "academic art" for both Duchamp and Dalí is that, if academic art means "art that is unaware of its medium," this seems clearly inapplicable to Duchamp. I will now argue that, in a different sense, it does not even work for Dalí. But Greenberg is not the only one who identifies the Dadaists and the Surrealists as belonging to one and the same current. Often enough we hear the phrase "Dada and Surrealism," though the link seems convincing primarily due to the shared irreverence of the two movements, and their joint incompatibility with Modernism in the Greenbergian sense. Nonetheless, it is necessary to distinguish the two, and numerous attempts along these lines have already been made. Consider the following passage by David Joselit:

> And this, perhaps, is why [Duchamp] never allowed himself to be officially associated with the surrealist movement even though he participated in many of its activities. For [surrealist leader André] Breton, the unconscious and the strategies of automatism in writing, painting, and *objets trouvés* [found objects] developed to gain access to it, held the promise of psychic liberation and revolution, whereas for Duchamp, the unconscious was the locus of constraint, repetition, and commodification.[7]

This is subtle, but I think too much so. Does the major difference between Dada and Surrealism really consist in their varying attitudes toward the unconscious? Must we go so far afield from the art itself into the factual techniques employed by the two movements, and their differing implicit attitudes to Freud? It seems to me that the distinction is simpler, notwithstanding the overlapping activities and membership of the two groups, and the often entertaining anti-traditionalism of both.

Generally speaking, Dada is a sort of globalist gesture. At least in the case of the ready-mades, it is an attempt to put a unified literal object in the usual place of an artwork, which I have argued is necessarily non-literal. Here I disagree with my friend Jackson, and on two separate counts. His first relevant passage runs as follows: "One can instantly evoke the lesson from Marcel Duchamp's Ready-mades, which refused to give art its autonomy and exposed the contextual systems that gave birth to it; the public's unexpected willingness to consider it 'as' art or the gallery that gives the anxious object its title and space" (AOA 146). And here is the second passage: "Duchamp was less concerned that 'any object' can be art, but on the contrary, the challenge of making something that *isn't* a work of art but a simple object" (AOA 146). Let's begin with the second. It is hard to see much of a challenge in the act of making something that is a simple object rather than art. On a daily basis, we prepare documents and purchase factory-made items; nothing could be easier. Yet only rarely, if ever, do most of us produce art. If Duchamp's goal had been the simple production of objects that were not art, he might have chosen an easier career path, such as textile or agricultural labor, or some sort of cottage shoemaker's craft. Thus I am inclined to the view that Duchamp was thinking along Dantoian lines before Danto: namely, there is no longer a *taxonomy* in which certain types of objects (paintings, sculptures) are automatically considered art, whereas others (bottle racks, bicycle wheels) are automatically excluded. The past half century has retaught this same lesson almost *ad nauseam*, even if the point is in some sense well-taken.

To my mind, Jackson's first passage is more consequential, though here again I disagree. Namely, I do not accept his claim that Duchamp "refused to give art its autonomy and exposed the contextual systems that gave birth to it." The point of the ready-mades, after all, is that they are objects *torn* from their usual contexts and displayed in autonomous isolation, something that is the norm in gallery and museum spaces, but is otherwise rarely encountered outside appliance stores. There is also the case of broken tools achieving isolation, described so famously by Heidegger. Jackson's point, of course, is that the art world provided the context that allowed even trivial everyday objects to be presented as art. This is reminiscent of George Dickie's "institutional" theory, which must be rejected on the grounds that the mere dicta of institutions assure nothing: they regularly house work that critics dismiss, sometimes rightly, as non-art, while excluding popular or eccentric phenomena that are sometimes seen later as the significant art of their time.[8] Van Gogh and Cézanne were clearly significant artists before being accepted as such in an institutional sense.

What happens with the ready-made, as I see it, is that the urinal or comb have a role analogous to those of the sensual qualities in a metaphor, but without any obvious real object-term. Stated differently, the implicit metaphor with ready-mades is "art is like a urinal," or "art is like a comb," and this is the metaphor the beholder performs. The gallery context certainly prepares us in a causal sense to enact such a performance: though if Duchamp had gone about it differently, he might have begun his exercise with "found" works on the street, inviting random pedestrians to experience them as artworks. Whether or not Duchamp succeeds and, if so, to what extent, is a question that can no more be answered *a priori* than "wine-dark sea" or "a candle is like a teacher" can be ruled in or out of play as metaphors prior to our experience of them. Stated differently, the artworld context for *Fountain* was a sufficient but not necessary condition for Dada to perform its labor. What remains is a lesson about literalism. By working with literal objects, which we have defined as nothing but bundles of qualities, Duchamp helps expose the fact that art might conceivably take place with no obvious underlying real object at all, thereby making it clearer than ever that the theatrical beholder is the primary agent in art. For although it is often said that Duchamp's point was that any object can be art, not just any object can be Dada: there are countless objects that would have failed as ready-mades, at least in the early stages of the movement. One example might be a found piece of thrift store art of the sort frequently exhibited in recent decades in a spirit of campy irony. Among my personal favorites is *Robot Bursts from Crate*, found in the amusing 1992 book *Thrift Store Paintings*.[9] Whatever we make of this whimsical low-grade painting today, it could not possibly count as Dada. The beholder would simply view it as bad or tasteless art, not as non-art striving to be art, and thus Duchamp's point would be lost from the outset. Another example would be an object that is too unfamiliar: an artifact drawn from an unknown culture would have been too mysterious in its own right to count as a bundle of literal qualities without an underlying object, and thus could not have had the effect of a ready-made. Still another would be a Surrealist painting: however much we grow used to saying "Dada and Surrealism" as a single phrase, there is no painting by Dalí or Magritte that could have functioned as a ready-made, since they are all too recognizable as attempted artworks to have the look of non-art that Dada requires. A final example would be an object of unusual complexity. If Duchamp had exhibited something called *Fountain* that was not a urinal, but a seventy-six-piece electric generator, the surfeit of detail would again have created a tension between the object itself and its numerous features, and the role of the beholder as a real object would thereby never have been brought into play. This is what I meant by calling Dada a "globalist" gesture: it requires a *literal* object, which really means just a bundle of Humean qualities without any separation from some underlying object. With the ready-made, therefore, the beholder is called upon to do all of the aesthetic work: a situation guaranteeing that in many or most cases, no aesthetic experience will occur at all.

Stated differently, the ready-mades can be interpreted as making the claim that any case of literalism (such as a urinal) can be converted *tout court* into an aesthetic scenario without any real object playing a role, since the literal urinal is merely a bundle of qualities and by no means an object apart from its qualities. The mechanics of Surrealism are entirely different. What happens here is that a literal set of elements in pictorial space, which Greenberg denounced as just more nineteenth-century academic illusionism, is punctuated by a number of out-of-context or unusual objects. It may be helpful to consider the different relations that a Dadaist ready-made and a Surrealist painting have to Heidegger's philosophy. I have already claimed that Heidegger, like Greenberg, ultimately takes the background of all experience to be a unified whole, which he calls Being. This is best revealed through certain basic moods. *Angst* is the most famous of these, though in other places Heidegger uses the examples of profound boredom, or joy at the presence of a loved one.[10] For Heidegger, these *Grundstimmungen* (fundamental moods) lead us to wonder "Why is there something rather than nothing?", which he takes to be the most profound of all philosophical questions. Note that in these moods, we are not brought to a sense of awe about Being through any *specific* breakdown in the network of worldly entities. Instead, just as with the ready-mades, literalism is undercut at a *global* level, invoking either the whole of reality (Heidegger) or the whole of a proposed artwork (Duchamp). It is different with Heidegger's tool-analysis, in which we are dealing with a case of one or more missing or malfunctioning entities that call attention to themselves rather than continuing to bleed silently into the entire context of entities that we take for granted. The tool-analysis, rather than the fundamental moods, is the Heideggerian parallel to Surrealism. For in both cases, it is the literalism of *something specific* that appears, and it can do so only if all or most of its surroundings continue to function in an unquestioned literal way. The breakdown of a hammer draws our attention to the hammer, not to all of its neighboring devices; likewise, in a painting by Dalí our attention is drawn to a finite number of unusual pictorial elements, not to the painting as a whole, since Surrealism still deploys a massive weaponry of literal, relational three-dimensional space, just as Greenberg complained.

Now, it is easy to see why readers of Heidegger generally take the various fundamental moods that reveal Being to be more profound than the strangeness of individual broken tools. These tools are local, after all, whereas a mood such as *Angst* seems to give us Being as a whole. There is an analogous reason, I think, for why Dada has had more intellectual prestige over the past half century than Surrealism, although the latter had a much faster start from the gate. Namely, Surrealist canvases might seem to produce nothing but local provocative stunts, while Dada seems to propose a deeper question about the nature of artworks as such. But just as I have argued against the superiority of unified Being in Heidegger and the unified canvas in Greenberg, I argue now that Duchamp's gesture is in many ways less interesting than the Surrealist one, which even Greenberg seems to place at a lower level than the Dada he grudgingly came to appreciate on a theoretical level.

As luck would have it, an interesting attempt has already been made to link Surrealism with OOO, in an article by Roger Rothman.[11] His general thesis is favorable to OOO, and emphasizes Dalí as the most object-oriented figure in the colorful Surrealist crew. This may seem surprising, given that "for many, including for a time Breton himself, Dalí represents Surrealism at its most embarrassingly superficial . . . [as failing] to guard [himself] against the spreading ooze of mass culture and its clichéd notions about art, creativity, and genius" (OOS 5). Nonetheless, Rothman's preference for Dalí over the other Surrealists strikes me as well-founded, and for the very reason he gives: "the most object-oriented thinker of the Surrealist movement was Dalí. Breton *overmines* objects by comprehending them as moments within the expansion of subjective experience and Bataille *undermines* objects by conceiving of them as evidence of material subbasement inaccessible to any and all 'attempts at symbolic inter-pretation'" (OOS 5). This should be convincing enough for anyone even loosely familiar with Breton and Bataille, but Rothman provides numerous citations to persuade the skeptical. Of great importance, for instance, is the following "dialectical" assertion by Breton: "Nothing that surrounds us is object to us, all is subject" (cited OOS 7), so reminiscent of Hegel's famous thesis that "substance is subject."[12] As Rothman summarizes Breton's position: "For Breton, the world of objects [is] animated by *human subjects*. In themselves, they are inert" (OOS 7). Now, someone might claim that Bataille is better attuned to an object-oriented approach due to his "materialism." But Rothman is well aware of the view – found in all OOO authors other than the pro-materialist Bryant – that materialism is simply idealism with a realist alibi.[13] If Bataille is in any sense a "realist," it is in a much weaker sense than the OOO thesis of a withdrawn reality beyond human access. On this point, Rothman amusingly notes that "to Bataille, the Kantian thing-in-itself is inaccessible not because of an epistemological limitation inherent in human perception and cog-nition, but rather because we are too *frightened* by what we fear this access will grant us" (OOS 7-8). In Bataille's own colorful language: "affirming that the universe resembles nothing and is only formless amounts to saying that the universe is something like a spider or spit" (cited OOS 8).[14] Note that Bataille is not even interested in spiders and spit as individuated base objects: his equating of them with the "formless" indicates that he takes them instead to be something like unarticulated sub-objects.

159

Rothman shows, convincingly, to my mind, that Dalí does precisely the opposite. Indeed, the mustachioed Spaniard comes off as something of a champion of objects: "For Dalí . . . objects mattered in themselves. The role of the artist was not to identify particular things that best serve the subject, but instead to liberate all things . . . from the minds that would control them" (OOS 11). Rothman goes so far as to claim that between 1922 and 1928, during the peak of Dalí's friendship with Federico García Lorca, "the painter initiated and developed his own ontology of objects" (OOS 11). Quoting from the Dalí–Lorca correspondence of that period, Rothman concludes that "what Dalí hated above all, was *subjectivity*" (OOS 13). He even reports the amusing fact that "Dalí liked to refer to those he despised as 'backward Kantians'" (OOS 14).[15] Beyond this, there is an animist-sounding passage in which Dalí asserts that Surrealist objects are "acting and growing under the sign of eroticism" (cited OOS 17), a far cry from Breton's reduction of the world to subjective human experience.[16] In Rothman's words: "*objectivity* was Dalí's method in much the same way as *automatism* was Breton's and *lowering* was Bataille's" (OOS 15). We should also note that at the beginning of Rothman's article, he made the observation that no less an authority than Walter Benjamin saw early that Surrealism is "less on the trail of the psyche than on the track of things" (OOS 1), even if Benjamin failed to realize that Dalí was actually the key figure in this respect.[17] Rothman does not force this thesis, and scrupulously notes several passages in which Dalí seems to veer toward idealism instead (OOS 17). Yet he notes correctly that this is not really a problem: for even if it turns out that Dalí was a full-blown idealist, it is possible to be an idealist and object-oriented at the same time, with the exemplary case being Husserl. In any case, the point of OOO is not to focus on non-human objects *instead* of human subjects, but to treat of both in a flat ontology that does not view humans as ontologically different in kind from cardboard boxes, atoms, or fictional characters. This has nothing to do with denying the existence of features that belong to humans alone. But by opening painting like never before to the emergence of weirdness from objects – the weirdness of an object deeper than its manifest qualities – Dalí combats the duomining strategies that would rely either on the subject-centeredness of Breton or the formless spider-and-spit-centeredness of Bataille.

We recall the earlier point that Surrealism – unlike Dada – makes an aesthetic point not about the art object as a whole, but only about certain of its elements. Stated differently, Surrealism begins with the broadly literal situation of illusionistic three-dimensional space, and relies on the sheer bulk of this literalism to gain our credence for a limited number of strange violations of it. This is why Surrealism would never succeed in a *Cubist* idiom, which already flouts our literal sense of space and why, conversely, the Cubist painters generally deployed such banal subject matter in order to call attention to the anti-literalism of their multi-planed *technique*. Even so, it is true that *Surrealism* is somewhat hard to pull off convincingly, just like its cousins in literature: magic realism, the weird, and fantasy. Remembering the bond between Surrealism and Heidegger's tool-analysis as forms of local astonishment, we find that the Heideggerian case will almost always be convincing: if a hammer can astonish us by breaking, this is because we were sincerely relying upon it in our everyday activity. In other words, the literal character of the pre-broken hammer (and "literal" is synonymous with "relational") is already guaranteed. But in the context of a painting or work of literature, the literalism must be painstakingly earned before anything out of the ordinary can be taken seriously by the beholder. Perhaps the best challenge to Surrealism I have read was written not by Greenberg, but by the fantasy writer J.R.R. Tolkien, of all people. In a neglected piece of criticism entitled "On Fairy-Stories," Tolkien hits the nail on the head: "In human art Fantasy is a thing best left to words, to true literature. In painting, for instance, the visible presentation of the fantastic image is technically too easy; the hand tends to outrun the mind, even to overthrow it. Silliness or morbidity are frequent results."[18] Though Tolkien understates the difficulty of pulling it off even in literature, we can take from this passage the useful formulation that Surrealism fails when "the hand outruns the mind." Producing a believable literal world in which deviations occur is in some ways more challenging than dreaming up the deviations themselves. The greatness of Lovecraft as a writer comes not just from his memorably inscrutable monsters, but above all from the convincing literal set-up provided by his usually plain-spoken academic narrators.[19] This is precisely why the opening paragraph of his tale "The Whisperer in Darkness," with its inexplicably hysterical tone, is a literary failure compared with the suitably bland reportage of the second.[20]

Conclusions

This chapter has tried to sort out the relative importance of the aesthetic and the literal in art, with a focus on the different ways this happens in Dada and Surrealism. My claim was that in Surrealism and related genres, the object/quality tensions are localized into individual elements of the artwork, made plausible by the bulky apparatus of literalist ballast that surrounds them: including, but not limited to, the three-dimensional illusionist space of Surrealist painting. Though it is easy to see why Greenberg found the Surrealists to be "academic artists," this is only true if we accept his view that the unified canvas background plane is the sole place where literalism can be counteracted. I have argued instead, using Surrealism and Heidegger's tool-analysis as evidence, that literalism can also be subverted locally in selected individual elements of an artwork. However, I argued further that this is hard to render plausible in the absence of a credible literal environment, which is why Dalí tends to go wrong whenever his paintings grow too cluttered or complicated, and also why he could never have employed the inherently non-literal cubist idiom for Surrealist purposes.

I made a related argument about Dada. While the ready-mades might seem like everyday objects shoved arbitrarily into a fine arts context, from a OOO standpoint they are not objects at all, but merely bundles of literal qualities. Yes, these sensual qualities already differ from their underlying sensual object as defined by Husserl, but this minimal rift is irrelevant for the purposes of art, and merely allows us to view ready-mades as the same object when viewed from different angles or distances. The point is that ready-made objects are too banal to suggest in advance any tension between their visible features and an underlying real object, whereas more familiar genres of art already press us down this path. In fact, ready-mades do not suggest real objects at all, unless and until someone manages to experience them aesthetically. Hence, the ready-mades have no other option than to shoot the moon and try to be experienced aesthetically in their entirety, just as Heidegger's *Angst* is meant to expose Being as a whole rather than this or that individual thing. If the different components of a urinal were somehow highlighted in their singularity and their mutual relations – which is not at all what happens in Dada – then we would have something more like Caro's syntactic modern sculpture. Yet this would require a pronounced work of abstraction that would take us beyond the mission of the ready-mades. While we can imagine a urinal-like piece by Caro called *Fountain*, we know it would look nothing like Duchamp's familiar prefabricated one.

We have now seen the opposition between the characteristic strategies of Dada and Surrealism. And despite the ostensibly radical

162

departure of one or both movements from the previous history of Western art, they resemble the works of that history in an important and necessary sense: namely, their respective attempts to aestheticize the literal without losing plausibility by throwing the literal completely overboard. The case might be made – and Kosuth has made it – that conceptual art finally escapes this tradition in the opposite way, by jettisoning the aesthetic rather than the literal. But this claim holds no water. We are surrounded in daily life by concepts of many kinds, yet we would never confuse them with conceptual art, unless someone were to frame them in an "art" way as Duchamp did with the urinal. Walter De Maria's *The Broken Kilometer*, which assembles 500 brass rods that jointly add up to a kilometer in length, is undeniably experienced in aesthetic terms, even if not solely visual ones. If the piece were simply called *500 Brass Rods*, it might not occur to anyone to wonder how long they would be in a single unbroken line: thus we can see how De Maria's actual title does extra conceptual work, but work that is aesthetic nonetheless. This does not violate Kant's ban on concepts in art, because what Kant meant is that no artwork can be *paraphrased* in terms of concepts. In other words, the fact that the concept of a kilometer plays a role in this work does not mean that the work can be exhausted aesthetically by explaining the concept behind it, and that is what leads the concept to have an aesthetic rather than logical role in this case. That is not because we encounter the "materiality" of the rods rather than just the idea of them: the same would be true even if De Maria had left the piece as an unactualized project. Stated differently, concepts in an aesthetic situation are no longer just concepts. Why not? Because they are not just concepts in the literal sense. It is possible to aestheticize any concept we please: justice, pi, existentialism, or the working class. But when this happens, they are no longer the same thing as they were in their non-aesthetic state.

We come to a final point I promised to address: Danto's claim that there is a vast difference between Duchamp and Pop, insofar as Duchamp was not part of a broader revolution in human culture and "did not celebrate the ordinary." The first point can be dispensed with, since we are considering the art itself rather than its social effects, which are an entirely separate issue. Social or political issues can be imported into artworks on a case-by-case basis, but only once they have been aestheticized in the same manner as a broken kilometer. Danto's second point is more interesting: Duchamp's supposed failure to celebrate the ordinary, as contrasted with Warhol doing precisely that. The problem with this claim is that a great deal of Warhol's work is clearly aestheticized. The famous portraits of Marilyn Monroe and Mao employ not only brilliant colors, but a deliberate repetition of images, quite aside from the fact that these two subjects were by no means ordinary people. The same holds for *32 Campbell's Soup Cans*, and for the same reasons. The real question is whether *Brillo Box* differs from Duchamp's *Fountain* in any essential sense. Is a urinal really less ordinary than a consumer supermarket product? It seems to me that Danto can only make such a case by retreating to his cultural explanation of the differing results of Pop and Dada, emphasizing the gap between Duchamp's prankish elitism and Warhol's often inflammatory presence in commercial media. Yet it does not follow, without further ado, that we can appeal to contextual factors that are not absorbed into the artwork itself.

What Pop does more effectively than Dada, in my view, is provide a vaster reservoir of literalism that lends additional credence to aesthetic modification. I noted that Duchamp could not have succeeded with an unfamiliar or excessively complicated object; for the ready-made to work, he needed something as simple and vacuous as a urinal or comb. Likewise, Warhol would probably have failed had he used fictitious celebrities rather than real ones, or non-existent consumer products instead of Brillo and Campbell's. In that case an additional and irrelevant mental labor would have burdened the beholder and deadened the effect. In this respect, there is an unexpected sense in which Pop and post-Pop draw more on Surrealism than on Dada, given that Surrealism employs a bulky literalist base in order to add strange spices at highly specific points. In more recent decades, the situation has evolved so that Pop literalism often ceases to be the *content* of art, but functions more as a convincing literalist base. I think of Tara Donovan, who does not just exhibit plastic cups and straws, as Warhol might well have done, but uses these highly familiar everyday materials to create strange and undeniably aesthetic results. I think also of my favorite piece from the 2012 Documenta show, Geoffrey Farmer's *Leaves of Grass*. A classic Pop artist might just have piled up all the *Life* magazines from 1935-1985 and called it art, or silkscreened selected photos from those issues. Instead, Farmer cut out thousands of images of people and objects from *Life* in those years, pasting them on sticks and arranging them on both sides of a sixty-foot table. *Life* is a well-known component of literal human existence throughout the decades in question, and thus can serve as a credible literal base for aesthetic adventures beyond that base. And if the spatial arrangement of all those images in a single room were not enough to provoke an aesthetic reaction in the beholder, the title *Leaves of Grass* – borrowed, of course, from Walt Whitman's great collection of poems – hammers the point home, like an ornament atop a skyscraper.

7

Weird Formalism

Philosophers are able to forecast the future of art even less than they can guess the future of philosophy. What they can do is illuminate those points on which debates in art theory have become bogged down in trench wars that have lost philosophical relevance, generate new ideas that may prove useful to artists, and point to some traditional ideas that may be less archaic than they seem. In this respect, my role *vis-à-vis* art is similar to my task at the school of architecture where I now teach, despite no professional training or experience as a designer. What I am fairly sure of is that significant new art is unlikely to emerge from any further banging of the anti-formalist political/ethnographic drum, or any continued rejection of aesthetics or even beauty. All of this belongs to the long 1960s from which art, like continental philosophy, has never really emerged. The differing contextualisms of deconstruction, New Historicism, and the Frankfurt School seem to me as a philosopher to be of little further use. A realist philosophy turning on an aesthetic axis is the number on which I have placed my professional bets, and a significant group of young artists and architects have done so as well. Let's do two different things in these closing pages of the book. First, let's take a look at how one expert observer views the current situation in art. Second, let's contrast this summary with some different possibilities that emerge once a new sense of formalism is introduced.

Bad New Days

It is hard to think of someone more different from OOO than the critic Hal Foster. Like Fried, albeit for different reasons, he is sus-

166

picious of thinkers I consider allies, such as Bennett and Latour.[1]
Unlike Fried, he openly favors a rampant politico-critical style of
art that runs counter to the renovated formalism endorsed in this
book. At the same time, Foster is obviously a well-informed observer
of contemporary art, to say the least. Taken together, these factors
make him a perfect foil with which to conclude our reflections. It is
common today to say that the art world has grown so complicated
and diverse that no generalizations can safely be made. Of course, the
same thing has often been said in the past – Greenberg was disputing
it in the early 1970s – and it strikes me as exaggerated. In *Bad New
Days*, published in 2017, Foster takes the admirable risk of trying to
boil contemporary art down to four basic tendencies that he openly
declares, along with a fifth that he never quite names but covers in
some detail. These tendencies are, in order: the abject, the archival, the
mimetic, the precarious, and – the one he never names – performance.
Since I happen to own Foster's book in the Kindle edition, the citations in what follows refer to Kindle electronic locations rather than
printed page numbers.

Foster's presentation of the abject begins with an appeal to
Lacanian psychoanalysis: "In the late 1980s and early 1990s, there
was a shift in much art and theory . . . from the real understood as
an effect of representation to the real seen as an event of trauma"
(*BND* 102). While this is no doubt true of the art world, this shift
must be rejected on philosophical grounds. I mean no disrespect
to Lacan, whose works can be endlessly fascinating. Nonetheless,
whatever use "trauma" has in Lacan's psychoanalytic conception
of the Real, it is merely a poor man's realism in philosophy. After
all, the real has many other things to do than traumatize humans;
among other things, portions of the real interact with each other
even when humans are nowhere on the scene. Failure to account for
this is the central idealist defect that spoils the otherwise energizing
philosophy of Žižek. Trauma may still have its uses in art as a local
effect, but it cannot claim to be hitched to a superior philosophical
conception of reality, and Lacan provides nothing of the sort. The
same holds for his supposed innovation of placing "the gaze" in the
world itself rather than in a mind, as in the example of the sardine
can already mentioned in the section on Krauss above. Though
Lacan and Merleau-Ponty are widely praised for proclaiming that
the world looks at me just as I look at it, this is not a genuine philosophical innovation, since it continues to place the same old modern
human–world couplet at the center of attention, if in a sexier way
than Descartes and Kant: the two terms at issue are still mind and

world. Granted that art and psychoanalysis require a human element in a way that physics does not, we still need to be aware of the wider ontological context in which they occur, and that means ceasing to believe that mere reversal of the subject-object relation does anything to escape familiar modern trench wars.

Foster reads the work of Cindy Sherman in part through this Lacanian lens: she "evoked the subject under the gaze, the subject-as-picture" (*BND* 150). He lists a number of other feminist artists – Sarah Charlesworth, Silvia Kolbowski, Barabara Kruger, Sherrie Levine, and Laurie Simmons – who also occupy the gaze as their "principal site" (*BND* 150). While there are other resources in these artists, I have already critiqued the built-in idealism of Lacan's position, and the gaze is not able to take us much further. More to the point, Foster sees a turn to the abject in Sherman's "challenge to the ideal figure" in her portrayal of figures "with scarred sacks for breasts and funky carbuncles for noses" (*BND* 170), or "a young woman with a pig snout . . . or a doll with the head of a dirty old man" (*BND* 174), or even "signifiers of menstrual blood and sexual discharge, vomit and shit, decay and death" (*BND* 174). Much of this work is obviously powerful, though its current philosophical justification is inadequate, as seen earlier in Rothman's skillful critique of Bataille as an underminer who makes impossible claims for the "formless" that are often just a pornographic or scatological version of Kant's sublime. Another key reference, of course, is Julia Kristeva in *Powers of Horror*, where "the abject is what a subject must get rid of in order to be a subject at all" (cited *BND* 197). Although I have been critical so far, there are obvious paths from the abject for escaping literalism, even though Kant held famously that the *disgusting* is the one thing that cannot be a subject of art, since "the object is presented as if it insisted . . . on our enjoying it even though that is just what we are forcefully resisting . . . ." (*CJ* 180). Perhaps counterexamples can be produced against Kant: I happen to find Bataille's pornographic *Story of the Eye* beautiful and not just interesting, despite a number of passages that inspire outright disgust. But here as with the sublime, it seems a mistake to assume that whatever eludes or frightens the human subject – even if it be spiders or spit – is actually formless. Each instance of the abject is specific, a particular terror, and as such it falls under the same canons that govern our judgment of tangibly crafted aesthetic form. In any event, I do not think the abject can claim privilege over less threatening artworks, for the same reason that Heidegger's globally world-negating *Angst* is really no deeper than the rupture of a single specific tool. And even if a work like Andres Serrano's *Piss Christ* need not be excluded *a priori* from the realm of art, it does face special challenges in getting there: disgust may not be a deal-breaker, but is certainly a deal-complicator in aesthetic terms. The call for artists to "touch the obscene real" (*BND* 238) is only compelling if we hold that the real is obscene, and this is more a dogma of Lacan and his followers than a compelling insight. Likewise, "the excremental impulse in abject art" may well serve as "a symbolic reversal of the first step of civilization" (*BND* 273), but this is of interest only if we fail to realize that the symbolic order is already pocked with holes. I see nothing especially oppressive in the near-universal human disgust at feces; sublimation occurs for good reason, and Maurizio Ferraris is right to call desublimation one of the chief dogmas of Postmodernism.[2] The Father is not so all-powerful that one needs to shit in his presence to make a point.

This brings us to the archival tendency, with Foster citing such artists as Thomas Hirschhorn, Tacita Dean, Joachim Koester, and Sam Durant, describing their work jointly as "an idiosyncratic probing into a particular object, figure, or event in modern art, philosophy, or history" (*BND* 378). One good example is Dean's *Sound Mirrors*, "a brief meditation in film on the huge acoustic receivers built on the Kentish coast of England between the world wars but soon abandoned as an outmoded piece of military technology" (*BND* 378). There is also Douglas Gordon's work, beloved even by Fried, in which – for example – Alfred Hitchcock's *Psycho* is slowed to a glacial 24-hour pace.[3] At its best, this kind of art does not just draw on existing collections of documents and facts, but produces new ones, thereby assembling conviction of a sort that Surrealism does not always achieve. Less favorably, if it merely "underscores the hybrid condition of such materials as found and constructed, factual and fictive, public and private ... [and] arranges these materials according to a matrix of citation and juxtaposition" (*BND* 435), it risks repeating the Postmodernist error of merely assembling signs and declaring them art by fiat, thus following Kosuth's injunctions in precisely the wrong sense. If the abject appeals too much to a formless and traumatic sublime, the archival risks relying too heavily on a collage-like technique that makes a dated philosophical point while failing to achieve cohesion. Foster reports that Hirschhorn "seeks to 'distribute ideas,' 'liberate activity,' and 'radiate energy' all at once" (*BND* 450). But when this goes wrong, Hirschhorn creates as much mental clutter as Dalí at his worst, and this time the clutter is not limited to canvas.

169

Foster introduces the mimetic form of contemporary art by referring to a Robert Gober installation called, not surprisingly, *Untitled*.
Among other things, the installation contains "a knotty plank of faux
wood in unpainted plaster"; "the folded shirt of a priest"; three dirty-
white slabs made of bronze that look like "chunks of old Styrofoam
that have washed ashore"; "a bag of diapers"; and "two glass bowls
filled with large pieces of fruit that look like plastic but are beeswax,"
along with newspaper clippings, a beheaded crucified Christ on the
wall who spews water from his nipples, a porcelain white chair
draped with a yellow latex glove, and some obscene beeswax torsos
(*BND* 808-842). It is noteworthy that Foster sees this work as a
hybrid of Dada and Surrealism: "Specific models like *Étant donnés*,
the peep-show diorama of painstaking facsimiles crafted by Marcel
Duchamp, come to mind, as do general precedents like the pictorial
paradoxes contrived by René Magritte" (*BND* 847-850). Foster adds
that "as usual with Gober, [these associations] are overshadowed by
topical allusions to events that are as epochal as 9/11 and as everyday
as a bath" (*BND* 850), before again invoking Lacan in a way that
is correct for Lacan but wrong – I have argued – for both art and
philosophy. Foster only refers to Dada and Surrealism in passing,
but I find it an interesting question as to which of these currents
Gober's work more resembles. On the one hand, there is an assemblage of unfathomable individual objects that Duchamp might well
have employed, but on the other, there is an attempt to provide the
literal ballast of an organized world through the references to 9/11
and even the Starr Report on President Clinton. Neither fish nor fowl,
or a new genre altogether? Adding further to the uncertainty, Foster
notes that the work "projects none of the sophisticated superiority
found in camp, and little of the secret support advanced in parody"
(*BND* 876).

What prevents *Untitled* from being just a mixed-media flea market?
Foster moves on to some works by John Kessler without solving
Gober's dilemma for us. Only later in the chapter, in connection with
Isa Genzken rather than Gober, does Foster give us a sense of what he
means by mimetic: "A hundred years ago, in the midst of World War
I, the Zürich Dadaists developed the strategy of mimetic exacerbation
at issue here: they took the corrupt language of the European powers
around them and played it back as a caustic nonsense" (*BND* 1092).
He concedes later that this runs "the risk of an excessive identification
with the corrupt conditions of a symbolic order," but adds that "with
a degree of distance created not through withdrawal but through
excess, mimetic exacerbation can also expose this order as failed, or

at least as fragile" (*BND* 1109). That is to say, mimetic art is "political" in a Dadaist sense of the term. I have no objection to exposing the failures of a corrupt symbolic order, especially when it is aesthetically transformed, as in many of the works Foster cites. But if we return to Danto's critique of mimesis – which I find more biting than the anti-realist one of Postmodernism – we recall that the problem Danto identified was the excessive focus of mimesis on content. There is a sense in which to parody something is to accept the very terms it establishes, yielding nothing but an inverted literalism. The pieces of parodied order achieve no genuinely new literal unity on which an aesthetic effect can be based.

The chapter on precarious art returns to Hirschhorn, who seems to be among Foster's favorite contemporary artists. The term "precarious" these days usually has a political meaning, referring especially to the increasingly fragile status of employment. In franker terms, Hirschhorn is quoted as referring to our shared contemporary reality as a "capitalist garbage bucket" (*BND* 1193), a situation he addresses in more than one piece by simply leaving its elements "on the street to be picked up by others" (*BND* 1198). Yet Hirschhorn soon concluded that precarity referred less to the status of his own works than to "a predicament of the people he wanted to address with it, with ramifications that are both ethical and political" (*BND* 1205) Complicating the premise of Bourriaud's affable relational aesthetics, Hirschhorn adds the interesting twist that "his activity might result in antagonism as well as fellowship" (*BND* 1236-1243). His primary goal is to stir things up: "Energy yes, quality no" (cited *BND* 1326). Clearly, the precarious is the most explicitly political of the forms considered so far. The issue I see here is less the old formalist credo that politics ought to be excluded from art, than the fact that political messages in art are unlikely to be new, and just as unlikely to have any effect beyond a cosmopolitan art scene already sweepingly opposed – in words if not deeds – to the capitalism Hirschhorn denounces. As Foster himself writes elsewhere, "to a great extent the left over-identifies with the other as victim, which locks it into a hierarchy of suffering in which the wretched can do little wrong" (*RR* 203). In short, the political value of art *qua* politics approaches nullity. Yet the reverse is not true: political issues do provide new material that can produce a literal base for aesthetic effects. Hirschhorn will not save the precariat from what he deems their garbage-bucket misery, but capitalism can give us a Brecht or Frida Kahlo by way of counterpunch.

After a fifth chapter denouncing the "post-critical" views of Bennett, Latour, and Rancière on grounds I find insufficient – such as the usual assertion that Latour is a "fetishist" for considering non-human objects – Foster adds a final chapter entitled "In Praise of Actuality." Though no specific art trend is named in the title, he focuses on performance. This is not performance in the broadly familiar sense. Foster speaks in particular about the frequent *restaging* of performances from the 1960s and 1970s: "Not quite live, not quite dead, these reenactments have introduced a zombie time into these institutions" (*BND* 1613). Yet his attention soon shifts to a group of more general problems. Above all, "why has the performative returned as an almost automatic good?" (*BND* 1665). One reason he offers is that performance, "like process ... is said to activate the viewer, especially when the two are combined, that is, when a process – an action or gesture – is performed" (*BND* 1675). Here I would object to the identification of performance with process. A performance, as seen in the theatrical interpretation of metaphor above, is as unique and autonomous as any physical object. By contrast, process is often used as a counterweight to the focus on objects, as in the "philosophies of becoming" found in Henri Bergson and Gilles Deleuze (though not, I insist, in Alfred North Whitehead).[4] There is a tendency in the School of Becoming to treat objects as though they were merely arbitrary cuts in an otherwise unbroken flow of continuous events, as even Bennett maintains.[5] Yet Foster is aware of the problem, adding that "this attitude can easily become an excuse not to execute fully ... [And moreover,] a work that appears unfinished hardly ensures that the viewer will be engaged" (*BND* 1675). What I have argued in this book is that the work is not supposed to be "unfinished," but that even in completed form, it must produce an object or objects that seduce the beholder into theatrical enactment of the work. Like Rancière, Foster sees that this need not involve anything more than looking: he rejects the assumption "that the viewer is somehow passive to begin with" (*BND* 1681). He also cites Bourriaud's claim that relational art is "an ensemble of units to be reactivated by the beholder-manipulator" (*BND* 1694), which falls short only of OOO's insistence that such an ensemble cannot be merely literal. But the real difference between Foster and OOO appears when he ends the book on the side of social practice art ("formal resistance") and Goberian mimesis ("mimetic exacerbation") (*BND* 1772). Coupled with his expressed wish that art should "take a stand, and do so in a manner that brings together the aesthetic, the cognitive, and the critical in a precise constellation"

(*BND* 1743), this indicates that he finds something missing when art fails to break through the walls and express views about society at large. Yet I have said that the alternative is to draw on outside forces as nourishment for a wider range of aesthetic achievement, rather than conducting a pretense of social heroism on the basis of already predictable slogans.

Foster's wide familiarity with present-day art, and his fearlessness in boiling down the contemporary scene into a few prominent tendencies, makes him a helpful guide to what has and has not been attempted in recent art. Of the five trends he discusses, three are explicitly anti-formalist or anti-autonomous in character: the archival, the mimetic, and the precarious. Though good work can be done in all three of these genres, there is the nagging problem of producing overly literal art that trades aesthetic authority for an unsurprising political kind. While this may serve to produce a sense of individual responsibility or guilt in the beholder, its challenges beyond the usual moral ones are few. The abject, though borrowing on what Bataille and Kristeva take to be repudiations of form, does so only through a formlessness that merely resembles a creepier version of the sublime. As for the kind of performance that Foster discusses, I have already defended the theatrical nature of art, though it need not take the form of the actual dance performances he cites. But above all, I fear that Foster misses the real point of the post-critical theory he rejects in his fifth chapter, and that is one of the topics of the final section of this book, to which we now turn.

Five Implications

The central idea of this book is no doubt also its strangest: the notion that beholder and artwork fuse jointly into a third and higher object, with the corollary that this third term is the key to shedding new light on the ontology of art. In this closing section, I will itemize no less than five specific implications of this idea, some of them already sketched in earlier chapters and others introduced for the first time here. But first, we need to establish a new piece of terminology.

Whereas Heidegger, Greenberg, and McLuhan's fixation on the medium refers to something hidden beneath the surface properties of the object, an even more important medium for OOO is the one located *above* beholder and work, which contains them like an unseen atmosphere. This is the point where we nearly agreed with Krauss, who also wanted to drag Greenberg's background to

173

the surface – though by calling it a "simulacrum," she gave it an unfortunate anti-realist twist. In any case, to unify beholder and work is to subvert the usual options according to which autonomy means either the independence of artwork from beholder (Greenberg, Fried) or of beholder from artwork (Kant), as if these were the only two basic kinds of things permitted to exist. Admittedly, they *are* the two basic ingredients of an artwork: beholders are needed for art just as carbon is required to form an organic chemical. But the interpretation of metaphor in Chapter 1 showed why theatrical enactment of the art object is required for aesthetic – and that means *non-literal* – experience to occur at all, and why theatrical enactment means a union of beholder and work. This has implications for much more than art, though these concluding pages are limited to art alone.

Now, it never happens that an idea is utterly new in the *ex nihilo* sense of having neither precursors nor parallels. My own thinking along these lines was initially inspired by Husserl's observation that intentionality is both one and two. That is to say, in a first sense my mind is something different from the various objects I perceive, judge, or enjoy, but in a second sense my relation with these things can be taken as a unified object in its own right. Yet once we view intentionality as a unit, it follows that I and the things meet as separate entities on the interior of that larger unit. This is the way in which Brentano's phrase "intentional inexistence" ought to be interpreted: not that intentional objects occur "inside my mind," but that they appear – and I exist – inside the new and larger object formed by my union with whatever I take seriously.[6] Mainstream phenomenology has not explored this implication, but has followed instead the usual idealist path of treating phenomena as if they occur inside a mind, despite the misleading assurance that we are "always already outside ourselves" when intending objects. For the point is not that we can step outside ourselves, but that we can never step outside the hybrid objects of which we form a part, and on whose interiors we inevitably dwell, unless it be to step into new ones.

Along with Husserl, there are two especially important parallels that run the same risk of idealism. The first is the autopoiesis theory of the Chilean immunologists Maturana and Varela, while the other is the social systems theory of the German sociologist Luhmann. In both cases there is special emphasis on how a system is cut off from the outside world, and all of these authors draw markedly pessimistic conclusions about the possibility of communication. OOO sees these theories as providing a needed counterweight to models that assume an easy ubiquity of communicative relations, such as Latourian ANT and Whitehead's philosophy of organism. Yet there are two significant ontological problems shared by autopoiesis and social systems theory as theories of closure rather than openness. The first is that, even in those moments when they do not think it impossible for communication to occur across the barriers between systems, they give no adequate account of how the outside is translated into terms graspable on the interior. The second, which repeats one of the defects of traditional aesthetic formalism, is that they tend to place the communicative barrier *taxonomically* in one particular location: the outer cell wall for Maturana and Varela, and the professional boundary for Luhmann, as if there were no problem of influence between things once whatever we take to be the perimeter is breached. Once we are inside the system, it is unclear how these theories avoid the very relational excess they claimed to forestall.

In any case, we need a term for the interior of an object, since I am not aware that the problem has ever been posed in quite this way: even Leibniz tells us little about the dynamics inside the monad itself. Beginning with my first book, *Tool-Being*, I have often used the term "vacuum," though this refers more to an object's separation from its neighbors than to the life of its own interior. For describing this interior the word "vacuum" will not suffice, since it wrongly gives the impression of emptiness, when in fact there is a great deal underway on the inside of any object. At the same time, Luhmann's term "system" leans too heavily in the direction of a total unified function, with insufficient autonomy left over for its individual elements. For this reason, I suggest that we provisionally turn to Maturana and Varela's vocabulary and use "cell" to describe the interior of an object: for just as a cell has numerous independent organelles, we will see that the inside of an object contains more than one independent entity. The only risk I see in speaking of cells is that, just as many idealists become irate over "anthropomorphic" metaphors for the actions of inanimate things, others are equally angered when biological metaphors are used outside the realm of living creatures.[7] But now as ever, we must reject all puritanism about metaphor, except in those cases that involve either clearly misleading comparisons or needless political offense. Let it be clear to the reader – if it is not already so – that by calling the inside of an object a cell, I do not mean that it is literally alive. On that note, we turn to the five implications of what I have called weird formalism: the sort in which it is neither the subject nor the object alone that is autonomous, but rather their union.

First implication: *Hybrid art forms can still attain closure.* We have seen that formalism in the arts generally hinges on one of two separate claims: (a) the autonomy of the artwork, or (b) the autonomy of the beholder. It is Kant who defends (b) most intensely, given his wish to protect the human experience of beauty from personal interest, conceptual explanation, practical usefulness, or whatever other externality might contaminate the purity of taste. Meanwhile, Greenberg and Fried tend in the opposite direction of (a) defending the autonomy of the artwork: Greenberg by appealing to the consensus of taste as a way of cancelling the beholder's subjective contribution, Fried by excluding the theatrical appeal of the work by way of an absorptive structure internal to the work and excluding the beholder. But by locating the autonomy of art in the union of beholder and work instead, we allow for a much wider range of genres to be treated as self-contained. The most conspicuous example would be any form of art involving explicit participation by the artist or beholder, which for Fried's sort of formalism could only be theatrical in the bad sense, but for OOO is theatrical in an unavoidable sense. A textbook case would be Beuys, who cannot be very important when viewed from where Greenberg or Fried is standing, though in my view his works achieve autonomous closure in several previously unnoticed ways. Object-oriented formalism is thereby able to make peace with much recent art – performance art in particular – that was excluded by the older formalisms.

Second implication: *Critical theory is not the path forward.* The typical anti-formalist dissident – whether of a Hegelian or Postmodernist stripe – will say that neither beholder nor work can be cut off from a wider socio-political, biographical, linguistic, or psychological context. This anti-autonomous gesture is precisely what Foster and others mean when they praise "critical theory." Rather than being naively attuned to our aesthetic experiences, we are asked to transcend our attachments and pass aloof critical judgment, usually on the basis of some widely familiar and suitably Left-leaning principle. In this way, we are supposed to dispense with Dante's or Scheler's attachment to objects and endorse a Kantian separation of the thinking subject from that with which it is involved. Ironically, this shows that critical theory is really just another variant of taxonomical formalism, one that takes the human being to be autonomously separable from its various sincere relations with objects. This is the attitude that enables the likes of Kosuth and de Duve to assert that the transcendent human artist gets to decide by fiat what counts as a work of art, as if the object had no say as to whether it was succeeding or failing. Among other difficulties, this assumption fails the test of Danto's chained cat, which reminded us that while we cannot say in advance where the sculpture ends, in a *de facto* sense it always ends somewhere in particular. Whether the sculpture turns out to be of a cat, a chained cat, or a cat chained to an iron railing, it is certainly not a sculpture of the universe as a whole: not even if the artist tries to stipulate that it is.

Third implication: *Anti-formalist art is not the path forward.* The major trends in contemporary art singled out by Foster are attempts to defy the closure of artworks by allowing either socio-political concerns or abject formlessness to bleed through their walls. I have argued that the abject fails for the same reason as its more aristocratic cousin, the sublime: there is simply no such thing as that which has no definite form. Spiders, spit, and menstrual blood are what they are, after all – not something else, and certainly not *nothing* else. As for socio-political content, this is generally so expected and banal when showcased in any artwork that I suggested the opposite procedure instead. Namely, rather than exporting messages from artworks into the political sphere, it is probably more fruitful for art to devour chunks of politics and give it an aesthetic life that might even be able to "redistribute the sensible," in Rancière's phrase. This seems more promising than simply denouncing capital or the surveillance state for perhaps the billionth time.

Fourth implication: *By excluding the outside of art, we emphasize the multiplicity of its interior.* To insist on the autonomy of the artwork only seems dull if we contrast it with the supposed infinite riches of the greater world surrounding it. Yet this extra-aesthetic world is so often boring, depressing, and stupefyingly familiar, which is generally one of the reasons we find ourselves seeking out art in the first place. As soon as we stop worrying so much about the surrounding context of art, and the generally futile demand that it be the salvation of that context, we are able to pay more attention to the internal diversity of whatever art we encounter. Formalist criticism in the arts does tend to have a holistic bias, as we have seen with Greenberg's lack of interest in the multifariousness of surface content. But if we ignore Fried's needless reliance on the linguistic holism of Saussure, his syntactic interpretation of Caro opens the way to greater attention to the loose interplay among individual elements. Against Greenberg's and Heidegger's unconvincing dualism of unified background and pluralized literal surface, I argued in favor of individualized backgrounds for every element in the work. If we consider an apple in a still-life by Cézanne, the apple is an object withdrawn behind its apple-profile, and need not look to the global canvas background to find its deeper medium. What this means is that every artwork has multiple media,

177

and not just in the Greenbergian sense of the multiple flat planes of cubist collage.

Fifth implication: *Since the multiplicity of the interior is not holistic, it is "cold."* Among media theorists there has been plenty of discussion, much of it negative, about what McLuhan terms a "cold medium."[8] With this term he refers to a medium in which insufficient information is given, so that some detail must be provided by the beholder, yielding an effect that is often hypnotic. For example, even though a fire in a fireplace is "hot" in the literal sense of temperature, it is a deeply cold medium in McLuhan's sense: for given how little information it provides, it requires that we add our own reveries to the experience of observing it. Here I would like to suggest the historical thesis that modernity was a period in which high art was generally dominated by hot media, in which a surfeit of information was already provided. I would like to suggest further that a surfeit of information always entails that the *relations* between various elements are overdetermined in a way that suppresses their autonomy.

In comparison with Byzantine icons, the decorative patterns of Islamic art, or the misty atmospheres of Chinese landscape painting – all of them ice-cold media – Western post-Renaissance illusionist painting depicts its elements in highly defined relations with all others. Since each of these elements occupies a definite point in depicted three-dimensional space, its relational existence is completely determined with respect to all other pictorial elements. The mind may be dazzled by the beauty of such paintings, but will never be hypnotized the way it is in front of a fireplace. In McLuhan's sense, illusionistic oil painting is a hot medium, whereas an abstract painting by Kandinsky, Paul Klee, or Pollock must count as hypnotically cold. In the case of literature, myths are cold media, since they stipulate little more than a finite number of characters and legends with room for variation in each retelling. The novel, by contrast, is as hot a medium as literature can possibly be, since every word is accounted for in an authoritative text, with no room for change between one reprinting and another. Film is a hot medium, since we are always given each shot in a highly specific way, with no leeway for looking at things from whatever angle we please: we always see Humphrey Bogart the same way in each scene, no matter how many times the film is replayed. Stated differently, there are no autonomous objects in film, but only objects overdetermined in their exact relations with everything else. By contrast, video art tends to be much colder, if only because the narrative is usually far less clear.

I mention this due to my suspicion that as we depart the modern era for whatever comes next – the Postmodern being more a smoking mess than a bona fide era – we will experience a cooling down of the many hot forms that dominated modernity. As Harold Bloom argues, not all genres are equally available in every era, and we should expect a shift in dominant aesthetic media as the century unfolds.[9] It is sometimes suggested that videogames may prove to be a colder replacement for cinema, though it is doubtful whether any have yet approached the status of art. Yet it may be a far older genre that takes the lead, one that philosophers have never much appreciated: I speak of architecture, which is inherently cold insofar as we wander it freely and never grasp it at once, meaning that it cannot be equated with any specific series of profiles in the manner of illusionistic painting, the novel, or film.

De Duve reminds us of the familiar historical trope that "every masterpiece of modern art . . . was first met with an outcry of indignation: 'this is not art!'" (*KAD* 303). Yet we would also do well to remember the opposite principle: that any style currently greeted by the exclamation "this is art!" is probably on the verge of toppling into the museum or into oblivion. The relational, the political, the stipulated, the non-aesthetic, the non-beautiful: all have been surfing the same wave for over fifty years.

Notes

Preliminary Note

1 Stephen Melville, "Becoming Medium," p. 104; Richard Moran, "Formalism and the Appearance of Nature," p. 117.

Introduction: Formalism and the Lessons of Dante

1 Graham Harman, "Aesthetics as First Philosophy," "The Third Table," "Art without Relations," "Greenberg, Duchamp, and the Next Avant-Garde," "The Revenge of the Surface," "Materialism is Not the Solution." See also Timothy Morton, *Realist Magic*.
2 Harman, "Aesthetics as First Philosophy."
3 Graham Harman, "On the Undermining of Objects," "Undermining, Overmining, and Duomining."
4 Harman, "The Third Table"; A.S. Eddington, *The Nature of the Physical World*.
5 Wilfrid Sellars, "Philosophy and the Scientific Image of Man."
6 Harman, "Greenberg, Duchamp, and the Next Avant-Garde"; Graham Harman, *Dante's Broken Hammer*; Clement Greenberg, *Late Writings*, pp. 45–49.
7 Robert Pippin, "Why Does Photography Matter as Art *Now*, as Never Before?", p. 60, note 6.
8 Claire Colebrook, "Not Kant, Not Now: Another Sublime," p. 145.
9 Melissa Ragona, personal communication, August 5, 2017. Cited with Ragona's permission.
10 Hasan Veseli, personal communication, December 4, 2016. Cited with Veseli's permission.
11 See especially Caroline Levine's wonderful book *Forms*.
12 No less a figure than Hal Foster slips into the "fetishist" trope in *The Return of the Real*, pp. 108–109. See also his related attacks on OOO allies Jane Bennett and Bruno Latour in Hal Foster, *Bad New Days*, Chapter 5. Another recent example can be found in the second paragraph of J.J. Charlesworth

and James Heartfield, "Subjects v. Objects." For a general response to the claim that realism about objects is a form of fetishism, see Graham Harman, "Object-Oriented Ontology and Commodity Fetishism."

13 David E. Wellbery, "Schiller, Schopenhauer, Fried," p. 84.
14 Dante Alighieri, *The Divine Comedy*.
15 Immanuel Kant, *Critique of Pure Reason*, *Prolegomena to Any Future Metaphysics*.
16 The classic example is Salomon Maimon, *Essay on Transcendental Philosophy*.
17 Immanuel Kant, *Critique of Practical Reason*, *Groundwork of the Metaphysics of Morals*.
18 Immanuel Kant, *Critique of Judgment*.
19 Virgil, *Aeneid*.
20 Bruno Latour, *We Have Never Been Modern*. There is another interpretation of modernity – or at least of its degenerate forms – that reads it in the opposite way as an improper *commingling* of thought with world. This can be found in the valuable polemic against "correlationism" by Quentin Meillassoux in *After Finitude*, which nonetheless resembles Latour's position in agreeing that thought and world count for the moderns as the two basic ingredients of reality. In this book I will focus on Latour's "purity" interpretation or modernity rather than Meillassoux's "impurity" version, since the Latourian stance is the one more relevant to Kant's aesthetics and formalism in the arts.
21 Dante, *The Divine Comedy*, *La Vita Nuova*.
22 Max Scheler, *Formalism in Ethics and Non-Formal Ethics of Values*.
23 Max Scheler, "Ordo Amoris."
24 Denis Diderot, *Diderot on Art*, Vols. I and II; Michael Fried, *The Moment of Caravaggio*.
25 Michael Fried, *Absorption and Theatricality*, *Manet's Modernism*.
26 Clement Greenberg, *Homemade Esthetics*; Michael Fried, *Art and Objecthood*.
27 See Bruno Latour, *Reassembling the Social* and Jane Bennett, *Vibrant Matter*. I had the opportunity to raise this issue with Fried in person on February 10, 2018 during his visit to Los Angeles, and he was helpfully direct in his response.
28 Timothy Morton, *Hyperobjects*, p. 60.
29 Alain Badiou, *Being and Event*; Meillassoux, *After Finitude*.

1 OOO and Art: A First Summary

1 David Hume, *A Treatise of Human Nature*.
2 Jaako Hintikka, "*Cogito, ergo sum*: Inference or Performance?"
3 Franz Brentano, *Psychology from an Empirical Standpoint*.
4 A good overview can be found in Barry Smith, *Austrian Philosophy*.
5 Kasimir Twardowski, *On the Content and Object of Presentations*.
6 Edmund Husserl, "Intentional Objects."
7 Franz Brentano, *On the Several Senses of Being in Aristotle*.
8 Martin Heidegger, *Towards the Definition of Philosophy*.
9 Martin Heidegger, *Being and Time*.
10 The most widely read account of this sort is Hubert Dreyfus, *Being-in-the-World*.

11 George Berkeley, *Treatise Concerning the Principles of Human Knowledge*; Maurice Merleau-Ponty, *Phenomenology of Perception*, p. 79 (his actual example is a house, not a mountain).
12 Martin Heidegger, *Kant and the Problem of Metaphysics*, pp. 251–252.
13 Graham Harman, *Tool-Being, Heidegger Explained*.
14 Hume, *A Treatise of Human Nature*.
15 Edmund Husserl, *Logical Investigations*.
16 G.W. Leibniz, "Principles of Philosophy, or, the *Monadology*," §8, p. 214.
17 For another discussion of the aesthetics of causation, see Timothy Morton, *Realist Magic*.
18 Dave Hickey, *The Invisible Dragon*, Kindle edn., location 163 of 1418.
19 José Ortega y Gasset, "An Essay in Esthetics by Way of a Preface."
20 See Graham Harman, *Guerrilla Metaphysics*, pp. 102–110; Graham Harman, *Object-Oriented Ontology*, ch. 2.
21 The poem, whose author is listed as "unknown," can be found on the popular Pinterest website at https://www.pinterest.com/pin/5079920329402 57456/?lp=true
22 This is another way to account for the difference between Kripke's theory of names (non-literalist) and those of Frege, Russell, and others (literalist). See Saul Kripke, *Naming and Necessity*.
23 For an unusually haunting meditation on the gap between art and knowledge, see Emmanuel Levinas, "Reality and its Shadow."

2 Formalism and its Flaws

1 Peter Eisenman, *Eisenman Inside Out, Written Into the Void*.
2 Bruno Latour, "On the Partial Existence of Existing and Non-existing Objects."
3 George Santayana, *The Sense of Beauty*.
4 Slavoj Žižek, "Burned by the Sun," p. 217.
5 Two of the most detailed works of OOO-influenced architectural theory to have appeared so far are Mark Foster Gage, "Killing Simplicity," and Tom Wiscombe, "Discreteness, or Towards a Flat Ontology of Architecture."
6 Harman, *Guerrilla Metaphysics*, pp. 134–141.
7 Timothy Morton, *Hyperobjects*, p. 60.
8 Plato, *Meno*.
9 Aristotle, *Poetics*.
10 See Graham Harman, *Weird Realism*, pp. 59–63.
11 Meillassoux, *After Finitude*.
12 Latour, *We Have Never Been Modern*.
13 The same question is raised and successfully answered by Manuel DeLanda, *A New Philosophy of Society*, p. 1.
14 Nicolas Bourriaud, *Relational Aesthetics*.
15 Moran, "Formalism and the Appearance of Nature," pp. 126–127.
16 Steven Shaviro, "The Actual Volcano"; Graham Harman, "Response to Shaviro."
17 Alfred North Whitehead, *Process and Reality*, p. 29.
18 Shaviro, "The Actual Volcano," pp. 288–289. The reference in the second paragraph is to Graham Harman, "On Vicarious Causation."

3 Theatrical, Not Literal

1 Michael Fried, *Absorption and Theatricality, Courbet's Realism, Manet's Modernism, The Moment of Caravaggio, After Caravaggio.*
2 Michael Fried, *Four Honest Outlaws, Why Photography Matters as Art as Never Before.*
3 The incident occurred during my keynote address at the Transmediale Festival at the Haus der Kulturen der Welt in Berlin on February 2, 2012. See ch. 8, "Everything is Not Connected," in Graham Harman, *Bells and Whistles*, pp. 100–127.
4 Knox Peden also rejects Pippin's Hegelian interpretation of Fried, though for different reasons related both to Merleau-Ponty's impact on Fried and to Peden's own fascination with Rancière. See Knox Peden, "Grace and Equality, Fried and Rancière (and Kant)," p. 192.
5 Harold Bloom, *The Anxiety of Influence.*
6 Rita Felski, "Context Stinks!"
7 Latour, *We Have Never Been Modern.*
8 Jean Baudrillard, *Simulacra and Simulation*; Graham Harman, "Object-Oriented Seduction."
9 Friedrich Nietzsche, *The Birth of Tragedy.*
10 Patrik Schumacher, "A Critique of Object-Oriented Architecture," p. 75.
11 Levi R. Bryant, *Onto-Cartography.*
12 Marc Botha, *A Theory of Minimalism.*
13 Ferdinand de Saussure, *Course in General Linguistics.*
14 Robert Jackson, "The Anxiousness of Objects and Artworks," "The Anxiousness of Objects and Artworks II."
15 Stanley Cavell, *The World Viewed.*
16 Brassier et al., "Speculative Realism."
17 Wolfgang Iser, *The Act of Reading*, pp. 9–10.
18 Bruno Latour, *Pandora's Hope*, p. 122.
19 Konstantin Stanislavski, *An Actor's Work*, p. 366.
20 Humberto Maturana and Francisco Varela, *Autopoiesis and Cognition.*
21 Niklas Luhmann, *Social Systems, Theory of Society* (2 Vols.).
22 Peter Sloterdijk, *Spheres* I, II, III.
23 Andrea Kern, "Aesthetic Subjectivity and the Possibility of Art," p. 218.
24 Theodor Lipps, *Ästhetik*, 2 vols.; Ortega y Gasset, "An Essay in Esthetics by Way of a Preface," p. 138.
25 Martin Heidegger, "Insight Into That Which Is"; Bruno Latour, *Reassembling the Social*, pp. 50 (note 48), 132 (note 187), 243–244.
26 Magdalena Ostas, "The Aesthetics of Absorption," p. 175, emphasis added. Beyond the sentence just quoted, the whole of Ostas' article is an important challenge to Fried's notion that absorption and theatricality are opposites.
27 Emmanuel Levinas, *Existence and Existents.*
28 Søren Kierkegaard, *Repetition*, p. 167.
29 Michael Fried, "Constantin Constantius Goes to the Theater," p. 258.

4 The Canvas is the Message

1 Clement Greenberg, *The Collected Essays and Criticism* (4 vols.), *Late Writings, Homemade Esthetics, Joan Miro, Henri Matisse (1869–)*.
2 José Ortega y Gasset, *The Dehumanization of Art*.
3 Graham Harman, "The McLuhans and Metaphysics."
4 Martin Heidegger, *The Basic Problems of Phenomenology*.
5 Graham Harman, *Tool-Being, Heidegger Explained*.
6 Martin Heidegger, "Insight Into That Which Is."
7 Martin Heidegger, *Ponderings II–VI: Black Notebooks 1931–1938*.
8 Martin Heidegger, *Contributions to Philosophy*, p. 6. I have modified the translation slightly for the sake of consistency with the rest of the present book.
9 Marshall McLuhan, *Understanding Media*.
10 Marshall McLuhan, *From Cliché to Archteype*.
11 Martin Heidegger, "The Origin of the Work of Art."
12 See the early pages of Martin Heidegger, *History of the Concept of Time*.
13 Marshall and Eric McLuhan, *Laws of Media*.
14 Cleanth Brooks, *The Well Wrought Urn*; Graham Harman, "The Well-Wrought Broken Hammer."
15 Heidegger, "Insight Into That Which Is."
16 Harman, "The Revenge of the Surface."
17 Heidegger, "Insight Into That Which Is."

5 After High Modernism

1 Tom Wolfe, *The Painted Word*, p. 98.
2 In the footnote following the word "tension."
3 After Sir Herbert Read intervenes on behalf of Rosenberg, he and Greenberg engage in further polemical dispute from pp. 145–149.
4 Berkeley, *A Treatise Concerning the Principles of Human Knowledge*. My esteemed friend and colleague Iain Hamilton Grant is among those who defend this "realist" reading of Berkeley, with which I cannot agree. See Jeremy Dunham, Iain Hamilton Grant, and Sean Watson, *Idealism*, p. 4. A more detailed discussion can be found in ch. 2 of Harman, *Speculative Realism: An Introduction*.
5 Steinberg's target here is Ortega, *The Dehumanization of Art*.
6 See the ultimately disappointing three-part exchange: T.J. Clark, "Clement Greenberg's Theory of Art"; Michael Fried, "How Modernism Works"; T.J. Clark, "Arguments About Modernism."
7 Harman, *Guerrilla Metaphysics*, ch. 4, "The Style of Things," pp. 45–58.
8 Rosalind Krauss, "The Originality of the Avant-Garde" and "Sincerely Yours," in *The Originality of the Avant-Garde*, pp. 151–194.
9 Saussure, *Course in General Linguistics*, p. 120, cited in Rosalind Krauss, *The Originality of the Avant-Garde*, p. 35.
10 Harman, *Object-Oriented Ontology*, pp. 209–217.
11 Harman, "Object-Oriented Seduction."
12 Jacques Derrida, *Of Grammatology*, p. 333.

13 Harman, *Guerrilla Metaphysics*, pp. 110–116.
14 Jacques Lacan, *The Four Fundamental Concepts of Psycho-Analysis*.
15 Jean-Luc Marion, *Being Given*.
16 Louis Althusser et al., *Reading Capital*.
17 Slavoj Žižek, "The Lesson of Rancière," p. 65. (Comma after "movement" added.)
18 Slavoj Žižek, "Carl Schmitt in the Age of Post-Politics," p. 18.
19 See Friedrich Schiller, *On the Aesthetic Education of Man*.
20 Friedrich Nietzsche, *The Will to Power*, p. 811.

6 Dada, Surrealism, and Literalism

1 Since Bogost has not been mentioned so far, allow me to recommend *Alien Phenomenology* as a good summary of his intellectual position in contrast with the other original OOO authors.
2 Judith Butler, *Gender Trouble*.
3 Alfred Jarry, *Exploits and Opinions of Dr. Faustroll Pataphysician*.
4 Greenberg, *Joan Miro, Henri Matisse (1869–)*.
5 Jorge Luis Borges, "Pierre Menard, Author of Don Quixote."
6 McLuhan, *Understanding Media*, pp. 22–32.
7 David Joselit, *Infinite Regress*, p. 185.
8 George Dickie, *Art and the Aesthetic*.
9 Jim Shaw, *Thrift Store Paintings*.
10 See Martin Heidegger, "What is Metaphysics?" (for *Angst*), *Fundamental Concepts of Metaphysics* (for boredom), and *Introduction to Metaphysics* (for joy).
11 Roger Rothman, "Object-Oriented Surrealism."
12 André Breton, *Surrealism and Painting*, p. 5; G.W.F. Hegel, *Phenomenology of Spirit*, p. 14.
13 Bryant, *Onto-Cartography*. For the idea that materialism is just a form of idealism, see Graham Harman, "I Am Also of the Opinion that Materialism Must Be Destroyed" as well as Bruno Latour, "Can We Get Our Materialism Back, Please?"
14 Georges Bataille, *Visions of Excess*, p. 31.
15 The reference to "backward Kantians" comes from Salvador Dalí, *The Collected Writings of Salvador Dalí*, p. 268.
16 Dalí, *The Collected Writings of Salvador Dalí*, p. 245.
17 Walter Benjamin, *Walter Benjamin: Selected Writings*, Vol. 2, p. 4.
18 J.R.R. Tolkien, "On Fairy-Stories," p. 15.
19 Harman, *Weird Realism*.
20 H.P. Lovecraft, "The Whisperer in Darkness."

7 Weird Formalism

1 Hal Foster, *Bad New Days*, ch. 5, "Post-Critical?"
2 Maurizio Ferraris, *Manifesto of New Realism*, p. 4.
3 Fried, *Four Honest Outlaws*.
4 For an explanation of why Whitehead is not a philosopher of becoming in

the manner of Bergson and Deleuze see Graham Harman, "Whitehead and Schools X, Y, and Z."

5 Jane Bennett, "Systems and Things," p. 227. For a critique of Bennett's monism, see Graham Harman, "Autonomous Objects."

6 Brentano, *Psychology from an Empirical Standpoint.*

7 No less an authority than Latour, for example, made this very critique of my 2016 book *Immaterialism.* For a response see Graham Harman, "Decadence in the Biographical Sense."

8 There is, however, a degree of ambiguity in McLuhan's use of the term "cold." See Graham Harman, "Some Paradoxes of McLuhan's Tetrad."

9 Harold Bloom, *The Western Canon*, pp. 20–22

Works Cited

Abbott, Mathew (ed.) (2018) *Michael Fried and Philosophy: Modernism, Intention, and Theatricality*. London: Routledge. Kindle edn.

Althusser, Louis, Étienne Balibar, Roger Establet, Pierre Machery, and Jacques Rancière (2015) *Reading Capital*, trans. B. Brewster and D. Fernbach. London: Verso.

Aristotle (1997) *Poetics*, trans. M. Heath. London: Penguin.

— (2018) *Rhetoric*, trans. C.D.C. Reeve. Indianapolis: Hackett.

Badiou, Alain (2005) *Being and Event*, trans. O. Feltham. London: Continuum.

Bataille, Georges (1985) *Visions of Excess: Selected Writings, 1927–1939*, trans. A. Stoekl. Minneapolis: University of Minnesota Press.

— (1987) *Story of the Eye*, trans. J. Neugroschel. San Francisco: City Lights.

Baudrillard, Jean (1994) *Simulacra and Simulation*, trans. S. Faria Glaser. Ann Arbor, MI: University of Michigan Press.

Benjamin, Walter (1999) *Walter Benjamin: Selected Writings, Vol. 2 (1927–1934)*, trans. R. Livingstone et al. Cambridge, MA: Harvard University Press.

Bennett, Jane (2010) *Vibrant Matter: A Political Ecology of Things*. Durham, NC: Duke University Press.

— (2012) "Systems and Things: A Response to Graham Harman and Timothy Morton," *New Literary History* 43, pp. 225–233.

Berkeley, George (1982) *Treatise Concerning the Principles of Human Knowledge*. Indianapolis: Hackett.

Bloom, Harold (1995) *The Western Canon: The Books and School of the Ages*. New York: Riverhead.

— (1997) *The Anxiety of Influence: A Theory of Poetry*, 2nd edn. Oxford: Oxford University Press.

Bogost, Ian (2012) *Alien Phenomenology, or What It's Like to be a Thing*. Minneapolis: University of Minnesota Press.

Borges, Jose Luis (1962) "Pierre Menard, Author of Don Quixote," in *Ficciones*, trans. A. Kerrigan. New York: Grove Press, pp. 45–56.

Botha, Marc (2017) *A Theory of Minimalism*. London: Bloomsbury.

Bourriaud, Nicolas (1998) *Relational Aesthetics*. Dijon, France: Les Presses du réel.

Brassier, Ray, Iain Hamilton Grant, Graham Harman, and Quentin Meillassoux (2007), "Speculative Realism," *Collapse* III, pp. 306–449.

Brentano, Franz (1981) *On the Several Senses of Being in Aristotle*, trans. R. George. Berkeley, CA: University of California Press.

— (1995) *Psychology from an Empirical Standpoint*, trans. A. Rancurello, D.B. Terrell, and L. McAlister. New York: Routledge.

Breton, André (2002) *Surrealism and Painting*, trans. S.W. Taylor. Boston: MFA Publications.

Brooks, Cleanth (1947) *The Well Wrought Urn*. New York: Harcourt, Brace, and World.

Bryant, Levi R. (2014) *Onto-Cartography: An Ontology of Machines and Media*. Edinburgh: Edinburgh University Press.

Butler, Judith (1990) *Gender Trouble*. New York: Routledge.

Cavell, Stanley (1979) *The World Viewed: Reflections on the Ontology of Film*, enlarged edn. Cambridge, MA: Harvard University Press.

Charlesworth, J.J. and James Hearfield (2014), "Subjects v. Objects," *Art Monthly*, Issue 374, March, pp. 1–4.

Clark, T.J. (1999) *Farewell to an Idea: Episodes from a History of Modernism*. New Haven, CT: Yale University Press.

— (2000) "Clement Greenberg's Theory of Art," in F. Frascina (ed.), *Pollock and After*, pp. 71–86.

— (2000) "Arguments About Modernism: A Reply to Michael Fried," in F. Frascina (ed.), *Pollock and After*, pp. 102–109.

Colebrook, Claire (2014) "No Kant, Not Now: Another Sublime," *Speculations* V, pp. 127–157.

Dalí, Salvador (1998) *The Collected Writings of Salvador Dalí*, trans. H. Finkelstein. Cambridge, UK: Cambridge University Press.

Dante Alighieri (1995) *The Divine Comedy*, trans. A. Mandelbaum. New York: Random House.

— (2004) *La Vita Nuova*, revised edn., trans. B. Reynolds. London: Penguin.

Danto, Arthur (1964) "The Artworld," *Journal of Philosophy*, Vol. 61, No. 19, pp. 571–584.

— (1981) *The Transfiguration of the Commonplace*. Cambridge, MA: Harvard University Press.

— (1997) *After the End of Art: Contemporary Art and the Pale of History*. Princeton, NJ: Princeton University Press.

— (2009) *Andy Warhol*. New Haven, CT: Yale University Press.

de Duve, Thierry (1999) *Kant After Duchamp*. Cambridge, MA: MIT Press.

DeLanda, Manuel (2006) *A New Philosophy of Society: Assemblage Theory and Social Complexity*. London: Continuum.

Derrida, Jacques (2016) *Of Grammatology*, trans. G. Spivak. Baltimore: Johns Hopkins University Press.

Dickie, George (1974) *Art and Aesthetics: An Institutional Analysis*. Ithaca, NY: Cornell University Press.

Diderot, Denis (1995) *Diderot on Art, Volume 1: The Salon of 1765 and Notes on Painting*, trans. J. Goodman. New Haven, CT: Yale University Press.

— (1995) *Diderot on Art, Volume 2: The Salon of 1767*, trans. J. Goodman. New Haven, CT: Yale University Press.

Dreyfus, Hubert L. (1990) *Being-in-the-World: A Commentary on Heidegger's Being and Time, Division 1*. Cambridge, MA: MIT Press.

Dunham, Jeremy, Iain Hamilton Grant, and Sean Watson (2011) *Idealism: The History of a Philosophy*. Montreal: McGill-Queen's University Press.

Eddington, A.S. (1929) *The Nature of the Physical World*. New York: Macmillan.

Eisenman, Peter (2004) *Eisenman Inside Out: Selected Writings, 1963–1988*. New Haven, CT: Yale University Press.

— (2007) *Written Into the Void: Selected Writings, 1990–2004*. New Haven, CT: Yale University Press.

Felski, Rita (2011) "Context Stinks!", *New Literary History*, Vol. 42, No. 4, pp. 573–591.

Ferraris, Maurizio (2015) *Manifesto of New Realism*, trans. S. De Sanctis. Albany, NY: SUNY Press.

Foster, Hal (1996) *The Return of the Real: The Avant-Garde at the End of the Century*. Cambridge, MA: MIT Press.

— (2017) *Bad New Days: Art, Criticism, Emergency*. London: Verso.

Frascina, Francis (ed.) (2000) *Pollock and After: The Critical Debate*, 2nd edn. New York: Routledge.

Fried, Michael (1988) *Absorption and Theatricality: Painting and Beholder in the Age of Diderot*. Chicago: University of Chicago Press.

— (1990) *Courbet's Realism*. Chicago: University of Chicago Press.

— (1996) *Manet's Modernism: or, The Face of Painting in the 1860s*. Chicago: University of Chicago Press.

— (1998) *Art and Objecthood: Essays and Reviews*. Chicago: University of Chicago Press.

— (2000) "How Modernism Works: A Response to T.J. Clark," in F. Frascina (ed.), *Pollock and After*, pp. 87–101.

— (2008) *Why Photography Matters as Art as Never Before*. New Haven, CT: Yale University Press, 2008.

— (2010) *The Moment of Caravaggio*. Princeton, NJ: Princeton University Press.

— (2011) *Four Honest Outlaws: Sala, Ray, Marioni, Gordon*. New Haven, CT: Yale University Press.

— (2016) *After Caravaggio*. New Haven, CT: Yale University Press.

— (2018) Personal communication, February 10.

— (2018) "Constantin Constantius Goes to the Theater," in Mathew Abbott, ed., *Michael Fried and Philosophy*, pp. 243–259. Kindle edn.

Funcke, Bettina (2014) "Not Objects So Much as Images: A Response to Graham Harman's 'Greenberg, Duchamp, and the Next Avant-Garde,'" *Speculations* V, pp. 275–285.

Gage, Mark Foster (2015) "Killing Simplicity: Object-Oriented Philosophy in Architecture," *Log* 33, Winter, pp. 95–106.

Greenberg, Clement (1948) *Joan Miro*. New York: Quadrangle.

— (1953) *Henri Matisse (1869–)*. New York: Harry N. Abrams.

— (1986) *The Collected Essays and Criticism, Volume 1: Perceptions and Judgments, 1939–1944*. Chicago: University of Chicago Press.

— (1988) *The Collected Essays and Criticism, Volume 2: Arrogant Purpose, 1945–1949*. Chicago: University of Chicago Press.

— (1995) *The Collected Essays and Criticism, Volume 3: Affirmations and Refusals, 1950–1956*. Chicago: University of Chicago Press.

— (1995) *The Collected Essays and Criticism, Volume 4: Modernism with a Vengeance, 1957–1969*. Chicago: University of Chicago Press.

— (2000) *Homemade Esthetics: Observations on Art and Taste.* Oxford: Oxford University Press.

— (2003) *Late Writings.* Minneapolis: University of Minnesota Press.

Greene, Brian (1999) *The Elegant Universe: Superstrings, Hidden Dimensions, and the Quest for the Ultimate Theory.* New York: Norton.

Harman, Graham (2002) *Tool-Being: Heidegger and the Metaphysics of Objects.* Chicago: Open Court.

— (2005) *Guerrilla Metaphysics: Phenomenology and the Carpentry of Things.* Chicago: Open Court.

— (2007) *Heidegger Explained: From Phenomenon to Thing.* Chicago: Open Court.

— (2007) "Aesthetics as First Philosophy: Levinas and the Non-Human," *Naked Punch* 09, Summer/Fall 2007, pp. 21–30.

— (2007) "On Vicarious Causation," *Collapse* II, pp. 171–205.

— (2009) "The McLuhans and Metaphysics," in *New Waves in Philosophy of Technology*, ed. J.-K. B. Olsen, E. Selinger, and S. Riis. London: Palgrave, pp. 100–122.

— (2010) "I Am Also of the Opinion that Materialism Must Be Destroyed," *Environment and Planning D: Society and Space* 28 (5), pp. 772–790.

— (2011) "Autonomous Objects," *new formations* #71, pp. 125–130.

— (2011) "On the Undermining of Objects: Grant, Bruno, and Radical Philosophy," in *The Speculative Turn: Continental Materialism and Realism*, ed. L. Bryant, N. Srnicek, and G. Harman. Melbourne: re.press, pp. 21–40.

— (2011) "Response to Shaviro," in *The Speculative Turn*, ed. L. Bryant, N. Srnicek, and G. Harman. Melbourne: re.press, pp. 291–303.

— (2012) *Weird Realism: Lovecraft and Philosophy.* Winchester, UK: Zero Books.

— (2012) "Some Paradoxes of McLuhan's Tetrad," *Umbr(a)*, No. 1, pp. 77–95.

— (2012) "The Third Table," in *The Book of* Books, ed. C. Christov-Bakargiev. Ostfildern, Germany: Hatje Cantz Verlag, pp. 540–542.

— (2012) "The Well-Wrought Broken Hammer: Object-Oriented Literary Criticism," *New Literary History*, 43, pp. 183–203.

— (2013) *Bells and Whistles: More Speculative Realism.* Winchester, UK: Zero Books.

— (2013) "The Revenge of the Surface: Heidegger, McLuhan, Greenberg," *Paletten* Issue 291/292 (2013), pp. 66–73.

— (2013) "Undermining, Overmining, and Duomining: A Critique," in *ADD Metaphysics*, ed. J. Sutela. Aalto, Finland: Aalto University Design Research Laboratory, pp. 40–51.

— (2014) "Art Without Relations," *ArtReview*, September, Vol. 66, No. 66, pp. 144–147.

— (2014) "Greenberg, Duchamp, and the Next Avant-Garde," *Speculations* V, pp. 251–274.

— (2014) "Materialism is Not the Solution: On Matter, Form, and Mimesis," *Nordic Journal of Aesthetics*, 47 (2014), pp. 94–110.

— (2014) "Whitehead and Schools X, Y, and Z," in *The Lure of Whitehead*, N. Gaskill and A. Nocek (eds.), Minneapolis: University of Minnesota Press, 2014, pp. 231–248.

— (2016) *Immaterialism: Objects and Social Theory*. Cambridge, UK: Polity.

— (2016) *Dante's Broken Hammer: The Ethics, Aesthetics, and Metaphysics of Love*. London: Repeater Books.

— (2016) "Object-Oriented Seduction: Baudrillard Reconsidered," in *The War of Appearances*, ed. J. Brouwer, L. Spuybroek, and S. van Tuinen. Amsterdam: Sonic Acts Press, pp. 128–143.

— (2016) "Decadence in the Biographical Sense: Taking a Distance from Actor-Network Theory," *International Journal of Actor-Network Theory and Technological Innovation*, Vol. 8, Issue 3 (July –September), pp. 1–8.

— (2017) "Object-Oriented Ontology and Commodity Fetishism: Kant, Marx, Heidegger, and Things," *Eidos* 2, pp. 28–36. http://eidos.uw.edu.pl/files/pdf/eidos/2017–02/eidos_2_harman.pdf

— (2018) *Object-Oriented Ontology: A New Theory of Everything*. London: Pelican.

Hegel, G.W.F. (1977) *Phenomenology of Spirit*, trans. A.V. Miller. Oxford: Oxford University Press.

Heidegger, Martin (1962) *Being and Time*, trans. J. Macquarrie and E. Robinson. New York: Harper and Row.

— (1965) *Kant and the Problem of Metaphysics*, trans. J. Churchill. Bloomington, IN: Indiana University Press.

— (1988) *The Basic Problems of Phenomenology*, trans. A. Hofstadter. Bloomington, IN: Indiana University Press.

— (1995) *The Fundamental Concepts of Metaphysics: World, Finitude, Solitude*, trans. W. McNeill and N. Walker. Bloomington, IN: Indiana University Press.

— (1998) "What is Metaphysics?," in *Pathmarks*, trans. W. McNeill. Cambridge, UK: Cambridge University Press, pp. 82–96.

— (2000) *Introduction to Metaphysics*, trans. G. Fried and R. Polt. New Have, CT: Yale University Press.

— (2002) "The Origin of the Work of Art," in *Off the Beaten Track*, trans. J. Young and K. Haynes. Cambridge, UK: Cambridge University Press.

— (2008) *Towards the Definition of Philosophy*, trans. T. Sadler. London: Continuum.

— (2009) *History of the Concept of Time: Prolegomena*, trans. T. Kisiel. Bloomington, IN: Indiana University Press.

— (2012) "Insight Into That Which Is," in *Bremen and Freiburg Lectures: Insight Into That Which Is and Basic Principles of Thinking*, trans. A Mitchell. Bloomington, IN: Indiana University Press.

— (2012) *Contributions to Philosophy (Of the Event)*, trans. R. Rojcewicz and D. Vallega-Neu. Bloomington, IN: Indiana University Press.

— (2016) *Ponderings II–VI: Black Notebooks 1931–1938*, trans. R. Rojcewicz. Bloomington, IN: Indiana University Press.

Hickey, Dave (2012) *The Invisible Dragon: Essays on Beauty*, Revised and Expanded. Chicago: University of Chicago Press. Kindle edn.

Hintikka, Jaako (1962) "*Cogito, ergo sum*: Inference or Performance?", *Philosophical Review*, Vol. 71, No. 1 (January), pp. 3–32.

Hume, David (1978) *A Treatise of Human Nature*. Oxford: Oxford University Press.

Husserl, Edmund (1970) *Logical Investigations*, 2 vols., trans. J.N. Findlay. London: Routledge and Kegan Paul.

191

— (1993) "Intentional Objects," in *Early Writings in the Philosophy of Logic and Mathematics*, trans. D. Willard. Dordrecht, The Netherlands: Kluwer, pp. 345–387.

Iser, Wolfgang (1978) *The Act of Reading: A Theory of Aesthetic Response*. Baltimore: The Johns Hopkins University Press.

Jackson, Robert (2011) "The Anxiousness of Objects and Artworks: Michael Fried, Object Oriented Ontology, and Aesthetic Absorption," *Speculations* II, pp. 135–168.

— (2014) "The Anxiousness of Objects and Artworks 2: (Iso)Morphism, Anti-Literalism, and Presentness," *Speculations* IV, pp. 311–358.

Jarry, Alfred (1996) *Alfred Jarry, Exploits and Opinions of Dr. Faustroll Pataphysician*, trans. R. Shattuck. Cambridge, MA: Exact Change.

Joselit, David (2001) *Infinite Regress: Marcel Duchamp 1910–1941*. Cambridge, MA: MIT Press.

Kant, Immanuel (1965) *Critique of Pure Reason*, trans. N.K. Smith. New York: St. Martin's Press.

— (1987) *Critique of Judgment*, trans. W. Pluhar. Indianapolis: Hackett.

— (2001) *Prolegomena to Any Future Metaphysics*, trans. J.W. Ellington. Indianapolis: Hackett.

— (2012) *Groundwork of the Metaphysics of Morals*, trans. M. Gregor and J. Timmerman. Cambridge, UK: Cambridge University Press.

— (2015) *Critique of Practical Reason*, trans. M. Gregor and A. Reath. Cambridge, UK: Cambridge University Press.

Kern, Andrea (2018) "Aesthetic Subjectivity and the Possibility of Art," trans. L.A. Smith-Gary, in Mathew Abbott (ed.), *Michael Fried and Philosophy*, pp. 206–224. Kindle edn.

Kierkegaard, Søren (1983) *Fear and Trembling/Repetition*, trans. H. Hong and E. Hong. Princeton: Princeton University Press.

Kosuth, Joseph (1972) "Art After Philosophy/Kunst nach der Philosophie," first part, trans. W. Höck, in P. Maenz and G. de Vries (eds.), *Art and Language*. Cologne: M. DuMont Schauberg, pp. 74–99.

Krauss, Rosalind E. (1986) "The Originality of the Avant-Garde" and "Sincerely Yours," in *The Originality of the Avant-Garde and Other Modernist Myths*. Cambridge, MA: MIT Press.

— (1993) *The Optical Unconscious*. Cambridge, MA: MIT Press.

Kripke, Saul (1996) *Naming and Necessity*. Cambridge, MA: Harvard University Press.

Kristeva, Julia (1982) *Powers of Horror: An Essay on Abjection*. New York: Columbia University Press.

Lacan, Jacques (1981) *The Four Fundamental Concepts of Psycho-Analysis*, trans. A. Sheridan. New York: Norton.

Latour, Bruno (1993) *We Have Never Been Modern*, trans. C. Porter. Cambridge, MA: Harvard University Press.

— (1999) *Pandora's Hope: Essays on the Reality of Science Studies*. Cambridge, MA: Harvard University Press.

— (2000) "On the Partial Existence of Existing and Non-existing Objects," in *Biographies of Scientific Objects*, ed. L. Daston. Chicago: University of Chicago Press, pp. 247–269.

— (2005) *Reassembling the Social: An Introduction to Actor-Network Theory*. Oxford: Oxford University Press.

— (2007) "Can We Get Our Materialism Back, Please?," *Isis*, Vol. 98, pp. 138–142.

Leibniz, G.W. (1989) "The Principles of Philosophy, or, the Monadology," in *Philosophical Essays*, trans. R. Ariew and D. Garber, pp. 213–225. Indianapolis: Hackett.

Levinas, Emmanuel (1987) "Reality and its Shadow," in *Collected Philosophical Papers*, trans. A. Lingis, pp. 1–13. Dordrecht, The Netherlands: Martinus Nijhoff.

— (1988) *Existence and Existents*, trans. A. Lingis. The Hague: Martinus Nijhoff.

Levine, Caroline (2015) *Forms: Whole, Rhythm, Hierarchy, Network*. Oxford: Oxford University Press.

Lipps, Theodor (1903) *Ästhetik: Psychologie des schönen und der Kunst*, Erster Teil: *Grundlegung der Ästhetik*. Hamburg and Leipzig: Leopold Voss.

— (1920) *Ästhetik: Psychologie des schönen und der Kunst*, Zweiter Teil: *Die ästhetische Betrachtung und die bildende Kunst*. Leipzig: Leopold Voss.

Lovecraft, H.P. (2005) "The Whisperer in Darkness," in *Tales*. New York: Library of America, pp. 415–480.

Luhmann, Niklas (1996) *Social Systems*, trans. J. Bednarz Jr. with D. Baecker. Stanford, CA: Stanford University Press.

— (2012) *Theory of Society*, Vol. 1, trans. R. Barrett. Stanford, CA: Stanford University Press.

— (2013) *Theory of Society*, Vol. 2, trans. R. Barrett. Stanford, CA: Stanford University Press.

Maimon, Salomon (2010) *Essay on Transcendental Philosophy*, trans. A. Welchman. London: Continuum.

Marion, Jean-Luc (2002) *Being Given: Toward a Phenomenology of Givenness*, trans. J. Kosky. Stanford, CA: Stanford University Press.

Maturana, Humberto and Francisco Varela (1980) *Autopoiesis and Cognition: The Realization of the Living*.

McLuhan, Marshall (1994) *Understanding Media: The Extensions of Man*. Cambridge, MA: MIT Press.

McLuhan, Marshall and Wilfred Watson (1970) *From Cliché to Archetype*. New York: Viking.

McLuhan, Marshall and Eric McLuhan (1992) *Laws of Media: The New Science*. Toronto: University of Toronto Press.

Meillassoux, Quentin (2008) *After Finitude: Essay on the Necessity of Contingency*, trans. R. Brassier. London: Continuum.

Melville, Stephen (2018) "Becoming Medium," in Mathew Abbott (ed.), *Michael Fried and Philosophy*, pp. 104–115. Kindle edn.

Merleau-Ponty, Maurice (2002). *Phenomenology of Perception*, trans. C. Smith. London: Routledge.

Moran, Richard (2018) "Formalism and the Appearance of Nature," in Mathew Abbott (ed.), *Michael Fried and Philosophy*, pp. 117–128. Kindle edn.

Morton, Timothy (2013) *Hyperobjects: Philosophy and Ecology After the End of the World*. Minneapolis: University of Minnesota Press.

— (2013) *Realist Magic: Objects, Ontology, Causality*. Ann Arbor, MI: Open Humanities Pres.

Mouffe, Chantal (ed.) (1999) *The Challenge of Carl Schmitt*. London: Verso.

Nietzsche, Friedrich (1967) *The Birth of Tragedy* and *The Case of Wagner*, trans. W. Kaufmann. New York: Random House.

— (1973) *The Will to Power*, trans. W. Kaufmann and R.J. Hollingdale. New York: Random House.

Ortega y Gasset, José (1968) *The Dehumanization of Art: And other Essays on Art, Culture, and Literature*, trans. H. Weyl. Princeton, NJ: Princeton University Press.

— (1975) "An Essay in Esthetics by Way of a Preface," in *Phenomenology and Art*, trans. P. Silver. New York: Norton, pp. 127–150.

Osborne, Peter (2013) *Anywhere or Not at All: Philosophy of Contemporary Art*. London: Verso.

Ostas, Magdalena (2018) "The Aesthetics of Absorption," in Mathew Abbott (ed.), *Michael Fried and Philosophy*, pp. 171–188. Kindle edn.

Parkinson, Gavin (2008) *The Duchamp Book*. London: Tate.

Peden, Knox (2018) "Grace and Equality, Fried and Rancière (and Kant)," in Mathew Abbott (ed.), *Michael Fried and Philosophy*, pp. 189–205. Kindle edn.

Pippin, Robert B. (2014) *After the Beautiful: Hegel and the Philosophy of Pictorial Modernism*. Chicago: University of Chicago Press.

— (2018) "Why Does Photography Matter as Art *Now*, as Never Before? On Fried and Intention," in Mathew Abbott (ed.), *Michael Fried and Philosophy*, pp. 48–63. Kindle edn.

Plato (2002) "Meno," trans. G.M.A. Grube, rev. J. Cooper, in *Five Dialogues*. Indianapolis: Hackett, pp. 58–92.

Proust, Marcel (2016) *À la recherche du temps perdu*, Tome 2: *À l'ombre des jeunes filles en fleurs*. Niort, France: Atlantic edns.

Ragona, Melissa (2017) Personal communication, August 5.

Rancière, Jacques (2004) *The Politics of Aesthetics*, trans. G. Rockhill. London: Bloomsbury.

— (2009) *Aesthetics and its Discontents*, trans. S. Corcoran. Cambridge, UK: Polity.

— (2011) *The Emancipated Spectator*, trans. G. Elliott. London: Verso.

Rosenberg, Harold (1994) *The Tradition of the New*. Cambridge, MA: Da Capo Press.

Rothman, Roger (2012) *Tiny Surrealism: Salvador Dalí and the Aesthetics of the Small*. Lincoln, NE: University of Nebraska Press.

— (2016) "Object-Oriented Surrealism: Salvador Dalí and the Poetic Autonomy of Things," *Culture, Theory and Critique*, Vol. 57, No. 2, pp. 176–196.

Santayana, George (1955) *The Sense of Beauty: Being the Outline of Aesthetic Theory*. New York: Dover.

Saussure, Ferdinand de (1998) *Course in General Linguistics*, trans. R. Harris. Chicago: Open Court.

Scarry, Elaine (1999) *On Beauty and Being Just*. Princeton, NJ: Princeton University Press.

Scheler, Max (1973) *Formalism in Ethics and Non-Formal Ethics of Values*, trans. M. Frings and R. Funk. Evanston, IL: Northwestern University Press.

— (1992) "Ordo Amoris," in *Selected Philosophical Essays*, trans. D. Lachterman. Evanston, IL: Northwestern University Press.

Schiller, Friedrich (2016) *On the Aesthetic Education of Man*, trans. K. Tribe. London: Penguin.

Schumacher, Patrik (2018) "A Critique of Object-Oriented Architecture," in *CENTER 22: The Secret Life of Buildings*. Austin, TX: Center for American Architecture and Design.

Sellars, Wilfrid (2007). "Philosophy and the Scientific Image of Man," in *In the Space of Reasons*, pp. 369–408. Cambridge, MA: Harvard University Press.

Shaviro, Steven (2011) "The Actual Volcano: Whitehead, Harman, and the Problem of Relations," in *The Speculative Turn*, ed. L. Bryant, N. Srnicek, and G. Harman. Melbourne: re.press, pp. 279–290.

Shaw, Jim (1992) *Thrift Store Paintings*. Venice, CA: Heavy Industry Publications.

Sloterdijk, Peter (2011) *Spheres* Vol. I, trans. W. Hoban. New York: Semiotext(e).

— (2014) *Spheres* Vol. II, trans. W. Hoban. New York: Semiotext(e).

— (2016) *Spheres* Vol. III, trans. W. Hoban. New York: Semiotext(e).

Smith, Barry (1995) *Austrian Philosophy: The Legacy of Brentano*. Chicago: Open Court.

Stanislavski, Konstantin (2010) *An Actor's Work*, trans. J. Benedetti. London: Routledge.

Steinberg, Leo (1972) *Other Criteria: Confrontations with Twentieth-Century Art*. Oxford: Oxford University Press.

Tolkien, J.R.R. (1939) "On Fairy-Stories." https://www.excellence-in-literature. com/wp-content/uploads/2013/10/fairystoriesbytolkien.pdf

Twardowski, Kasimir (1977) *On the Content and Object of Presentations*, trans. R. Grossmann. The Hague: Martinus Nijhoff.

Veseli, Hasan (2016) Personal communication, December 4.

Virgil (1981) *The Aeneid*, trans. A. Mandelbaum. New York: Bantam.

Wellbery, David E. (2018) "Schiller, Schopenhauer, Fried," in Mathew Abbott (ed.), *Michael Fried and Philosophy*, pp. 64–63. Kindle edn.

Whitehead, Alfred North (1979) *Process and Reality*. New York: Free Press.

Wiscombe, Tom (2014) "Discreteness, or Towards a Flat Ontology of Architecture," *Project* 3, pp. 34–43.

Wolfe, Tom (1975) *The Painted Word*. New York: Bantam.

Wollheim, Richard (1980) *Art and its Objects*, 2nd edn. Cambridge, UK: Cambridge University Press.

Žižek, Slavoj (1999) "Carl Schmitt in the Age of Post-Politics," in Chantal Mouffe (ed.), *The Challenge of Carl Schmitt*, pp. 18–37.

— (2004) "The Lesson of Rancière," in Jacques Rancière, *The Politics of Aesthetics*, pp. 65–75.

— (2006) "Burned by the Sun," in *Lacan: The Silent Partners*, ed. S. Žižek. London: Verso, pp. 217–230.

Index

abject, tendency in contemporary art,
  167–168, 173
absorption, 7, 49, 50, 67–68, 73–82,
  94, 107, 136
abstraction, 52, 89, 95, 99, 102,
  114–120, 128, 153
  Abstract Expressionism, 89, 111,
  120, 121
academic art, 10, 95–96, 99, 104,
  115, 122, 144, 154, 162
actor-network theory (ANT), 8, 33,
  70, 174
aesthetics, definition of, xi-xii
allure, allusion, 30, 39, 46, 67, 68
analytic philosophy, 1, 17, 31
animals
  mistreatment of in modern
  philosophy, 37–38
anti-formalism, aesthetic, x, 31, 57,
  87, 93, 138, 166, 173, 176, 177
anti-realism, 33, 116, 127, 134, 171,
  174
architecture, 92, 134, 166, 179
  criticized by Kant, 38–39
archival, tendency in contemporary
  art, 167, 169–170, 173
Aristotle, 15, 16, 43, 128
  Poetics, 152
  Rhetoric, 149, 151–152
art, definition of, xii
Artaud, Antonin, 63, 71, 136
autonomy, 32–33, 45, 56, 75, 110,
  113, 119, 123, 135, 136, 172

in aesthetics, x, 8, 44–45, 50, 53,
  66, 75, 100, 104, 109, 112, 113,
  117, 138, 139, 141, 173, 177
as central term of Kant, 5
of objects from their contexts, 3, 7,
  33, 125, 138, 178

Badiou, Alain, 9, 14, 131, 132
Bataille, Georges, 159, 160, 173
  Story of the Eye, 168
Baudrillard, Jean, 61, 126–127
beauty, 5, 24, 33–40, 41, 136, 140,
  141, 142, 166, 176
  as patterned contrasts, in
  Whitehead, 46
  no science of, 43
  opposite is the literal, not the ugly,
  8
beholder of art
  human being as, 9, 45, 53, 55, 57,
  58, 68–69, 71, 74, 77, 79–82,
  120, 136, 156, 157
Bennett, Jane, 64
  criticized by Foster, 167, 172,
  180n11
  criticized by Fried, 8, 181n27
  monism of, 186n5
Bergson, Henri, 172, 185n4
Berkeley, George, 18, 116, 151
  read as realist by Grant, 184n4
Beuys, Joseph, 3, 73, 84, 176
  *I Like America and America Likes
  Me*, 113

196